PRAISE FOR

BECKY LYNCH: THE MAN

"A treat for fans of The Man and pro wrestling, with plenty of peeks behind the curtain."

—*Kirkus Reviews*

"An endearing debut memoir . . . [Quin] grounds her accomplishments with candid discussions of body image issues, her unglamorous pre-wrestling days as an Aer Lingus flight attendant, and moments when she acted like a 'jerk'. . . Such honesty sets her account apart from other professional athlete memoirs. Even non–wrestling fans are likely to enjoy this."

—*Publishers Weekly*

"Becky's writing style is infectious and contagious. Just like her personality. From hard times and hard decisions, to changing the landscape of sports entertainment, the self-described 'underdog' has always been destined to do great things. I'm sure there is more to come. And that's the bottom line, because Stone Cold said so."

—"Stone Cold" Steve Austin

"Quin's story is one of perseverance, humility, and raw emotion. Her authenticity allows us to feel her struggles and mature alongside her as the story unfolds. Anyone who's ever wondered what it takes and what it's like to become a WWE superstar will not be able to put this down. It might just be the new Underdog's Guide to the Galaxy. A trailblazer, a groundbreaker, and a great example of my three favorite words: Never Give Up."

—John Cena

"Effortlessly authentic, poignant without ever trying too hard, and a little rough around the edges—that's my lovely wife, and it's also her lovely book. I am so proud and so inspired. Between being a full-time WWE Superstar, a full-time mother, and a GOAT life partner, my one and only somehow casually found the bandwidth to pen a perfect memoir . . . because of course she did."

—The Man's Man, a.k.a. Seth Rollins

"*Becky Lynch: The Man* is the story of a remarkable woman who had the guts to put it all on the line. Taking risks that would take her from flight attendant to one of the biggest WWE Superstars in the world, Becky Lynch defies every stereotype. The crowd loves her because she is vulnerable and real, and I have no doubt you will too!"

—Stephanie McMahon

"If you don't know why they call Becky Lynch 'The Man,' you will after reading this book. Becky is my friend, but I had no idea about her unreal journey. From emigrating from Ireland to helping to orchestrate the ascension of women's wrestling, this is a must-read for any WWE fan but also for anyone with big dreams and odds stacked against them."

—Maria Menounos

"*Becky Lynch: The Man* is one of the finest wrestling books—or memoirs of any kind—I have had the pleasure to read. Actually, it was equal parts honor and pleasure; Becky allowed me in on the ground floor of her creative process, and I read with great joy as she found her voice as a writer. I am so glad she has chosen to share that voice and her remarkable life story with all of us."

—Mick Foley

"My whole life I've searched for a badass ginger role model, and finally found one in the great Rebecca Quin. Enjoy her incredible origin story and learn how she became a real-life superhero."

—Seth Green

"Becky Lynch—A.K.A. Rebecca Quin, A.K.A. The Man—has written a memoir that's deeply personal, legitimately hilarious, and truly inspiring. She's a gifted storyteller both in the ring and on the page. Multiple times I found myself saying 'Damn, Becky, I had no idea' out loud to no one in particular. Most people would be satisfied headlining WrestleMania, changing the face of women's wrestling, and pulling off a flawless Cyndi Lauper on network television. Thankfully for Becky that was all just a precursor to this freaking masterpiece of a book."

—Brian Gewirtz, author, former head writer of Raw, and SVP of Development at Seven Bucks Productions

"Such a beautiful read. Becky doesn't just tell a story, she lets you sit shotgun as she relives a journey of triumph, family, heartbreak, and crippling self-doubt. Her honesty and accountability is beyond refreshing. This is a story written by a dreamer for other dreamers with the enduring message that if she can reach the top of the mountain, we can too."

—James Roday

BECKY LYNCH

MAN

NOT YOUR AVERAGE
Average GIRL

REBECCA QUIN

THE

Gallery Books

New York Amsterdam/Antwerp London Toronto Sydney New Delhi

G

Gallery Books
An Imprint of Simon & Schuster, LLC
1230 Avenue of the Americas
New York, NY 10020

First Gallery Books trade paperback edition March 2025

GALLERY BOOKS and colophon are registered trademarks
of Simon & Schuster, LLC

For information about special discounts for bulk purchases,
please contact Simon & Schuster Special Sales at 1-866-506-1949
or business@simonandschuster.com.

The Simon & Schuster Speakers Bureau can bring authors
to your live event. For more information or to book an event,
contact the Simon & Schuster Speakers Bureau at 1-866-248-3049
or visit our website at www.simonspeakers.com.

Interior design by Silverglass

Manufactured in the United States of America

10 9 8 7 6 5 4 3 2 1

Library of Congress Cataloging-in-Publication Data is available.

ISBN 978-1-9821-5725-8
ISBN 978-1-9821-5726-5 (pbk)
ISBN 978-1-9821-5727-2 (ebook)

Dedicated to my dad, whose unconditional love
allowed me to be everything I am.

To my mom, who only ever wanted the best for me.

To my brother, who gave me a dream.

To wrestling, for making those dreams come true.

To my husband, Colby, and my daughter, Roux, for giving
me a life and love beyond those wild dreams.

*If you bring forth what is within you,
what you bring forth will complete you.
If you do not bring forth what is within you,
what you bring forth will destroy you.*
—my dad, but also the Bible (kinda)

CONTENTS

SEASON 2: **THE WANDER YEARS**

SEASON 3: **WELCOME TO THE BIG TIME**

AUTHOR'S NOTE

All contents in this book are strictly from my point of view, as I remember it. Which means I may have misremembered a whole bunch of stuff, or at least skewed it towards my own personal bias. I like to think I'm pretty self-aware and, as much as possible, do know when I'm the jerk. But maybe not; I suppose we'll see. Sometimes I might change a name here and there in an effort to protect the innocent.

In any case, don't take any of it too seriously: "It's life, and life only." I think Bob Dylan said that.

PRESHOW

When I was five years old, my dad said to me, "Make sure you keep a journal. I wish I had. Back in my day, a quarter pound of sweets cost five p; now it costs fifty p. It would be interesting to keep track of that."

I'm sure there are more interesting things I could have kept track of than the price of sweets, but that's where my lifelong love affair with writing began. I've journaled my whole life, in the hopes that when I began writing my memoir I could draw from a well of information and memories. It didn't quite work out that way, however. In researching this book, I discovered that my journals were more like the repetitive ramblings of a madwoman. Maybe not a madwoman, but certainly a lost girl trying to find her way in this crazy world—tormented by bad relationships, teen angst, and repeating the same problems over and over again.

Despite my diligence in recording how I was feeling at *all times* (and the price of sweets, of course), I wrote down very few actual stories or memories. One thing that my journals make abundantly clear, though, is how much wrestling changed my life forever. It got into my bloodstream early on—and I don't believe it could be eradicated even if I were to get a complete transfusion.

You probably know me as Becky Lynch. If not, maybe I served you in a bar in New York City or handed you peanuts high above the Atlantic. Maybe you saw me kill a man with a shield on *The Vikings*, or watched me reach octaves reserved only for Cyndi Lauper as I played her on NBC's *Young Rock*. My professional life has been turbulent either way, and I hope to be able to recap the most interesting parts here for you. At times, I wish Rebecca Quin were more like the character I play on TV. Instead, she's vulnerable, often foolish, and a whole lot more complex. But I like that about her.

THE
GROWING
YEARS

SEASON 1

THE ENTRANCE

It was April 2020. I was the longest-reigning Raw women's champion. And I was pregnant.

With the world shut down for covid and nothing to do, the least I could do was create human life. If ever there was a time to sneak a kid into the wrestling family, I decided this was it.

My fiancé, Colby, and I had just gathered our snacks, taking a break from our *Game of Thrones* marathon to watch the biggest wrestling event of the year, WrestleMania 36. The showcase of the immortals. The Super Bowl of sports entertainment. An event so big, it sells thousands upon thousands of tickets before even a single match is announced. Only this year's attendance, precisely zero. And I was wrestling on it. Again, pregnant.

We had pretaped the event two weeks earlier, covid protocols calling for us to travel as little as possible, meaning we taped several shows at a time, weeks in advance.

Vince McMahon, our almighty overlord and the chairman of WWE, would rather die than cancel a show. That man believes in what he does and what WWE means more than anything. At a time when people were scared and confused, not knowing what the future held for them or their loved ones, people needed a distraction more than ever.

Vince, the almost mythical billionaire, could be a terrifying figure. He was never one to shy away from controversy or tough decisions. He even remains one of the few people to take on the

United States government and win. WWE was his baby. But how the hell was he going to feel about my baby?

As I chomped down on my cheese puffs, I watched my opponent Shayna Baszler throw my expecting ass around like I was a kite on a windy day. I had recommended that she take the title from me at WrestleMania. Not because I was with child, but because I had been a babyface champion for so long and could feel the audience beginning to turn on me. I had gone from underdog to top dog, and such a situation can't overstay its welcome. Plus, we needed to make more female contenders, and what better way to do that than having them win the title on the grandest stage of them all? Everyone wins.

Except me, whose request was denied. I wanted to lose, but I would actually win, so it was a loss. . . . Sigh. Wrestling is confusing.

"How am I gonna tell Vince?" I turned to Colby, realizing that beyond our immediate family, the most powerful man in wrestling needed to be the first recipient of our news.

"You're just gonna have to tell him," he responded.

"You think he's gonna yell at me? Fire me?"

"I don't *think* so. But he'll probably be upset."

"Ugh."

I waited till the hullaballoo of WrestleMania weekend was over. All things considered, it was a success. Or as much of a success as a wrestling event can be when taped in front of absolutely no one, with only the grunts of our pain and effort to interrupt the awkwardness.

"You're just going to have to call him," Colby advised, looking at my anguished face while I was in the midst of something resembling a workout. "Just rip the Band-Aid off."

"Okay. Okay, yeah. I can do that."

"You sure?"

"Yeah. Yeah. I'll tell him how I can still keep working. You know, maybe I can . . . I could make a documentary about all this. Or I could maybe be a consultant on the creative team or something?!" I said as I scrambled for ways to save my job.

"I think you're going to be fine," Colby comforted me.

"Yeah, I'm The Man," I said facetiously. "I'm gonna call him now." Then I stepped outside to make the biggest phone call of my life.

Brrring, brrring. Brrring, brrring.

There was a light drizzle as I stood outside Colby's Iowa gym, waiting for Vince to answer.

Brrring, brrring. Brrring, brrring.

I began to kick up the dirt on the ground, making patterns with my foot. My anxiety overriding my nausea.

Brrring, brrring.

It's just life, Rebecca. You can have it all. The family and the job. The men do. Why not you? It's not fair for anyone to ask you to choose. And it's none of their business, I reasoned with myself.

Brrring, brrring. Click.

I reentered the empty gym.

"He didn't answer," I relayed, more relieved than disappointed.

"Probably in a meeting or somethi—"

"Oop! That's him!" I yelled as my phone rang.

The drizzle had turned to a downpour as I ran outside, seeking refuge in my fiancé's Tesla.

I took a deep breath before pressing the illuminated green phone button.

"Hi, Vince!"

"Hello! Sorry, I was just in a meeting. How are you doing?" Vince's signature gravelly voice sounded like the embodiment of a death sentence.

"Oh, I'm, eh, I'm good. I'm calling you because, well, we have a little bit of a problem," I began, searching for any signs of my big-girl pants in the car so I could put them on and get through this conversation.

Just say it, Rebecca. Just fucking say it. Okay, here it goes.

"Sir, I'm five weeks pregnant, and so I was thinking maybe we could . . ." I kept talking so that maybe he'd miss the gravity of the first part of my sentence and concentrate on this award-winning documentary I was somehow going to make.

Without waiting for me to finish, and with zero hesitation in his voice, he responded with the last words I expected to come out of his mouth. . . .

"Congratulations!"

Huh? I came here ready for a verbal ass kicking.

"Oh my god, Rebecca! That's fantastic news. Wow! I'm so happy for you!"

I sat there stunned, tears beginning to stream down my face. Relief, joy, hormones. Of all the possible outcomes, this was the most surprising.

I had done a few things in my life. But this was about to be the biggest, and it was far from the way I was brought into this world. . . .

I made my prompt and elegant entrance into the world on January 30, 1987, in Limerick, Ireland.

My mother, having just uprooted her life to accommodate my father's new job, learned midlabor that he had lost said job. As she pushed me out in the grimy Limerick hospital, the radiator repairman unceremoniously interrupted to complete his final task of the day.

"I beg your pardon, ma'am. Just a little jammed here. Hope you haven't been too cold. That's all fixed now."

"Get out!"

"Of course, of course. Goodbye now and congratulations, by the way. That's a beautiful little girl you have there."

It wasn't long after the radiator repair man had wished us well that Mom picked up and moved back to Dublin City.

When I was growing up, my mother was the most beautiful woman I had ever seen. I know just about everyone says that about their ma, but I had validation. External validation. Professional validation.

She was a model.

In fact, when the term "milf" was first coined, it seemed like the entirety of popular culture had been designed specifically to taunt my older brother, Richy, and me.

When modeling proved less stable, she traded in being a calendar centerfold for the equally glamorous (at the time) life of being a globe-trotting flight attendant.

Her head-turning good looks gave me hope that I might one day achieve this esoteric superpower whenever the puberty fairies would bestow their blessings upon me. However, these fairies seemingly missed the "make her a stunner" portion of their growth dust.

Or rather, my invention of the potato waffle and cheese white bread sandwich had my taste buds in a stranglehold from the age of nine and trapped me in their starchy, creamy prison, keeping those cellulite bumps on my thighs fed and happy, living their best lives.

It wasn't just that I revered my mom because she was drop-dead gorgeous. She had a humility about her, almost as if she was unaware of the attention she garnered at every turn. She was also a hard worker and a staunch realist to boot.

It was all of these attributes that made her marriage to my father utterly confusing.

Don't get me wrong: my dad was an absolute legend. He was a dreamer, a charmer, a man with his head in the clouds who valued imagination and originality above all else. He was constantly inventing the next revolutionary thing. But his ideas always seemed to exceed his execution. He never really found his footing in life, but the one thing he was most proud of was me and my brother.

My brother was an angel, but I, on the other hand, was Satan with a poorly cut bob. I could be bashing my brother over the head with a frying pan and my dad would reprimand Richy, "Just leave her be! She's expressing herself."

I don't think I've ever met two more diametrically opposed people than my parents. My dad valued independence and autonomy. The first words I remember my mom telling me were "Be normal." Even at five, I knew I was going to break her heart. My dad was in and out of employment for most of his life. My mom always had the steady job. The one thing, and possibly the only thing, they could agree on, however, was that they loved me and my brother more than anything and we should always come first.

To me, their contrasting personalities were a blessing. My dad gave me the courage to dream. My mom gave me the practicality to go out and work for it. My mom gave me hope I was going to grow up to be a babe. My dad diluted the gene pool enough for me to know I had to work on my personality.

By the time I was just a year old, they decided to call it quits and separate, which, in Catholic Ireland, where divorce wasn't even legal yet, was immensely frowned upon.

It didn't affect my life too much. (A) I was too young to know what the hell was going on, and (B) by the time I was four and old enough to realize my dad wasn't around, my mom allowed Dad to move back into our house in an act of highly admirable parenting. A victory on all accounts.

We could have our dad, and she had help when she had to go away on longer trips.

Sure, living with your ex sounds like a downright nightmare, and they hardly talked or had much interaction at all and there was an undertone of tension in the house at all times that we were too young to understand. But they were civil enough to do everything as a family. Vacations, dinners, gatherings, you name it.

For Richy and me, everything was hunky-dory as our parents continued their separate celibate lives under one roof—which is the wistful assumption of all kids anyway.

It also meant we didn't have to take time away from our quintessential lower-middle-class Dublin neighborhood, where every day was a kid party. There were about seventeen of us young hooligans all close in age running around together, causing havoc, with little drama ever breaking out among us.

Until we were infiltrated by the British in the summer of 1997. One of the neighbors had their English grandson Robbie come to stay while school was out. The kid had the charisma of Dwayne "The Rock" Johnson packed into his tiny sixty-pound frame. He danced and sang to the amusement of everyone on the block. Everyone but me. I never liked this guy. I don't know what it was about him. Maybe I was jealous of how beloved he was among my peers. Maybe I envied his rhythm and his angelic singing voice. Or maybe, just maybe, this kid was a little prick.

One day, while Robbie sat perched in a tree above me in the communal green area of the hood, likely performing a perfect rendition of "Bohemian Rhapsody," I swung from our makeshift swing below. It was essentially a rope hanging from a branch with a small plank to sit on. Our many hours of dragging our feet in the same spot had worn a dent into the packed ground underneath.

Suddenly the rope snapped! I landed on my ass with a loud thud.

"She's so fat she broke the swing!" Robbie yelled, and laughed uproariously.

All my friends laughed along too.

I sat there humiliated, trying not to cry.

Eventually, when the urge had left my eyes and forcing any bravery I could garner, I got up and brushed myself off. Only to reveal that I had landed right on top of the indentation on the ground.

"She put a *dent* in the *ground*! *Hahahahahaha!*"

Everyone laughed again.

"I did not!"

"Then how did it get there? Hahaha!"

I couldn't stop the tears this time and ran inside crying.

The next day, as every day, the whole gang was playing outside. I decided today was a seesaw kind of day—doubly so with the swing now out of commission. In addition to the swing, we had constructed a seesaw from a large plank of wood balanced haphazardly on a brick wall.

"Who wants to go with me?" I asked as I jogged towards the wall where the seesaw awaited.

"No, Becky, stop!" one friend shouted.

"What's your problem?" I asked as I reached my teeter-totter destination.

I looked down at the plank of wood and quickly discovered their problem. Written in bold letters were the words:

BECKY'S GOT A BELLY LIKE A SACK OF POTATOES

accompanied by a sketch of me with a sack of potatoes–shaped belly, which, in fairness to the culprit, had been rendered with some skill.

The plank was literally *covered* in Becky-themed insults.

"Who . . . wrote this?" I demanded, before the finger-pointing started:

"It was her."

"It was not!"

"It was him; he made us do it!"

How could I have such a wildly different interpretation of our friendship?

I grabbed the plank and once again ran home in floods of tears. Then and there, I vowed to lose weight so I might have a chance of actually being like my mom when I grew up. But then I got hungry and sad and just wanted pizza. Beauty was my mom's domain. Pizza was mine.

THE JUMP START

The perks of my mother being a flight attendant meant that even though we had little spare cash, we were able to travel for pennies. She took my brother and me with her on transatlantic flights quasi-regularly, and one year we even got to spend Christmas in New York. Literally on the set of *Home Alone 2*, there was an undeniable magic to the city. Pizza slices as big as my belly, spending Christmas Eve wandering FAO Schwarz and ice-skating in Central Park—I fell in love with America there and then.

When my mother offered to take me to Boston a few years later, I jumped at the chance. Generally, flight attendants get an allowance for each day they're in a particular destination and Mom would usually spend hers on my brother and me. She had saved up her per diems over several trips so I could pick out some clothes. I always felt a bit special getting my clothes from America. I might as well have been wearing Gucci for how fancy I felt sporting a new hoodie from The Gap.

I was ten years old and my, ahem, "growth spurt," shall we say, had me bulging out of my trousers in all directions, so naturally it was time to invest in pants of the stretchy variety. Boston wasn't quite as awe-inspiring as Manhattan at Christmas, but the shopping was great. We had walked the length and breadth of the city, it seemed, when my chunky little legs couldn't take any more and I wanted to stop for some food.

"Can we go to McDonald's?" I begged like most red-blooded ten-year-olds, and I was delighted to be answered in the affirmative.

Upon arrival, I waddled up to the counter and radiated anticipation.

"May I get a Quarter Pounder with Cheese meal, please?"

"Medium or large?"

"Make it a large," I said. This was my time and I was balling.

"Would you like to supersize it?"

"What does that mean?"

"Bigger drink and more fries than a large."

What in the world? I thought, *You bet your ass I want to supersize it!*

"Wow!" I gasped as the spotty teenager put my meal on a tray and pushed it towards me.

I had never seen such a triumph of delicious golden fries in all my days. I took my tray and swaggered to a seat near the window, chuffed with my gluttony.

I was so engrossed in my food and the conversation with my mom that I didn't think it weird when a man came in without ordering anything and just sat across from us.

"Show me the jeans you got!" my mom enthused.

I bent over to look in the bag when my eyes landed upon the strange man. *That guy has a weird-looking thumb*, I thought, *and why is he stroking it?*

I resurfaced with my new jeans in hand when it dawned on me: that might not be his thumb!

"How about the top you got?"

I leaned over again and caught a second glance.

Yep, definitely not *a thumb!*

"I'm not hungry anymore!" I exclaimed as I jumped from the table and ran to discard my previously coveted food.

My sudden movement startled the man, making him jump up and run out the door.

Throwing out food was out of character for me, so my mom followed quickly behind asking "What's wrong?"

"That man was stroking his . . ." I whispered, "penis."

That event soured my view of Boston for a while. And penises even more so.

Maybe my mom's good looks weren't all they were cracked up to be.

Despite my negative Bean Town experience, I jumped at the opportunity when my mom suggested a trip to New York a year later, just before my eleventh birthday.

This time we went post-Christmas, and the cold rain and absence of fairy lights illuminating every tree made it a lot less magical than before as we spent our time wandering around in a jet-lagged haze, our feet soaked from puddles. On our final day, after breakfast, we came back to our Times Square hotel, exchanging the bright billboards that overwhelmed our senses for our darkly lit room with its mustard-yellow walls and old must, like the sheets and walls had been stained with years of cigarette smoke.

"I have something to tell you," my mom began.

This isn't good, I thought. No one says "I have something to tell you" before delivering *good* news. My mind raced with a plethora of possibilities. First to my brain was that she and my dad, in a strange turn of events, had been getting along lately, talking and even laughing. Very weird behavior for them altogether. *What if she is going to tell me they are getting back together?* Even at ten I knew that would have been a terrible, terrible mistake.

"I've started seeing someone," she continued.

Well, shit, this isn't what I wanted to hear either!

I stared at her blankly, trying to fight the tears that would soon roll down my face.

"His name is Chris and he's a pilot."

"Do Dad and Richy know?" I asked, bereft of any other questions. I didn't want details.

"Yes, they've both taken it well. Your dad said he was happy for me and I deserve it."

She *did* deserve it, but that didn't stop me being upset! Our whole lives, my brother and I had been the sole beneficiaries of all her love and affection. I wasn't ready to share it. I had never even known her to go on a date. She actually used to wear her wedding ring so people wouldn't ask her out. Clearly, that didn't deter this Chris fella.

"You actually answered the phone when he called around Christmas," my mom admitted.

This asshole was calling around Christmas?! What a homewrecker, I thought as I immediately searched for any reason not to like him.

"He's divorced; he lives in Bayside; he has two boys, Alistair and Kenneth. Alistair is two years older than Richard and Kenneth is two years older than you."

She took a deep breath before cooing dreamily, "He's the one."

Well, fuck.

"But nothing's going to change around here," she promised.

A promise she couldn't keep.

THE UNDERDOG

Two years into her relationship with Chris, my mom was already burnt-out. She was working full-time, flying around the world, nurturing a blossoming romance, and parenting an absolute asshole of a teenager. (That would be me.)

She decided to look for houses located closer to Chris in Bayside, Dublin, about thirty minutes from where we lived. She may as well have wanted to move to India for how far away that seemed to my thirteen-year-old self. And, of course, this meant *everything* was about to change!

I'd have to leave the house I grew up in. I'd have to change schools. I'd have to leave all of my friends. My dad would have to move out.

"Why can't Chris just move closer to where we live?" I bargained.

"Because his kids' mother lives closer to him and he has to see his kids too."

I didn't like any of this! I felt like our family was getting the shaft, while his was being catered to.

In adult reality, my mom was looking for a way out of the tension-ridden house that in many ways had kept her captive in her own home—as one might expect when cohabitating with one's ex-husband. Plus, Chris was an amazing man who had proved to be an incredible partner for my mother and it was about time they progressed this damn inconvenient thing. She also didn't want to move in with him either, worrying that living with someone who wasn't our dad would be difficult on my brother and me. And I'm sure sparing Chris my teenage wrath.

After my mother had searched for months on end, as if by some great miracle the house next door to Chris came up for sale, and my mom instantly made her move.

It rained on moving day, perfectly encapsulating my mood. We'll ignore the fact that it rains most every day in Ireland.

As I left the only home I had ever known, I yelled at my mom that I hated her—with a venom I don't think I've spit out since.

My dad attempted to comfort me as he guided me to the car, but I was too far gone. He hated her too. The last nearly ten years had worked well for him. He loved his kids more than anything and now he had to move away from them. He wasn't able to afford much in terms of housing, which automatically disqualified him from majority custody.

Mom's new house was a fixer-upper verging on dilapidated. The previous owners clearly dabbled in pharmaceutical sales of the street variety, as they left behind their triple-beam scale and a constellation of burn marks all over the carpet.

The stress I was putting my mom under was taking its toll on her. She began wasting away to nothing, unable to eat, and gagging at the dinner table when she tried. She only ever wanted to be a good mother, raise good children, and live a good life. But somehow, no matter how many masses she attended, things weren't working out that way for her. And unfortunately, for the next few years, I was only going to get worse.

What's more, the new neighborhood was a maze of dodgy side alleys and nettle-filled fields, with a random ancient graveyard smack-dab in the middle of it. Perfect for delinquent teens—of which there happened to be an abundance. Which facilitated my newfound hobbies of street drinking and pot smoking that I had picked up to cope with all of these thirteen-year-old emotions.

On the plus side, me and my brother were becoming closer, bonding over our shared disdain for our current situation. Richy was four years my senior, and though I had annoyed the ever-living shit out of him for most our lives, he had the patience of a saint and, ultimately, all I wanted was to be like him. He is one of life's good guys, an old soul with an innate wisdom about him.

Richy also excels at anything he puts his mind to. While I never had many interests beyond hanging with my friends and watching television, he was always doing something productive—karate, playing guitar, playing rugby—but ultimately his greatest love was creating art. He was gifted from a young age, drawing comic book characters or pulling tar up from the roads on hot summer days to make his own action figures. And though he was older, smarter, and more accepting than I was, he was struggling with this family deterioration too, maybe even more so as he attempted to balance his own grief with also being my shield of armor. When my parents' fighting was at its peak, he bore the weight so I would be less impacted.

Through all of these changes, we found solace in two things.

Number one: wrestling. Of course we were all Hulkamaniacs in the early nineties, singing along to "Real American" as the balding, bandana-clad hero flexed his twenty-four-inch pythons to the sheer delight of all watching. But once I had passed the age of five, it was no longer hip to love wrestling. After a long period of abstention from all things WWE, my brother rekindled a love for the sport, and that meant I, inevitably, was soon to follow suit. It was the height of the Attitude Era, where wrestling was bold and brash, beating up your boss only led to making more money, the objectification of women was strangely celebrated, characters were outlandish, and it had just become cool for teenagers and folk in their twenties to re-indulge, while classrooms were filled with kids giving one another the middle finger and telling their teachers to "suck it."

But I wasn't just going to accept wrestling's coolness willy-nilly. It would have to prove itself to me. Because clearly I was the authority on cool.

"That stuff is for babies," I jeered my brother as he watched. "Don't you know it's all fake?" I was the worst.

"Actually, it has gotten really good," Richy replied cool as a cucumber, completely unbothered by my insults.

And while I was doing my own thing around the house, listening to Nirvana or detailing my woes in journal entries, I kept one eye on the television—due to one captivating performer.

His name was Mick Foley and he was involved in an angle with Triple H. Mick, a large and hairy man, missing half of an ear and with the physique of a springtime bear, had a particular way of speaking that I was mesmerized by. With his slightly high-pitched and cracking voice, there was something about the way this madman told a story that would not allow me to look away. He had intensity and warmth in equal measures. He was brave but vulnerable and also had incredible comedic timing. More than anything, he was authentic. Through my TV screen I could tell he was a wonderful human.

In my teenage disarray and feeling like I didn't belong, I could relate to Mick. Like me, he wasn't naturally gifted. He wasn't an athlete, but he made up for it by taking huge risks in the ring and I wanted those risks to pay off for him so badly.

I began to instruct my brother, "Just call me when Mick comes on!"

Mick would come on the telly and reel me in—and, well, after that I was there to stay. It would become one of my life goals to one day give Mick Foley a big bear hug. And while I don't want to give away the ending of this book . . . (but tick ☑).

Wrestling is a funny thing. Once you get into it, you can't seem to shut up about it. Or at least I couldn't. The spectacle, the story lines, the conflict and resolution. The athletic maneuvers, the stunts, good prevailing over evil and even if things aren't going well for our heroes there could be a win around the corner. It had everything: drama, comedy, romance, adrenaline, excitement. Above all, it had hope.

I revered the effort, training, dedication, and toughness that it took to become a WWE superstar. Even though I myself knew nothing of discipline, I could live vicariously through my idols.

I wanted to talk to everyone about wrestling. I wanted to break down the nuance in the ring and the gossip outside of it. And I found a place I could go on endlessly, which brings me to number two: the Central Bank. I'm sure you're thinking, *That's an odd thing for a thirteen-year-old to be into.* It wasn't actually banking I was into, but the location of the bank. It was in the middle of Dublin City and became the hangout spot for misfits of all kinds. The goths, the hippies, the rockers, and the emos would all go there on the weekends to drink away our common misery, bonding over our dysfunctional families and love of alternative music and of course wrestling.

We weren't the bad kids, but we were the kids sneaking vodka into our Coca-Cola bottles and drinking in the bathroom of the cinema, or stealing the chocolate bars on the bottom shelf in the local corner store when no one was looking. At the same time, we thought about the state of society and the world, and wanted peace, love, and harmony. Well, mostly.

There was, amidst us, a twenty-four-year-old man named Zippy who had spent time in prison and had emerged unreformed and who would inspire fear amongst us teens whenever he entered our orbit. However, he adored one of my friends, Steven. Steven and I had connected over our mutual love of wrestling. He was a smart, dashingly handsome lad with beautiful long, flowing blond hair—and to top it all off, he was in a band. Swoon.

Steven got along with everyone. And thus, even the most feared thug in the group, Zippy, wanted to impress him.

While discussing wrestling one evening, all three of us walked through the center of the city. We had just descended a set of concrete stairs leading to a large courtyard when we came across a kid no older than sixteen.

"What's your name?" Zippy asked as we approached him.

"Who, me? I'm—"

Suddenly, with no warning, Zippy scooped under the kid's arm, hoisted him up into the air, and rock-bottomed him flush on the concrete, his skull hitting the ground with a most disgusting thud.

The kid, miraculously still conscious, got up and scurried away as quick as his shaky legs could carry him, blood coming from his head, as Steven and I looked on with wide-eyed horror.

As much as I loved wrestling, I didn't want a live impromptu show. Especially when one of the participants wasn't consenting. I abided by the "Don't try this at home" WWE warning. I wished this full-grown dodgy man would too.

Back in my new neighborhood, I had acquired a group of friends. We all had the same love of getting stoned and hanging around the mean streets of Bayside. Everyone was slightly older than I was, so it made purchasing alcohol even easier.

With my mom being gone on overnights on weekends, our place became the party house. Most weekends were fairly tame, but occasionally the wrong person would invite a group of wrong people. Then my brother and I had to prevent fights from breaking out and stop people from setting fire to our furniture.

My mom could smell the stench of smoke when she walked into the house, jet-lagged and exhausted from working through the night. She'd start frantically cleaning, disappointed in us and worn-out by our irresponsibility and recklessness.

We, of course, would deny everything emphatically. Innocent until proven guilty! And she had no concrete evidence that there were hordes of delinquent youths utilizing her home as if it were the local nightclub.

My aunt, noticing my wildness—and probably thinking she could extinguish the flames, considering she was a former wild woman herself—took me away to Italy with her and her family for two weeks during the summer, with the hope this would give me some grounding and life experience.

The first week was filled with sightseeing and historical excursions. Getting to travel through the city of Pompeii, imagining the world two thousand years ago and the horror people experienced as their town was covered in molten lava, reminded me of the insignificance of my problems and that maybe things weren't as bad as they could be. Especially when I was spending the evenings eating authentic Italian pizza and the world's best gelato.

However, when we came to the relaxing, sitting by the pool part of the vacation, I was less than enthused. My rotund fourteen-year-old body and frizzed-up mop of hair had me rather self-conscious, so I would do all I could to avoid wearing a bikini in public.

One day while I sat next to my aunt, trying awkwardly to cover up my body, she did her best to comfort me. "Oh, Becky darling," she said with sincerity, "there's far too many blond beauties around here for anyone to be looking at you."

Oh, gee, thanks. That makes me feel fucking great.

She quickly found out that I really was as difficult as my mom claimed. I pouted all day long, secretly smoked my cigarettes, and hoarded alcohol in my room, unwilling to socialize with anyone. But Italy really is beautiful in the summertime.

When school recommenced, I had fully retracted into myself, showing little interest in anything other than getting high in the bushes during lunch break. I even failed PE, which, by the way, I thought you passed just by showing up. And I was there, bloodshot eyes and all, refusing to do anything. I was worried I looked stupid when I ran. To be fair, high as I was, my worry was most likely valid.

By the time the parent-teacher meetings rolled around, my mom left the school in tears after being waterboarded with stories of how lazy and unmotivated I was, how I was falling behind and something needed to be done.

I knew I wasn't doing well and I had no aversion to making my mom cry myself, but when someone else made her cry on my behalf, that was different. It felt like maybe, perhaps, there was a small chance that I was, in fact, the problem and needed to do something about it.

As I sat in my dismal bedroom, contemplating the meaning of everything and whether school mattered or if a better way to cope with this confusion was to find myself a can of beer and chill out in the graveyard by the house, I had an epiphany. I had to turn my life around once and for all right now.

But how?

THE BABYFACE

I walked into the computer room to find Richy staring at a black-and-maroon website.

"What's NWA Hammerlock?" I asked, reading the letters at the top of the screen. It sounded like either a rap band or an especially unfriendly shark. Maybe both.

"It's a wrestling school in the UK."

"Oh, cool!" I said as I wondered if he was reconsidering his art career.

Earlier that week, we'd watched a new show by WWE called *Tough Enough*, where contestants with no prior wrestling experience learned the craft from scratch. The training was gruesome and the bumps looked painful. But most stuck with it, because two winners—one male, one female—would be selected to join the promotion.

It was frustrating to watch, because these aspiring stars would constantly drop out of fitness tests or complain about being sore or hurt. "Stop being a little bitch!" I'd yell at the television. "This is your dream, people!!! You're so lucky! How could you show any weakness?! It's the WWE, for Godsake!"

Richy and I knew we could do better (my athletic shortcomings were simply a side note), so I figured that's why he was looking up NWA Hammerlock.

"I wrote to them and told them I want to train. I said I'm not a dreamer, I know the hard work that it will take, but I feel like I would regret it if I never tried," Richy explained as he scrolled through the website, landing on the talent roster.

"Look! There's two Irish lads on their website," he pointed out as he clicked on their profiles.

"Paul Tracey"—a tall, slightly smug-looking, largely pale, gingery blond lad.

"Fergal Devitt," who was dark-haired, with piercing blue eyes and an unbelievably ripped body.

"That Fergal lad looks like a real douchebag," I jeered.

Even though I was sure I could do better than the people on *Tough Enough*, the thought of actually pursuing wrestling had never crossed my mind. But now there was a pit of envy in my stomach—that Richy was most likely going to get to do this and I wouldn't.

At nineteen, he was a full-grown adult, but there was no way my mom was going to let my fifteen-year-old-self fly over to England to train to be a wrassler.

A few days later the owner of Hammerlock, Andre Baker, wrote back to accept Richy's application. In a delightful turn of events, he announced that Paul Tracey and that douchey-looking Fergal Devitt would be opening a wrestling school in Ireland in May.

"That's two weeks from now! Where is it going to be?"

"In Bray"—which was a simple one-hour train ride from us.

"I want to go!" I beamed.

"You can't. You have to be sixteen," he said as he tried to sway me away

"I'll lie!"

"You're not coming. I don't want to have to look after my little sister."

"You won't have to." My lies had already begun.

My brother wasn't going to get behind my newly found wrestling ambitions just yet, and neither would my mother. In fact, if she ever came into the room when we had wrestling on, she would shriek, avert her eyes, and run quickly out of the room as if she had caught us watching some depraved porno. It was for that reason she wouldn't even get the chance to object—as I told her I was going to do Brazilian jiu-jitsu, which sounded much more exotic.

Luckily for me, my dad was always a supporter of whatever eccentric whim would pop into my noggin.

Training would commence at 2:00 pm on Sunday, so the Saturday night before I stayed with my dad.

"Dad, they're opening a wrestling school in Bray. I really want to go."

"That's great, Becks! Sure, you'll be only marvelous." I could have told him I was going to be a competitive sewer diver and I'm sure he would have said the same thing.

"Would you be able to give me a lift?"

"Of course, madame," my dad said with a certain sense of austerity.

As we drove up the next afternoon with *Tough Enough* fresh in my mind, I fully expected to pull up to a warehouse with a giant metal sign over the door that would read: "NWA Ireland."

I would walk in and be dwarfed by muscle-bound men and women all ready to prove their fortitude. It would be darkly lit except for a single spotlight that would shine down upon a wrestling ring in the center of the room, fitted out with bright red ropes and a black canvas. I was giddy with anticipation.

"This looks like the spot," my dad announced as we pulled up twenty minutes early to the school, which was actually just the gymnasium of a local primary school. Needless to say, there was no giant metal "NWA Ireland" sign hanging over the door.

"Don't come in!" I instructed my dad as I got out of the car. Nothing would have been as uncool or a dead giveaway to my youth as my dad chaperoning me on my first day.

"As you wish, missy."

I jumped out of the car and ran across the grounds, trying to avoid getting soaking wet on this classically rainy Sunday. I kept my hoodie over my head to prevent my freshly dyed red hair from running down my shirt as I pulled up my baggy pants so that the bottoms didn't get drenched in the grass.

I walked up nervously, pushed open the double doors, and turned left to enter the hall. Now was time for my master plan. *If I say I'm sixteen, they'll be onto me. They might even ask for ID and that would be mortifying. I'll say I'm seventeen and they won't suspect a thing!*

"Hello," a singsongy voice greeted me. It was Fergal Devitt, and his profile picture had not done him justice. He was stunning, engaging, confident, and one of those types you couldn't help but be drawn to; there was a knowing that he would go on and do big things one day—which he has, as Finn Balor in WWE—and more than anything, he was not, in fact, the least bit douchey. He sat at a table with a sign-up sheet in front of him: name, age, contact number, money.

"Rebecca Quin, 17, January 30th, 1985, 0868918980," a neatly folded ten-euro bill courtesy of my pops.

"Go ahead," Fergal said without asking for ID as he guided me into the hall, proving my master plan a success!!

I'm a goddamn genius!

I looked around the brightly lit room. It was nothing like I had pictured. There were no behemoths leering over me. Just about twelve teenage boys, some tall and gangly, some short and skinny, some with their hair half-grown-out in that really awkward stage. Some a bit rotund, one or two who looked like they lifted a few weights but also loved a burger and a beer. I did a double take. I was also the only girl in the class. It was strangely comforting. I had gone from being the least fit girl in my PE class to suddenly being the most fit girl in my wrestling class. Absolute worst-case scenario, no matter how bad I might be at this, I would still be the best girl here.

Most shocking of all, there was no spotlit wrestling ring with bright red ropes and a black canvas. In fact, there was no wrestling ring at all! Just six blue padded mats on the floor.

A few minutes later my brother walked in the door, his hair and clothes wet from walking the twenty minutes from the train station.

Sucker, I thought, while simultaneously being comforted by his presence.

I could tell he was annoyed to see me, his annoyance growing in relation to my awkwardness as I inevitably wanted to be glued by his side.

"Get away from me," he growled through clenched teeth, trying not to draw attention to the fact that I was following him around like a lost puppy.

When everyone had arrived, Paul and Fergal welcomed the class.

"We don't have a wrestling ring yet; it should be here in the next few weeks. In the meantime, we'll get you started with the basics."

"Basics" was right. We began with a short and simple warm-up, which was a few air squats and jumping jacks, nothing like the fitness tests I had seen on *Tough Enough*. I came here ready to puke, for crying out loud!

Next up: bumping. I had seen people struggle with this on TV. I wasn't going to be one of those people. I wasn't going to be a wuss about it. Just fall backwards, tuck your chin, land on the upper part of your back, and slap the mat. Simple as that. How hard could it be?

My brother, who had now put as much space between us as he could, volunteered to go first.

His first bump was flawless, as if he had been doing it since birth. Just came out of the womb and hit a perfect flat back. Asshole.

Next in line was a short, skinny boy named Kenny who bore a shocking resemblance to Frankie Muniz and couldn't have weighed more than one hundred pounds. He also landed perfectly.

I knew this shit would be a piece of piss, I thought, their competence giving me confidence.

They were then followed by a tall, gangly lad.

That's *a long way to fall*, I thought.

He obviously thought so too.

He fell to the ground awkwardly as he tried to protect himself. I began to coach him in my head, like the armchair expert I had become: *Just commit! Land on your back; what are you doing, sissy-boy?*

He couldn't hear my telepathic instructions so he kept landing on his elbows or otherwise attempting to break his fall in the most painful ways possible. *How shameful*, I thought.

"Who's next?"

That was my cue to jump in. Something I have learned from failing at most things is, take your turn when it seems like the bar is at an all-time low. That way, there's nowhere to go but up!

"I'll go!" I volunteered enthusiastically.

I stood on the blue mat. Arms across my chest, ready to hurl myself backwards and—for the first time in my life—be a pure natural at something.

Thud, thud, thud, thud. I landed unimpressively—not smoothly on the upper part of my back, but on my lower back, followed by my elbows, then my upper back, and, finally, my head. My hands didn't slap the mat like I expected. More like gave it a feeble high five, Napoleon Dynamite–style. Also: *Ouch! That fucking hurt.*

"Not quite . . . kick your legs out and try slapping the mat," Fergal coached.

That's what I was trying to do!!

"Yeah, yeah, of course," I whimpered.

I tried again. This time just three thuds. My back, elbows, and the back of my head. The slap was equally waif-like.

"Give it a go again."

Thud, thud. Ooooof. I had winded myself this time. The mats didn't provide much cushion, considering there was concrete just an inch below.

"All right, we'll come back to it."

"Yeah, cool," I uttered painfully as I hobbled to the back of the line.

Next up were front bumps, i.e., falling forward, which came a bit easier. Something about being able to see where I was going was helpful.

Then we moved on to side bumps. We were instructed to crouch down, then throw ourselves to the side and land with our whole side body flush to the mat while simultaneously slapping it.

More mat slapping . . . I did not have a knack for mat slapping.

Again my brother landed everything perfectly and with intensity. For me, not so much. I was more like an old lady slowly falling to the side with no way to stop herself while letting out an understated howl as her face plummeted closer to the ground.

After falling repeatedly with little cushion to break our falls, I was delighted when Paul pulled out a giant crash pad and declared, "You're going to learn flip bumps next."

Essentially you do a somersault, but instead of landing on your feet, you land on your back.

Shockingly, I didn't stink up the joint this time. Sure, I barely made it over—but I made it over, and that's the main thing.

We were only thirty minutes in and I already had a pounding headache and sore, tender ribs.

"All right, that was bumps. We're going to drill them every week so you get them down perfectly. They're the most important things you'll do, so you need to be able to do them well."

Okay, no big deal that I didn't have them down perfectly yet. Lots of time to work on them. But also: *Fuck, I'll have to fall down lots to get the hang of this thing—and it really, really hurts.*

"Now I want you all to pick a partner and we're going to show you how to lock up," Paul continued.

My eyes searched eagerly for Richy, who was actively avoiding my stare and had already joined up with someone close to his size.

I had to be paired with a stranger.

"You go with him," Fergal said, pointing to Kenny, that tiny little flawless bumper.

Paul and Fergal demonstrated a perfect, aggressive-looking lock-up. Stomping their feet simultaneously as they locked arms.

"Anyone have any questions?"

"No!" several voices yelled.

Not that I was going to speak up anyway, but . . . *what did they just do? Which arm went where? What foot how?*

"How do we do this?" I meekly asked Kenny. Luckily, he was

kind as he guided my arms where they needed to go and showed me which foot to lead with.

I was abysmal at this, but it was exhilarating. I had never broken down the mechanics of what I had seen on TV. To be able to do that here, so that one day I might be able to have an actual wrestling match, was thrilling.

Not that I had any ambition to be in WWE. Like my brother had said of himself earlier, "I'm not a dreamer," and that would be such a faraway, lofty, exaggerated dream. I wanted to do something stable, like my mother. Maybe I could become a lawyer or something? Fight for the underdogs of life. You know, if I started studying and stopped smoking away my brain cells.

When the class was finished, we had learned how to bump, lock up, exchange a few holds, and even do a little demonstration match at the end.

Bad as I was, to my comfort—or at least I told myself—I wasn't the worst person there. Poor, gangly fucker.

Waking up the next day, my body was aching. My neck creaked from the repetitive whiplash, but I couldn't wait to get on the bus to school and tell my friends all about it.

I had found something that I loved. I wasn't good at it, but I wanted to be, and that seemed more important.

But now I had to look the part. Get jacked, stacked, ripped, lean, and mean. Gainzzzzzzzzz, baby! Except I didn't have a clue about nutrition. I only knew that jacked people drink protein shakes. So I bought my very first tub of protein powder. Bye-bye, flabville—muscletown, here I come.

I eagerly opened the white tub and gagged at the waft that followed. It smelled like a two-thousand-pound man who lived on a diet of eggs and moldy cheese had caged his farts into this powder substance I was about to consume. Pinching my nose and choking back the thick, gloopy beverage, I tried desperately not to vomit. There must be a better way.

I wanted shoulders and abs like my hero Lita, the spunky female spitfire I had watched busting out backflips on TV, but maybe not that badly yet.

I decided my best bet was to cut out my drinking and smoking and join in the fad at the time and stick with a low-fat diet, which would consist solely of bread, pasta, rice, and more bread. I was going to build a body from the gods, loaf by loaf.

STINGER

After I trained every weekend for two months, the day had finally come. I walked into the school hall, my eyes widened with disbelief to see what was before me: a real-life wrestling ring!

I had never seen anything more beautiful. Paul and Fergal were standing at the edge, arms draped casually over the top rope.

"Congratulations, lads. Today you get to see what a ring is all about," Fergal announced.

I was going to run the ropes in a wrestling ring. Like I had seen on TV. I couldn't stop smiling in anticipation.

But first things first, practicing our bumps. This time: in a ring!

We all lined up. The group's excitement was palpable. I stepped up onto the ring apron and threw my leg over the middle rope, envisioning myself as a long-legged Stacy Keibler. As I crotched myself on the second rope, I realized that probably wasn't the entrance for me.

Making my way to the center of the ring, flabbergasted I was here, I savored every footstep. It wasn't the crash pad I imagined it would be. While there was some amount of cushion under my feet and a spring in each step, it was by no means a soft landing. I took my first bump. The sound of my once-waiflike slaps had turned into slightly less waiflike-sounding slaps against the plywood and steel supporting my weight. This was fucking cool.

I exited the ring high on life, awaiting our next line of instructions.

Paul and Fergal demonstrated running the ropes. Being scared of looking funny when I ran was a large component in me failing PE. But this was different. This was in a wrestling ring. There was no amount of silly I wouldn't look for this thing. Even if it meant something like, I don't know, doing an embarrassing awkward Irish jig on my TV debut that would live on forever. I'm kidding; I would never sink *that* low.

"Three big steps, that's all it should take to clear the ring, pivot, back flat against the top rope, grip it with your right arm, big step out," Paul instructed.

Easy peasy. I got back in the ring, going over the bottom rope this time. *Three big steps*, I told myself.

I gripped the top rope with my right arm. Already off to a good start. Then came the footwork. I was more like a baby deer than a stealthy gazelle. I would take two to three steps to everyone else's one step. And pivoting was much easier said than done. I stumbled, tripped up over my own feet, and damn near fell flat on my face. What a rush!

One thing you may not have heard is the day after you've run ropes for the first time you get bruises all over your back and arms. No one is immune to this. Add in taking a few turnbuckles too and you look like a beaten-up peach.

At home, I forgot to hide this from my mother and sauntered downstairs in a string top.

"How did you get those marks on your back?" she asked.

"Emmm, well, ehhhhhh . . ."

I couldn't think of a lie quick enough, so I had to defer to the goddamn inconvenient, about-to-get-my-ass-in-trouble truth. I hadn't actually been practicing Brazilian jiu-jitsu as I told her weeks ago to explain my absence for four hours every Sunday. I was learning to be a wrassler.

There was an all-out war in Bayside that night. My mom thought wrestling was the lowest form of class in entertainment. Considering she couldn't even stomach watching it, there was no chance she could stomach her kids doing it. I should be more specific and say she couldn't stomach *me* doing it. In her defense, at the time it wasn't the most savory of sports to imagine your daughter getting into. The women were mostly treated like side pieces or sex objects. They weren't seen as the athletes and storytellers that we are today.

She didn't see the art that I did. She saw the bra and panties matches and mud-wrestling bouts that I vowed I would never participate in. Not that anyone would want to be looking at me getting rowdy in a pair of knickers anyway. There was nothing I could point to and show her: "That is what I want to do." Because, frankly, it didn't exist yet.

After a wailing and gnashing of teeth at each other, with me calling her a snob and her calling me underhanded and sneaky, we were able to meet at an appropriate talking volume.

"You lied to me."

"You wouldn't have let me do it."

"Is this what you want to be doing with your life?"

"It's not my career choice, Mom. I'm still going to college. I'm going to be a lawyer. I just love this. It's helping me get fit. I get along with everyone and it's keeping me focused."

"You could break your neck."

"I could do that with anything I chose to do. I could get hit by a car in the morning; that's no reason not to do something. We train so we can do it safely."

Wrestling *had* made me more focused and disciplined. It gave me goals and something to work towards. There's a saying that goes "How you do one thing is how you do everything," and that rang true here. I started doing better in school and eating better (or at least what I thought was better). Between wrestling, workouts, and studying harder, I had stopped partying with my friends. There was no more going out on weekends. I wanted to be fresh for wrestling on Sundays.

But of course it wasn't entirely without incident either.

The moves were getting more complicated and I was having a hard time picking them up. Luckily, with my growing comfort among the boys, I had no problem going again and again, trying to get it right. It didn't even dawn on me that I would be holding up the rest of the class. I just wanted to get better.

My brother was picking everything up effortlessly and had finally accepted that I wasn't going to quit.

Richy being so good came in handy, as did his natural ability to teach just about anything. Meaning he could spend time coaching me in our back garden as I attempted to drill various techniques.

My favorite move was a pinning maneuver, and the closest thing to high flying that we had learned so far. It was a crucifix into a sunset flip. You would duck under someone's arm when they were trying to hit you with a "clothesline," wrap both of your arms around their shoulder, and kick your legs so they would wrap around their other arm so it looks like a crucifix. With your legs secured, you would release your arms and drop your head between their legs, forcing them to fall backwards and allowing you to pin them. I must have practiced it over a hundred times in our back garden, eager to show off my improvement in class.

Sunday came and at the end of class I was paired up with someone new for practice matches. I wanted to finish with my new, super, high-flying finishing move. He threw a clothesline, I ducked, hooked a most beautiful crucifix, released my arms, and was heading down south to complete my pin.

Crack.

He didn't wait for me to tuck my head and sat straight on my head.

Oh no. This wasn't good. I sat down on the benches along the wall clutching my neck. I could still feel all my extremities, could still walk. I might make it. But I would probably have to get it checked out, only I couldn't tell my mom. She had literally *just* told me, "You could break your neck."

Last thing you ever want to do is affirm your parents' perfectly rational fears.

Luckily for me, my dad wasn't much of an alarmist, so the next day he picked me up and brought me to see one of his friends from the pub who was a sports doctor.

We entered the front door of a regular semidetached house in walking proximity to my dad's local pub. The front room had been converted to an office, with various certificates lining the wall, affirming the legitimacy of my dad's friend, even though I'm pretty sure he had just consumed a couple of pints at the local establishment.

Doctor: "What happened ya?"

Me: "A lad sat on my neck."

Doctor: "What he do that for?"

Dad: "She's training to be a wrestler!"

Doctor: "A what?"

Me: "A wrestler."

Doctor: "Like in the Olympics?"

Me: "No, a professional wrestler."

Doctor: "Are you getting paid?"

Me: "No, that's just what they're called."

Doctor: "Well, you're not a professional if they
     don't pay you."

Dad: "Well, not yet anyway!"

Doctor: "So you're an amateur wrestler."

Me: "No, that's what Olympic wrestlers are. Look, could you
     check out my neck?"

Doctor: "Oh yes, yes. Give us a look at you here."

After running a series of tests on me, he came to a diagnosis and said, "A stinger. Lots of rugby players get them. Basically, your vertebrae have been compressed. Would you consider rugby instead?"

Me: "I tried it once, didn't like it much. So am I going
    to be okay?"
Doctor: "Ah, you'll be grand; just rest it a bit now
    for a few days."
Me: "Thanks, Doc."
Doctor: "I suppose I'll be seeing you on the telly soon. . . ."

Crisis averted, my wrestling training would continue—and I was ready to take it to the next level.

THE HAMMERLOCK

Now, my mother is a religious woman, so God himself must have had a word with her—because against all hope she let me go to the wrestling summer camp held by Hammerlock in the UK that August. Being at camp gave us a chance to drill the sport day in, day out for a full week, with different instructors and varying styles. Thankfully, I had the guidance and protection of my brother to keep me in line.

We got off the train after a two-hour journey from the airport at Sittingbourne, Kent. Richy pulled out the directions he had written on a sheet of paper and led us down a shifty-looking alley until we came to an equally shifty-looking side door. There right in front of us was a wrestling ring that had most certainly seen better days. Like in '72, when it was probably new. We were in the right spot.

To the right of the ring was a bar, with about three or four small dark wooden tables in it. The room was filled with dodgy-looking geezers. The most dodgy-looking of them all was the owner, Andre Baker, like he had popped straight out of a Guy Ritchie movie and into this dingy gym. He was bald, short, and wide, covered in awful tattoos, with eyes that bulged out of his head like a pug's. Despite Andre's menacing look, there was a warmth and charisma to him. He was a dodgy geezer, but a nice dodgy geezer. The bar was for wrestlers only. I can't imagine Andre had a liquor license. But it allowed him to make some more money, and for all of the wrestlers to unwind after a day of practice, and no one was going to be snitching anyway, because Andre was an intimidating lad.

Hammerlock had been featured on a TV show called *Faking It*. The premise was that people from different walks of life would train under a certain discipline for four weeks. At the end of the show, they would show off their newly learned skills alongside three actual professionals in that chosen discipline.

To my fifteen-year-old self, anyone who appeared on it looked like an A-list celebrity.

As different roster members would pop in during the day, we would nudge one another as if John Cena himself had walked into the room. One was a tall, blond, strikingly handsome twenty-one-year-old guy who was jacked out of his mind. I had seen him on *Faking It* and was instantly in love. Or I thought he was hot—same difference at fifteen. Turned out he took a liking to me too. That or I was the only option, once again being the only girl in the camp.

After our first day of training, I spent the evening in the filthy side lane, flirting with the British stud. And after a few drinks from the bar and no reservations, we were making out in the middle of a roundabout up the road. I loved this camp! Not only was I getting to do the thing that I loved and improve at it, but for the first time in my life, attractive men were paying attention to me and I didn't even have to stalk them!

The days were long—nine hours of wrestling in a hot gym in the middle of summer with no air-conditioning. Sleeping on the mats or in the ring or under the ring, or, if you were really lucky, you'd get to sleep on the crash pad. After we'd been up until three or four in the morning drinking, our wake-up call came at 8:00 am in the form of a pit bull named Chester with the biggest pair of testicles I have ever seen on a mammal. Chester would come in bounding across our lifeless heads, teabagging anyone unlucky enough to have their mouth open.

Then the bright lights were turned on and it was time to head to the bar again. Only this time for small plastic cups filled with crappy instant coffee. Then to the mirror to see if anyone had shaved off your eyebrows in the middle of the night. Ribbing was alive and well in the NWA UK culture of wrestling.

Over the course of that one week, the class banded together to tie one lad up in red duct tape and hang him upside down like a giant fish as we posed for photos. I witnessed one guy shave his pubes and stuff them into another's open mouth while he was sleeping. The owner of a large bottle of cider left it unattended for a pee break, only to return and, after taking a large, satisfying swig, realize someone had taken a pee break in his cider bottle.

Thankfully, my brother and I returned home unscathed but exhausted. A full week of that schedule—combined with little more nourishment than some French fries from KFC and Dooley's toffee liqueur—hadn't exactly done our bodies a service. But my wrestling had improved dramatically.

I went back to school a few weeks later with all the excitement of a summer's worth of wrestling brimming in me, plus a newfound confidence that comes from dedicating yourself to a skill.

Even more exciting was that Paul and Fergal announced that we were going to have our very first wrestling show! In front of a real crowd. After wrestling for a little over six months, November 11, 2002, would be the date of my first show. My training was going to be kicked into high gear. My diet of bread and water would be strong—no veering off course now, Becky, the time has come!

As someone who had never really tried at anything in life, except maybe chasing boys, I found it was rewarding to learn that hard work does indeed pay off.

The week before the show, Paul and Fergal gathered the class to announce the card. We all stood around the ring eagerly waiting for our names to be called. Only when they got to the main event, my name hadn't been called.

I didn't get a match, and my consolation was to be a valet for my brother, who now went by the (awesome) name Gonzo de

Mondo. I didn't want to be a valet. I wanted to be a wrestler. And I'm sure my brother didn't necessarily want to babysit me in his debut match either.

I was, however, put in the commiseration battle royal. That's where they put the people who sucked. Along with almost everyone else—who'd already had matches—in an effort to fill out the numbers.

I was crushed.

I tried to reassure myself that it was just because I was the only girl. It might send a bad message to have a guy beating up a girl. But Chyna got to do it, damn it! And just a few more years of my brioche-based diet and I was gonna have muscles like her!

I had bought new baggy pants to wrestle in and was given a spot at the end of my brother's match where I would do a hurricanrana off the top rope (you jump and wrap your legs around the opponent's head and flip them over as you fall to the side) to his opponent in an effort to cost him the victory. I was just a blatant rip-off of Lita at this stage, just without the abs, shoulders, tattoos, or moonsaults—i.e., I was the "what comes in the mail" Lita, versus the "Instagram ad" Lita.

The day of the show, the audience of family and friends buzzed outside the curtain as we all got ready to go out and wow them with the best wrestling they had ever seen. I looked around at the congregation of young lads in tight booty shorts greasing themselves up with baby oil, making jokes as if they had done this before. Was no one else deathly afraid of what was beyond that curtain? Social rejection? Public humiliation?

As I questioned how I would fare should I have my own singles match one day, my brother was gearing up to make his entrance, as chill as if he were about to order a McDonald's Happy Meal. I, on the other hand, could feel my lunch starting to reappear at the bottom of my throat.

"I'm gonna be sick," I confessed right as the poorly played version of Richy's entrance music rang through the large peach-colored hall. You see, Fergal had asked his brother's "band" to play the entrance music for all the wrestlers that night. And by "band" I mean it was his brother on the drums and another lad with an untuned guitar attempting to play "Walk This Way" by Aerosmith.

My brother busted through the curtain nonetheless, swaggering confidently as if he was born to this. I tailed closely behind, hoping to pick up some charisma fumes that he might have left in his wake.

As I cheered generically at ringside, Gonzo wowed the crowd with his strength and finesse.

At last, it was time for my big moment. I hit my maneuver, not completely terribly. To put it any other way would be a lie. Kindly, the crowd went mad! It was enough for Gonzo to hit him with his finisher, the Demondo Driver!! *One, two, three!! It's all over!! So this is what winning feels like.*

But I still had to go out for this battle royal! Normally with a battle royal, the winner is decided when all other opponents have been tossed over the top rope, leaving one person standing alone in the ring, victorious.

The problem with the battle royal in this case, apart from being mostly filled with the class's rejects, was that we hadn't yet learned to go over the top rope. Considering that ineptitude, the stipulation became that if you landed on your back you would be eliminated from the match. It quickly became hard for the audience to understand, as the ring was crowded with awkward bodies pretzeled around each other. Several times people tripped or botched their own moves, landed on their backs, and would hop up hoping no one noticed. Everyone noticed. And no one was impressed.

I took a body slam from a larger gentleman and rolled outside unceremoniously with a certain amount of relief.

Battle royal aside, I was on a high. The thrill of performing, the fact that we had more than two hundred people in the crowd and they had actually cheered for me. For Becky with the belly like a sack of potatoes.

Wrestling was in my bloodstream now and it wasn't going anywhere.

I was now a professional wrestler. Sure, I hadn't made any money, but I was a performer and I couldn't wait for the next one.

This time, though, I wasn't going to settle for being a valet or being in a nonsensical battle royal, even if it meant I had to fight for it.

"I want a match," I told Paul.

"We just don't have any girls for you to wrestle, and I'm not sure it sends the right message."

"I work as hard as anyone," I pleaded.

"I'm not saying you don't; we just don't have any other women, Rebecca."

"That's not my fault, though. It's not fair that I won't get the chance to have a match because I'm the only girl."

Whether I hounded him just the right amount, or they were a person short, or the ghost of wrestling past visited Paul Tracey in his sleep, but he gave me my first real wrestling break by booking me in a tag match at the next show. He might as well have told me I was about to main event Monday Night Raw against "Stone Cold" Steve Austin for how much it meant to me.

However, as life goes—that is to say, all over the place—I ended up banging my head pretty badly taking a simple body slam early the day of the show during practice.

"I'm just going to go look at the trees for a second," I announced to the class as I stumbled outside, trying to figure out how I had gotten down there and what day of the week it was. *Where the hell am I?*

I started a full medical examination in the privacy of my own head.

What's your name?

Rebecca Mary Quin—born January 30, 1987.

Seeeee, I'm fine. I'm fine, guys. It's all good; I'm fine.

Where do you live?

Glasnevin. No, wait, that's not right! You moved—remember?
Oh yeah, where was that to again?! Sutton? Howth?

Bayside, you idiot!

Oh yeah yeah yeah. Cool. You're fine, Rebecca. Pick your chin
up and go inside and don't you tell a damn soul you're fucked-up.

There was no way I was going to let forgetting where I was come
between me and my big break.

Backstage, all of the lads were seasoned veterans now, with their
one match under their belts. I had begged and pleaded to get this
match and I wasn't about to be seen as the rookie with the soft head.
Show no weakness, I coaxed myself. And actually, my residual loop-
iness may have taken a bit of the edge off.

I was partnered with a big, burly man named Davey. A delightful
Dub with all the strength of a silverback gorilla. We were the good
guys (in wrestling terminology, the babyfaces).

Standing in the opposite corner was a heel (bad-guy) pairing of
posh, ginger boys. One being the tall, gangly guy I mentioned earlier.

Davey was the perfect partner for me. Tagging with him was how I
imagined it might be having a trained pet bear. I could taunt and rile up
my opponents and he would come in and maul them to pieces. When
they were incapacitated, he gorilla-pressed me and body-slammed me
onto the evil villains, eventually allowing me to pick up the victory as
the crowd gave this odd couple a big ol' standing ovation.

I had just done my first proper match. And I had proved I could
hang with the boys.

I wasn't very good, but the crowd didn't seem to care; they cheered
regardless. Whether it was out of pity or respect for this young girl
trying to hold her own with the lads, I felt like we had a connection.

It is that connection that would carry me further than I ever could
have possibly imagined later in my career.

HART ATTACK

Hammerlock had tours across the UK every February. They were considered a big deal, because not only would you get to wrestle every night for a week straight, but these tours also included a huge star, usually someone who had once wrestled for WWE. On this particular tour, Andre had booked Jim "The Anvil" Neidhart—a former WWE tag-team champion and one half of the Hart Foundation. One of WWE's greatest tag teams.

These tours didn't pay anything except priceless experience, but Andre thought it would be a good idea to have a match that represented the new affiliate, NWA Ireland.

Paul and Fergal were tasked with hand selecting two people who consistently put on the best matches and, naturally, my natural of a brother was picked, along with another trainee by the name of Carl.

"Can I come?" I asked my brother.

"No," he responded with zero hesitation.

"Please," I begged.

"No."

I can see why. I had literally hijacked his wrestling journey thus far—even down to him being saddled with me for his first match—but as you might see in this book, I am pretty good at finding my way into things.

I just wanted to learn and improve. To be immersed in the wrestling world and take every opportunity given. Even if those opportunities weren't necessarily given to me. Really, I was just like Robin Hood. Stealing from the opportunity rich (Richy) to give to the opportunity poor (me). I tagged along like a nagging injury.

I even somehow wrangled my way onto the card and valeted for Fergal and Paul. Of course this time I took no offense to being a valet, knowing I was already pushing my luck being there. Plus, who knew when a bigger opportunity might pop up.

Turns out it wouldn't be long. On the last day of the tour I got booked in a six-person tag-team match! I was scheduled to team up with Fergal and Paul, to take on the dastardly team of Danny Williams, Ciara Wilde, and *Jim "The Anvil" Neidhart*!!!!

At sixteen years old and with eight months of wrestling experience, I was going to be facing a WWE superstar. Only problem was, I didn't know what the hell I was doing.

At the beginning of the match all three of us attacked Jim. In my haste, I kicked him square in the kneecap, sending his giant ham of a leg twisting in the wrong direction. Out of rightful fear of losing an ACL, he gave me a firm shove, scolding me in his thick American accent, "You don't kick people like that!" with a voice that came from the very pit of his diaphragm.

All my excitement turned to mortification as I slunk back and rested by the ropes, hoping I wouldn't mess anything else up or injure anyone else. My first real opportunity and I had nearly kneecapped the star of the show.

The match ended and I rushed shamefully to the back and awaited Jim to return so I could apologize profusely for nearly putting him in the hospital.

Thankfully, he had calmed down in the short walk from ring to curtain. As he came through, a massive pile of red flesh covered in sweat and hair, I timidly approached.

"Sir, I'm so sorry. I didn't mean to hurt you."

"Oh, honey," he said in his sweetest dad voice. "That's okay. Let me show you how you hit people."

He took me to the side out of view of everyone.

"You see the leg doesn't bend that way, so you're better off hitting here—like this."

Despite his colossal frame, he gave me a club to the back that felt like I was hit by a marshmallow.

My fear of him blacklisting me dissipated. Thank god, because this week had been a blast and I couldn't wait to get at it again.

It was a turf war. A battle for dominance. Like Springfield versus Shelbyville in *The Simpsons*. We were the first school and promotion on the block. For someone else to come in and try to purloin our market was downright treachery.

We were NWA Ireland. The OG. The first.

They were Irish Whip Wrestling (IWW). The imposters. The frauds. The promotion for the Dublin bitches who didn't have the balls to take the train down to Bray to learn how to become real professional wrestlers. And I hated them. I hated what they stood for. I hated their stupid name and everyone who wrestled for them.

Even worse, I hated that they were running their first show in my school hall! A crime akin to treason in most parts of the world. They may as well have walked up to my house, opened the windows and doors, and had every one of their "wrestlers" piss on the furniture.

And more than that, these frauds had the audacity to bring American and Canadian wrestlers over to promote their show as if they were a bigger deal than they were. (You leave Jim Neidhart out of this!)

Of course the perception in Ireland that anyone from America was somewhat of a big deal was alive and well in the early 2000s—still plugging away from the auld success of Bill Clinton where the fascination of all things USA was at a fever pitch. Canada, naturally, got the rub, 'cause who can even tell the difference?

In an act of sheer spite, masked in faux support, a band of us Springfield folk went to the show to check out our competition, ready to scoff at their shabby attempts to woo a crowd or slap on a proper wristlock.

We got there early to make sure we got the good seats, so they could hear us yell our overly enthusiastic cheers and mess with their heads. Were we genuine? Was this mockery? No one could accuse us for certain. But let there be no qualms about it. This was an infiltration.

The show started. The sleazy ring announcer came out looking like an evil circus master ready to announce his stars for the night.

Unfortunately for us, these fuckers actually had potential.

The first match of the night included a man named Joe Cabray, who had biceps akin to Hulk Hogan's twenty-four-inch pythons. What was a kid like this doing in a promotion like that? Didn't he want to come and train with the real wrestlers? The good wrestlers? The tough wrestlers?

Sure, some of our lads had some muscles. But some of their lads were mostly muscles, with heads popping out of their thick necks.

One such muscle-bound freak—six-three, so pale he was practically transparent, with hair as orange as a clementine—went by the name of Sheamus O'Shaunessy.

We scoffed at the pure Irishness of it. Like he was trying to get Vince McMahon's attention all the way from this school hall with the two hundred people in attendance.

"Pffft. As if. Bet he can't work for shit," we sneered as if we were the authority on working, regular Dean Malenkos we thought we were.

We quickly shut up as we watched him club the ever-living shite out of some poor young fella. Knowing full well that if this Sheamus fella did stick to it, he would be snapped up by WWE in a heartbeat. *What a sellout.*

I also got to take a look at my direct competition. Much like I was the only female in NWA Ireland, they also had their token lady, a tiny, thick woman by the name of Alex Breslin. I detested her. It was primal. The audacity of her to compete in my town. I was the only girl wrestler in Ireland. This was my land. My kingdom. Who did she think she was? I was going to take her down here and now the only way I knew how. With fake kindness.

I cheered for her with everything in my body lest it be known that I was seething with jealousy.

She'll never make it, I thought to myself. *She doesn't have the toughness.*

This island wasn't big enough for both of us. Only one of us could make it. And it sure as fuck wasn't going to be her.

Their main event was their trainer Blake Norton—a "Canadian" Simon had brought in to try to take down our promotion (or at least that's how we looked at it)—versus another Canadian superstar by the name of Scotty Mac. A jacked and tanned pretty boy who had more real-life charisma than any other human being I had ever seen in my life up until that point. As it turned out, Blake Norton wasn't actually Canadian. He had just gone to train in Calgary for the guts of six weeks and came back with a Canadian accent. He was quickly exposed for not actually being as experienced as he had claimed once IWW began to run shows and established wrestlers uncovered how bad he was.

When the show was over, we stuck around to introduce ourselves as the competition we were. Clearly, our fake niceness was confused for real niceness, as Scotty even invited me to the after-party that night.

Sure, I'll cavort with the enemy. Let this ignorant Canadian know the error of his ways. He's just talent for hire. He doesn't know that he could have, in fact, been wrestling for the greatest wrestling company in all of Ireland. You know, if we had money to pay him. Or anyone, in fact. But that didn't matter. It was the principle!

But my principal interest was now in making a new Canadian friend—who would genuinely become a great friend over the next few years.

I sat in a brightly lit white locker room on a green bench. There was an overarching smell of sweat, mildew, and Lynx spray deodorant wafting around the concrete walls.

It had been two years since my first training session, and finally I was starting to feel like I knew what the hell I was doing.

My brother and I had just teamed up, playing the villains against a happy-go-lucky duo. And for the first time it didn't feel like Richy was saddled with me. We were two equals, doing what we do well. The small Kildare crowd berated us and yelled insults. One old lady tried to hit me with her bag that allegedly concealed a brick. We were rocking.

Elbows on my knees, I looked down at my makeshift gear of neon-blue shorts, pink fishnets, and luminous pink tank top. I didn't have the money or means to get proper gear made, so whatever obnoxious clothing I could find in thrift stores became my wrestling attire.

I looked up at my brother sitting across from me.

"This is what I want to do for the rest of my life. I want to make a career out of this."

"So do it."

"I will."

This felt like destiny.

I had denied that I wanted to make a living out of the sport since I began. It seemed like such an absurdly ambitious goal. That this unimpressive, unathletic girl from Ireland could actually earn money from wrestling. If WWE at the time was anything to go by, the odds were already stacked against me. But I wouldn't know unless I tried.

At seventeen, I finally accepted that I was, indeed, a dreamer. I found something I was good at and I was getting better at by the week. I could change the game. I was the one to do it—I knew it in my heart of hearts.

I didn't tell anyone except my brother. The fear of failure, being judged, having to listen to all the opinions on why I wouldn't make it was far too great. My mom would have lost her shit. My dad would have been encouraging, but to quote the man himself, "If you talk too much about your dreams, they get lost in the wind."

I had to make sure I made it. My dad was a dreamer who never did. None of his dreams ever came into being. I couldn't be that. But maybe his dreams did just get lost in the wind.

Even in my own wrestling gym, I was surrounded by certain dreamers daily—the ones who talked about how they were going to be the biggest thing in wrestling. They were going to move to America and train with ["insert legend X" here]. But they would never so much as lift a dumbbell. When they wore a tank top, it looked like two noodles dangling out of the armholes.

No, sir. I had to be the dreamer who did.

I did go to college, but it was only to make my mom happy and get free access to a well-stocked gym. I had no interest in studying or making friends or anything that related to college life. I had already done my partying years earlier, and now I was fixated on delayed gratification—as opposed to the instant kind found at the bottom of a keg.

I couldn't wait until the October school break. While everyone was excited to get their Halloween costumes sorted, I was busy looking for more wrestling costumes.

I was going back to tour in the UK.

Only I wasn't tagging along this time: I had been invited.

I had shown enough promise, despite nearly taking out Jim Neidhart, that Andre even allowed me to stay at his house during the tour, with Paul and Fergal. Every day we would get up and train, drive to a new town or city, wrestle, and drive back to his home that night.

I had picked out the new, rather generic name of Rebecca Knox and was honing my skills as a heel, working every night in a mixed tag-team match in front of rambunctious crowds.

On the drives and in between shows, I was getting to know Fergal better. He had, in the space of a week, gone from mentor and trainer to friend.

We chatted about life and wrestling, and everything in between. We would go for walks and shop together. He was the perfect combination of thoughtful, insightful, passionate, creative, and hilarious, all wrapped up in a beautiful bundle with perfectly chiseled abs.

I know what you're thinking. *Sounds like you were falling for him, Becky?* Noooooo, I wasn't falling for him. Not me, not the wrestler formerly known as "Becky with the belly like a sack of potatoes."

But there was a connection; surely there was a connection. Okay, maybe I *was* falling for him. But I buried it deep down in my soul and maybe secretly wrote "Becky ♥ Fergal" in a diary entry or two.

On the final night of the tour we had returned to Andre's and were served up pizza as a postwrestling treat. I was never one to turn down pizza, but this was vegetable pizza. Who on earth orders vegetables on their pizza? Up until this point I had only ever had a plain cheese, or cheese and pepperoni, or on the odd occasion ham and pineapple when I was feeling spicy. But never vegetables. *Why* for all that is good and sacred would you ruin something so delicious by throwing a bunch of healthy crap on top of it?!

Anyway, while I picked mushrooms off my tasty cheese-bread, there was a knock on the door. *Strange*, I thought, considering it was now close to 3:00 am.

Andre opened the door to a stringy, disheveled man with long, black hair and a large hooknose. As the man moved shiftily into the living room he explained why he didn't have Andre's money.

Wait, what?! Money for what?! What's going on here?! I asked silently with curiosity, though I dared not make a peep.

"What 'appened to your friend when he didn't 'ave my money?" Andre asked, ominously calm.

He got an extension? I answered in my head, curiosity now turning to nervousness.

The hooknosed man mumbled something inaudible.

"I said, what 'appened to your friend?" Andre repeated himself, voice raised.

I stared wide-eyed at the congealed mushrooms I had picked

off my pizza, now lying derelict in the grease-stained box. I feared that soon this man would meet a fate unbearably similar to that of the picked-off mushrooms.

"He got kneecapped, didn't he?" Andre prompted helpfully.

Maybe "kneecapped" means something different in England. Maybe he got cute little hats to keep his knees warm.

Inner monologue aside, I instinctively grabbed Fergal's arm to the right of me.

"Yeah . . . he did, didn't he? Now, what's stopping me from having these two boys 'ere 'old you down an' I snap every one of ya fingas?"

Eh, morality? Conscience? Catholic guilt? The law? Dear Lord, let something stop you! My mind racing, I instinctively grabbed Paul's arm to the left of me.

The hooknosed man was now visibly shaking. As was I, feeling like two tectonic plates had collided in the localized area of my seat cushion while I imagined the forthcoming wails and accompanying crunching of breaking bones. I was not ready to be an accessory to a crime.

Luckily, Andre granted this degenerate some grace and he had until Monday to come up with the money, and I do hope he came up with the money. But by then, I was safely home in Ireland.

The wrestling business had its ugly side too and I had unwittingly witnessed it firsthand. The message I took was keep your head down, focus on the love of the sport, and maybe avoid staying at the promoter's house.

THE DECISION

If I was going to drop out of college to pursue my wrestling career, the perfect time would be when my mother was halfway across the planet, so she couldn't yell at me.

Luckily for me, that exact opportunity arose in January 2005 when she and Chris took a trip to Australia to visit my stepbrother.

To reassure her, I told her that I would switch college courses, maybe to something more sports related, seeing as I had miraculously become some version of an athlete in the last two years. But while I'm waiting, I may as well get some life experience, make some towns, see if there's hope for me beyond the borders of my wee island.

But where? America or Canada? Both had plush wrestling scenes and America had the biggest promotions in the world.

Wrestling in Japan had become my ultimate goal. In contrast to American wrestling, where women had a substantial history of being treated as side acts or sex objects, Japanese promotions showcased their women as the performers and fighters they were. I only owned one Japanese women's wrestling VHS tape but it was my most coveted possession: a golden chalice of plastic and metal containing the outline to my future. The women were better than any man I had seen. They were high flyers and they hit hard and fast. I had no idea if I could ever come close to their abilities, but I sure as hell wanted to try. However, I had no clue where to start. Plus, I didn't speak the language. So that brought me back to my first two options.

Getting a visa for America was harder, and realistically, going over there on my own and not knowing anyone, having just turned eighteen, seemed a bit scarier, what with all the guns and all.

I didn't really know anyone in Canada either, but I had met Scotty Mac at the IWW show a year earlier, when he had spent much of the evening boasting of the wealth and popularity of promotions in British Columbia.

And if things really went south, I had a cousin who lived on Vancouver Island. Sure, I had only met him once when I was twelve, but family is family.

Vancouver was a go! With this bedrock foundation of two people I barely knew.

I was determined to make something of myself.

If I didn't succeed by the end of the year, I would come back and go to college as I had promised my mom.

With time running out before leaving for the adventure of a lifetime, I began saying my goodbyes to all my friends and family who had offered me eighteen years of memories. I felt like the more final I made this, the more pressure I put on myself, the more likely I would be to make it.

There were three days left when I met up with Fergal in town to say goodbye. After all, I wouldn't have even had this dream if it hadn't been for him opening the school in Bray. We had been getting closer and closer ever since the UK tour where we almost became accessories to a crime. We would talk about wrestling and our ambitions, knowing that we wouldn't get to where we wanted by staying in Ireland. We had to take risks, travel, go out on a limb, put ourselves out there.

And I suppose as we laughed and flirted all day around town, we were putting ourselves out there. Just in a different way. After four hours of fun and anticipatory butterflies had passed, it was that terrible time of day when we were due back to our respective homes in their separate directions. As we stood at the train station and I looked to the electric board above, warning me of the four minutes I had left to make a move or be doomed to travel to the Pacific Northwest with a suitcase full of what-ifs, I went for it right there, kissing him in the middle of Dublin's busiest station, my knees almost buckling with glee.

But now that I had love on the brain, the *last* thing I wanted to do was leave!

The time that was meant to be dedicated to packing and preparing was promptly replaced by going on hikes and sitting at the beach, gazing into each other's eyes, sharing those loving tender moments that leave a lingering sense of magic in the air as young love does. The need to leave and the desire to stay pulled me with equal force as if I might split in half. Yet at the same time it felt like everything I could ever want in life was happening.

I now had a boyfriend I had once thought was way out of my league. I was about to travel to do the thing I adored more than anything and take a massive leap of faith.

I knew I was on the brink of something big. I was terrified but kept thinking, *It will either be a great adventure or a great story, but either way, it might make a decent memoir one day.*

THE JOURNEYMAN

My mom saw me all the way to the gate at the airport. She cried; I cried.

"Are you sure you have to leave? You don't have to go. You don't have to do this, you know."

"I do, Mom; I have to do this." The part of me that wanted to stay was now being decimated by the dreamer.

Looking back now, I can't imagine the bravery it took for my mom to let her often-reckless daughter go across seas to pursue the unknown. But in regards to raising children she had always said, "Give them roots and give them wings." And I was about to fly. Both literally and figuratively.

My brother had passed me an envelope to open on the flight.

"Don't read it until you're in the air," he instructed, and I dared not dishonor his word. I took my middle seat, unpacked my Discman, books, and journal for the flight. Once I was airborne and my ears had popped, I took out his note.

It was a sketch he had done of me from when I was maybe six or seven years old. On the back he wrote how far this kid had come and how much further she was going to go and reminded me, above all else, to keep my integrity.

He even enclosed a fifty-euro bill, though he didn't have much money himself. Again the tears streamed down my face. Knowing I had his support and belief in me felt like I was wearing a parachute. Either I would be able to achieve everything I set out to do or I'd float back home safely on the love he had always given me.

Despite the fact that Richy was twenty times the wrestler I was, he never wanted to pursue it as a career. He was a fine artist, and that was what he wanted to dedicate his life to. But without him, his love for wrestling, and his patience in helping me, this journey would have never begun.

As I stepped onto the jet bridge in Vancouver the heat of the summer hit me like a left hand to the face. I had that cactus-like prickly feeling you get from traveling so long, and I felt further exhausted from being up chatting with my new boyfriend, Fergal, the night before I left.

I stood in the long immigration line, waiting to be questioned.

I always feel mildly criminal as I walk up to the booth, where some stern lady or man is there to ask me about all of my evil plans to destroy Gotham City—or Vancouver, as the case may be. And suddenly I'm afraid I've somehow accidentally smuggled a honey-glazed ham into my luggage. As I stutter over my answers, becoming increasingly clammy and anxious, I'm aware of every side eye and lingering moment on the computer.

Lo and behold, I escaped through, imaginary ham and all, and proceeded to the baggage claim, where upon luggage collection I would meet my future roommates whom I acquired online. Fergal joked that they could be serial killers, which, ya know, was funny in that it-could-be-true kind of way. Luckily for me, it appeared they were not, as they greeted me with smiling faces and hugs while they led me to their car.

I could have ended up anywhere, because research wasn't my forte at this point in my life—or, I suppose, at any point in my life. But somehow I had landed myself in Kitselano, a ritzy, safe part of the city. We pulled up and walked down to a basement apartment that was bereft of light and contained only a minimal amount of furniture. It was the perfect humble abode for yours truly for the next twelve months.

I woke up the next morning ready to explore my new surroundings, smiling to myself all the while. My roommates hadn't killed me in my sleep and the world was my oyster! *Everything is coming up Becky!* I thought in my best Milhouse voice.

As I walked up the street to get groceries, my head was bobbing from side to side, in the manner that one does when they are full of joy, gratitude, hope, and new love. It felt like anything was possible, like I was going to achieve every aspiration I had ever summoned, like the universe, or God, or whoever is in charge of all of this was setting me up for a win.

My cousin, Kev, even happened to be in town that day. His positivity reminded me of my dad's, and Kev loved the idea of chasing a dream. An immigrant himself, he had come to Canada some twenty years earlier. Now he was married with a kid, a fine big house, and a respectable job.

Though there was a large age gap between Kev and me, one big enough that he could credibly be my father, we were kindred spirits: a couple of renegades who had left the nest in search of the promised worms.

It was a few days before I discovered the location of the wrestling school of the promotion Scotty Mac had raved about. Making my way by train, bus, and foot and trekking through a new transportation system proved treacherous. It rained as if it thought it was Ireland, the bottoms of my pants were soaked, and my mascara ran down my cheeks.

I eventually rocked up to the door, looking like an insane Irish banshee that had followed Scotty across the pond. He surely must have been startled. But Canadians will be Canadians, so I was welcomed with open arms as he immediately invited me to join the class, rain-soaked pants and all.

I instantly felt bonded to the other trainees as we rolled around exchanging holds and techniques. It was as if I had found my new wrestling family, which was confirmed as they invited me for lunch at Subway.

Over footlongs and Diet Cokes, I listened to stories about the promotion's most notorious characters. With names like Ladies' Choice, El Phantasmo, and Moondog Manson, I couldn't wait to meet these people, and I wouldn't have to wait long. They had a show coming up that weekend, which they were certain they could get me booked on.

ECCW didn't have many women, which was common at that time, but there was one lady I could wrestle, although everyone described her as "the drizz" (short for "drizzling shits," i.e., bad, real bad). Challenge accepted. A goal of mine (which I still have) is that I want to make anyone I share a ring with look good. That, to me, is the mark of a truly seasoned professional wrestler. It is what all the greats do remarkably well. Ric Flair, John Cena, Seth Rollins.

It is doubly important to me, with women's wrestling still in its infancy in terms of favorable positioning, and thus I believe it is my duty to enhance everyone with whom I step in the ring, so that the sport can continue to grow.

With this mindset, or just my exuberant existence, I was booked. I was about to make my Canadian debut.

Scotty Mac collected me from the train station in his rusted burgundy pickup truck. His white teeth gleamed as he smiled, contrasted against his equally burgundy skin. While most wrestlers used sun beds, Scotty could often look like he lived in one. He was a twenty-seven-year-old pretty boy, with spiked-up golden hair and a perfectly formed physique, and he ruled the Vancouver wrestling scene.

We cruised along to Bridgeview Hall, the location of my debut. Scotty Mac did the rounds, greeting everyone and making sure I was introduced, like he was the "King of ECCW" that he was.

With pro wrestling having had much deeper roots in the culture of Canada than Ireland, it was a departure from the younger scene I was used to. Most of these people were full-grown men, with full-grown muscles and full-grown mustaches, and had years of experience in the biz.

The wrestlers were as welcoming here as they had been at the school. Ladies' Choice had already captivated me with his raspy voice, long blond hair, and golden tan. The guy looked like he was straight out of a 1970s porno, in the best possible way. He jested about my future opponent's inexperience, making me feel like we already had inside jokes and were the best of pals. Yep, he was the "Ladies' Choice" indeed.

About an hour after I arrived, I noticed a woman with an enthusiastic face, attached to a platinum-blond headful of hair, come bounding through the front door. This was the famous Miss Chevius.

I was almost disappointed in how she had been sold. I expected a sea urchin who had crawled out of a rock cavity and into the ring, ready to put my skills to the test. What I found was a gorgeous and polite young woman who was eager to work and have a good match. As we talked ideas, I consulted the journal full of wrestling spots I had written down over the years and slotted in her move set, then mine, and kept it simple.

When the time came for us to go out for our match, the whole roster congregated at the curtain in delightful anticipation of a potential disaster.

After all, they hadn't seen me work. I could have been "the drizz" too.

The crowd applauded Miss Chevius like the local hero she was—before I, the cocky, brash, shrill heel interrupted their party—as they showered me with a chorus of boos.

The crowd, clearly regulars, was excited by this new, foreign face before them—but stayed loyal to their hometown girl, willing her to whup that arrogant, alien ass.

After much back-and-forth and a valiant attempt by Miss Chevius, I eventually stole the win, boasting all the way to the back. My music, MC Hammer's "Can't Touch This," played as I sang along—having proved that you could not, in fact, touch this.

As I Hammertimed through the curtain, I was met with a round of applause from the rest of the ECCW roster.

"That was great!" enthused Scotty Mac.

"Best match I've seen her have," Ladies' Choice added.

"Good job, kid," Michelle Starr, the booker, said, impressed.

My first outing and I hadn't stunk up the joint. Things were off to a hot start. As I began to take my boots off Starr slipped me an envelope. "It will be bigger next time."

I opened it to see thirty dollars. He might as well have handed me $1 million. After spending three years paying to wrestle, I was finally making money. All told, I would do it for free. Anything more was a bonus.

I quickly became a regular at the training school and shows. My pay almost doubled to fifty dollars. But even with this great surge in wealth, Vancouver was expensive and it was hard to get by. Not to mention, I spent most of my money on calling cards to talk to Fergal back home as our long-distance relationship continued to blossom. I relied on a tub of protein and a bag of oats to keep me fed, essentially living like a juiced-up racehorse.

But if I wanted to keep a roof over my head, I was going to have to do the unthinkable. I was going to have to get a real day job.

My roommate got me a job at a telesales company in downtown, raising money for charity, so it didn't seem so soul sucking. Though bonuses *were* handed out to whoever had raised the most money, which seemed counterintuitive.

Aren't we doing this for charity? Shouldn't they get the money? Is it wrong to solicit for charity if it is for personal gain? I pondered with one foot already out the door.

After the third day, I was given a talking-to for not raising enough cash. I wasn't pushy enough, apparently. But forcing people to give away money they might not have or want to give away—knowing that it was for my own financial profit—seemed a bit seedy and more soul sucking than I initially thought.

Later that day, I rang someone who clearly didn't want to be bothered but was Canadianly polite enough to engage.

"Time to put my pushy pants on!" I relented to my orders.

Rebuttal one: "Now's not a good time."

Rebuttal two: "I said it's really not a good time."

I, not taking no for an answer, pushed a third time, to which the lady exclaimed, "My husband just died!" and slammed down the phone.

That was it for me. I walked out at lunch and never went back, forgoing my check. Now I had an even greater hunger to make a living out of wrestling. Of course, hunger wasn't going to pay the rent, and I had to leave my cushy basement apartment that had afforded me shelter and convenience for a solid two months.

Realizing this, Scotty kindly allowed me to move into his house in Surrey. Which he had appropriately named the MacMansion. My room had nothing but a mattress on the floor, but it beat sleeping on the actual floor or a park bench.

GET THE TABLES

After just one month of working with ECCW, Starr approached me to let me know that things had been going so well that they were going to put on an all-female show—branded as SuperGirls. Of course, it couldn't be a two-hour iron-man match with me and Miss Chevius, and there weren't many other women on the scene, bar a couple of new trainees. So they would have to fly women in from all over Canada and America.

Feeling like I was the nucleus of essentially a new promotion would have blown my mind—if I hadn't somehow generated a strong belief in myself in the last few years.

What's more, Starr informed me, I was about to become their first champion and I was about to win my first championship— defeating Miss Chevius for the honor.

Elated by the fact that I had finally made it, I was presented with the most horrendous-looking title belt ever made, with all due re-spect to WWE's 24/7 title. It had your standard silver hard plate, but it was mounted on a furry, albeit partially matted, zebra-print strap, looking like something you'd find in between couch cush-ions after years of neglect, congregating with popcorn kernels and lost pennies. But I was going to wear that sucker proudly like the main eventer I was about to become.

Several days before the big event, as if things weren't already on the most exhilarating trajectory, I got an email from a wrestler called Sumi Sakai. We had worked on the same show once and she had graciously taken my contact information. I stared bug-eyed at the screen, mouth agape in sheer disbelief. A friend of hers was looking for foreign female talent for his new all-Japanese women's promotion.

This can't be real, could it? No way can a real-life Japanese promotion be looking to book me? After only a mere few months of betting on myself?! What in all of the universe's great power is this sorcery?!

I snapped back to the present, reading the contents of the email:

Wrestling promotion called "International Women's Grand Prix" showcasing female champions from all over the world.

Though Japan was an entirely different entity, all-female promotions had begun to blow up the world over. Likely due to the lack of actual women's wrestling on mainstream television, leaving a gaping hole in the market for female athletes who could actually go.

Truth be told, I didn't care much about whether the promotions were all-female or not. I just wanted to be seen as a great wrestler in my own right, gender be damned. And I didn't care whether there was one women's match or ten. I just wanted to be great.

Back in ECCW, it was time for the debut of SuperGirls. Starr even got me a new luminous pink leather strap for my belt. Talent was brought in from all over. Many of the girls had much bigger names and followings than I did, and way more experience. One such name was that of Natalya Neidhart, the daughter of Jim Neidhart, whom I had nearly kneecapped two years earlier. Nattie, who came from the most legendary family in all of pro wrestling—the Hart family—was just about the friendliest person you could ever meet.

What's more is she was also going to be part of the International Women's Grand Prix in Japan in November.

Despite the experiential edge that most of the SuperGirls roster had over me, shockingly I did not feel out of place. And not just because most of the women were as lovely as Nattie, but contrary to how I started my journey in this business, I had all the confidence in the world. I thought I was the best and only getting better, and was out to prove it. No one could match me in technical finesse, sheer charisma, or swag.

Years later, I would wish I could return to this confidence and, well, arrogance, but for now, I was owning every second of my brilliance on this all-lady show. Well, mostly all-lady show. Scotty Mac was my valet to the ring that night.

In a world where hot women are usually the accompaniment to the top male superstars, it felt quite poetic for this female champ to have a smoldering side piece walk her into battle. My formidable opponent for the night was named LuFisto. She was a tiny French Canadian hard-core wrestler who had made her name by going toe-to-toe with some of the toughest men on the continent.

We decorated our match with hard-hitting strikes and suplexes on the concrete floor, going all out to try to make this match feel worthy of a main event, regardless of gender.

I had hit her with everything I had, but it wasn't enough to keep the good woman down. Reaching my wits' end, I ordered Scotty Mac to hoist a table into the ring.

While I distracted the ref, Scotty superkicked LuFisto through the table, allowing me to pick up the win and escape with my title still intact.

I had won my first main event. I felt at home there. The show was a considerable success. I say "considerable" considering it was only considered a success by the considerably small crowd in attendance. I hadn't changed the business—not yet anyway—but every journey to change starts with small steps in the right direction.

I was also about to move in a new direction geographically. After successfully defending my title, I was leaving the floors of the MacMansion and shipping off to a new home in the wilderness on Vancouver Island.

Because I was making so little and struggling to stay above-board, my cousin Kev invited me to live with him, his wife, Loretta, and their eight-year-old daughter, Courtney, rent-free, while I pursued my dream.

The house was big and beautiful, overlooking the ocean, giving views you'd see on a postcard, and from time to time you might see an orca pop its head up from the water. It was a little slice of heaven and far from sleeping on floors or in the dark little basement apartment that I had become accustomed to.

Kev and Loretta took me in with open arms, asking nothing in return, except maybe for me to pick Courtney up from school from time to time if either of them was working.

I liked the exercise and I loved Courtney and there wasn't much else to occupy my time on the island. With all this free time I began to train like a complete and utter maniac twice a day in a small spit-and-sawdust gym about a twenty-minute walk from their house.

Loretta, who just so happened to be a former bodybuilder, helped dial in my nutrition by writing up a diet for me and spent the evening cooking us all healthy culinary masterpieces.

I really had landed on my feet.

And everything was gearing me up to being a full-time professional wrestler.

CUSTOMS

Fergal had family in Boston, so in early October 2005 he moved in with them while he pursued wrestling stateside. With our relationship still blossoming, I flew down to Boston to stay with him at the end of the month. The autumn air was crisp and his new, quaint Massachusetts neighborhood gave off a sense that Michael Myers could pop out of a bush at any moment. Fergal had gotten in with NWA New England, and thus I was welcomed aboard the roster also. Female wrestlers were sparse and hard to come by. Even more so if they were half-decent, allowing me to get booked on shows easier than most.

After spending a week in Boston with Fergal's family, we flew down to Florida to meet up with Lexie Fyfe, whom I had met at a wrestling show a year or so ago. Lexie was a short, stocky lady who had been wrestling for many years and looked like an all-purpose human, as if she could do anything from wrestling an alligator to fixing a drainpipe to saving a cat from a burning building.

She was eager to share her knowledge of the business with us youngins. She ran what were called customs, a shady part of our business. A client with, say, a certain proclivity would message Lexie with a request for a specific type of match (for example, a barefoot match) or working a specific type of hold (for example, the midsection) and they would pay a hefty fee for the service. Lexie would then find wrestlers to facilitate said request, tape it, and send it on to the consumer. Odd, yes. But a quick way to make a buck for a struggling wrestler.

My naivety at the time allowed me to believe that it was an easy way to get paid to do what I loved and there was nothing perverse about it. In reality, it was a fetish site. And hey, man, whatever floats your boat and doesn't sink mine is A-okay with me. But this was definitely not what I set out to do—and I would wager this was the kind of stuff my mother would dread when the concept of professional wrestler was brought her way.

For me, I got to wrestle; it didn't matter the means. Sure, it was barefoot, with holds being applied to my belly, in a warehouse with no fans, but I was substantially richer leaving than when I got there, allowing me to do the thing I loved even longer. Looking back now, I shudder; however, it would be rare to find a struggling independent wrestler who hasn't done their fair share of customs.

Before our trip to Florida had ended, Lexie and her husband generously gave us our first Disney World experience. We got to chatting about the future of the business and where our ambitions would take us.

"I want to wrestle in Japan, maybe NWA TNA; they have a great women's division," I said, glowing with possibility.

"What about WWE?" Lexie questioned.

"I don't think that's for me," I dissented.

"Yeah, they don't want girls like us; they want fluff," Lexie affirmed.

Fuck that, was my first thought. *They would want me if I wanted them to want me.* The contrarian in me rose up, without any probability for cause whatsoever.

Lexie wasn't trying to be offensive; in a way, she was being complimentary. She was saying that I was a wrestlers' wrestler, like her, and in fact, she was very right. I was nothing special from a physical standpoint. I was a little soft, with a fairly decent set of arms; my face looked not totally awful when you put a bit of makeup on it, but nothing you'd put in or on a magazine; and certainly I wasn't filling out anything past an A cup.

I hadn't even wanted to go to WWE based on their treatment of women.

But now that I was challenged and told I couldn't make it, I wanted to change the whole damn industry.

If there is one thing that fires me up more than anything, it's being told that I can't do something or I'm not good enough. As much as I doubt myself from time to time, or even most of the time, the rebellious spirit in me thrives on a challenge.

Once I had gotten out of Ireland and was gaining confidence wrestling in different places, it never crossed my mind that I "wouldn't" be wanted somewhere, even if it was WWE. I truly believed so much in myself that I thought I could go anywhere.

I boarded my Japan Airlines flight in Vancouver, meeting Nattie at the gate. For all the confidence I had amassed in North America, uncertainty met me at that gate like an old pal.

My dream was to wrestle in Japan like all of my heroes. *What if I'm not ready? What if it's too soon? What if I fuck it up and fall flat on my face? What if I can't keep up?* Sure, I felt like I was the best female wrestler on my circuit, but the women over there were on a different level.

I wrote in my journal endlessly for the duration of the twelve-hour flight to Narita Airport, trying to give myself pep talks and reminding myself it would all be okay. When the fear would begin to cripple me, I would look at the time left on the flight and say to myself, *Okay, you've eight more hours to get nervous. You're safe now,* and it would calm me for the next five to ten minutes.

We arrived in Tokyo with one hiccup. We were visa-less.

The company we were working for didn't spring for work permits, so we had to act like we were tourists. Here came that feeling of being a complete criminal again, akin to smuggling a ham.

We walked up to the customs table where the stern officers were thoroughly searching foreigners' bags. My bright pink championship belt was in there, offering no bigger giveaway that we hadn't simply come to sample the sushi.

If they knew we were coming over to work without a visa, we could be kicked out of the country. Barred for life. Put in jail. The dream, and the revolution, would be over before it began.

They dug through the bags with great vigor, hand searching relentlessly through all compartments and crevices as I looked on, smiling, trying to keep my composure. Saying some Hail Marys in my head and at least one round of "Our Father." Somehow, by some great miracle, or my divine prayer, they missed the championship belt. I smiled at them as if everything were normal while internally fist-pounding the air and doing a celebratory dance. No Japanese jail for this gal.

We walked out to the arrivals hall to meet with Shima, a gaunt, serious-looking Japanese man with glasses and a high-neck-collared trench coat. He had that standoffish air of a man not to be fucked with.

He led us to a black SUV, his intimidating aura having zero effect as I smiled so wide that my tiny mouth felt like it connected to my hairline. I remained gleefully gobsmacked as I looked out of the window in awe of the skyscrapers and bright lights of Tokyo.

Shima, apparently charmed by my enthusiasm, even cracked a smirk from time to time as I cooed over the Land of the Rising Sun. He even threw me a compliment—I looked like Britney Spears allegedly. I didn't, but I was a young Caucasian girl with blond highlights, and according to one Japanese bartender I met en route, all us white girls have the same face.

We pulled up to a beautiful, ornate hotel in the electronics district.

The rooms, spacious and modern, disappointed me, in a way. I had seen movies and documentaries about tiny, cramped Tokyo hotel rooms and I wanted the full Japanese experience, darn it! Even if that meant sleeping in a hotel room the size of a sardine can. Alas, I would have to make do with my full-size room, complete with fancy intimidating toilets.

I bounced out of bed bright and early the next day, too high on life for jet lag to reach me. It was our first big show in the famous Korakuen Hall.

Wrestling here was a rite of passage for anyone who considered themselves a wrestler's wrestler, and that's what I wanted to be. All my favorite matches had taken place here: the Dynamite Kid versus Tiger Mask, Kobashi versus Misawa, and so many more.

Here I was. Rebecca Knox. The girl who, only four years ago, there were too many blond beauties for anyone to be looking at. Tonight, they'd all be looking.

I entered the arena, taking careful consideration to be mindful of every step I was taking. This step was where Eddie Guerrero and Terry Funk had stepped. The locker room where Mick Foley got ready. I climbed the stairwell that led to the main hall. On the grey wall were the signatures of everyone who had ever performed there. It was like wrestling's version of the Hollywood Walk of Fame— albeit low-budget.

After standing dumbfounded and quasi-starstruck in front of the wall for what seemed like hours, I signed my own name among those of the greatest legends to ever grace a wrestling ring.

The IWGP roster was a hodgepodge of men and women from all over. Some were legends in their home countries of Mexico and Japan; some were people like me—total unknowns. However, Shima was so good at promoting me, you'd think I was the biggest star to walk out of Ireland since Bono. And I felt like it too when I went out for my first match. I was partnered with Nattie in an intergender tag taking on two of the Japanese male stars. Despite the promotion's name—International Women's Grand Prix—it was not actually an all-women's promotion. The men were graciously willing to bump around for us and make Nattie and me look like badasses!

Upon our entrance the crowd showered us with streams of ribbon, littering the ring as if it were Mardi Gras.

Wrestling in front of a Japanese audience is a full departure from wrestling in front of Western audiences. The Japanese don't yay and boo and chant in the same way, and so for a first-timer it can be rather jarring as they sit there silently and occasionally clap politely as you try to wow them with your most impressive maneuvers. I like the challenge—it's akin to courting a person with an air of mystery to them. You're not sure if they're into you or not.

And I suppose the Japanese crowd were into us, because after the match, ladies rushed the ring brandishing stunning bouquets of flowers for us.

Wrestling in Japan had already exceeded my high expectations. There was nothing like it.

Shima vowed to make me a star. Regardless of the fact that I couldn't even afford proper ring gear yet.

One night in and it was already working.

"*Rebecca-San!!!!!*" a loud yell came from behind me. I turned to see dozens of fans closing in on me, screaming at the top of their lungs as if I were Harry Styles exiting Madison Square Garden in a feathered boa.

What the actual fuck?

I was trying to leave the arena, but they kept coming from different directions, asking for pictures and signatures, offering me gifts. I was no one, but the impression that I was a big deal had sent these people into a frenzy.

I wanted to bask in it as long as I could, giving everyone a photo until the crowd became too overwhelming in size and security yanked me from the mound of fans and guided me to the bus.

The sacrifice of leaving Ireland and my family and Fergal behind was paying off. I could hardly believe how quick this was all happening.

The next day, the press was abuzz with praise for this champion by the name of Rebecca Knox. I had found the pot of gold at the end of the rainbow and it was wrestling in Japan.

However, it seems that once we left Korakuen I tripped, stumbled, and fell, sending those golden coins flying, with the pot eventually rebounding and hitting me in the head.

Over the next two weeks, as we toured the country, the crowds dwindled. So did my confidence.

I was put in the main event every night, partnering with two wrestling icons, Gran Hamada and Aja Kong, facing Los Brazos, a Mexican trio of burly brothers who had gigged* themselves so much that it looked like a miniature replica of the Grand Canyon had been carved into their foreheads.

Shima wanted me to be a high flyer (something I was not particularly good at), so he put me opposite Brazo de Platino, who was an excellent base and would throw me up, catch me, and maneuver me in such a way that made it look to the audience like I was doing all the work.

That's one of those illusions of wrestling. Often the credit is given to the flyers when in actual fact it is the person standing steady and taking the move who's doing the hard work.

Since I came to Canada I had made my name by being a good technical, ground-based wrestler. I was completely out of my element in the air. I was scared. I was a fraud and I knew it. Not being in tune enough with the temperature of the group, I vocalized my frustrations too much to some of the other girls on the tour, who were already salty over my very obvious preferential treatment and main event spot.

I was the chosen star of the show. I got the attention, was brought out by myself for dinners with sponsors—a situation unique to star performers in Japan, who are often treated to lavish meals and experiences. It was causing resentment, especially because I wasn't even grateful for it. I'd piss and moan about not wrestling the way I wanted to when I was being given everything. Midway through the tour I could tell I had made some enemies.

....

* In wrestling lingo "gigging" is a term used to describe intentionally cutting oneself to provoke bleeding—and while that practice may sound barbaric, there's wrestlers who specialize in it, and even enjoy it!

Being so young, with a fear of failing at my dream of wrestling in Japan and knowing I wasn't particularly good in this new high-flying main event role, I lacked couth and humility. Sometimes I would do fine; most times I would fall flat and Shima would reprimand me.

"Give sixty percent, seventy percent. Not one hundred percent. You try too hard. You no good. You go sixty percent you can go up. You go one hundred percent you only go down."

I didn't know how to give it anything but my all. Even now, I could never aim to give a performance less than my best.

Which, in fairness to Shima, is an observation I am guilty of. I *do* try too hard. I so badly want to entertain the people who came to see me, and prove to myself and the world that I am the best. But ultimately, what trying too hard is is a confession that you don't completely trust yourself to be good enough yet. And in this moment in Japan I certainly did not.

By the time we had done our last show and it was time to leave, I was relieved. I had wanted to love this experience more, but I left feeling dejected.

Regardless of my own feelings of inadequacy about my performance over the last couple of weeks, Shima's marketing of me was clearly effective. As soon as I returned to Canada, I opened my email to get the biggest offer of my life:

Dear Rebecca-San,

We are writing to you as one of Japan's biggest advertising agencies. We saw you wrestling in Japan and we think you are very good

champion. We would like to represent you and make you big star.
We will make you Maria Sharapova of wrestling. Making you
make pop music single. We pay you $8000 in 4 installments.
We also pay airfare. You tell us how much you charge per match
and we get you money.

> *We look forward to your correspondence.*

If these people were legit, I was about to be the biggest thing the wrestling world had ever seen. Especially in Japan, which was where I wanted my future to be anyway!

My mind was blown. This was more than I had ever gotten paid for anything in my life!

I signed on the dotted line and awaited stardom.

THE HEAT

Even with this brand-new unbelievable offer, after being admonished so many times by Shima I felt like I had failed in Japan.

As a result and on brand, I began to try even harder. My matches started to become more complicated. Now that I had wrestled in Japan (albeit badly), I acted like I was better than I was and tried things I couldn't pull off. I attempted difficult spots without fully grasping the psychology behind them. Nonetheless, faking it till I could make it, I was continuing to build hype around the world.

Fergal had moved across the country to train at the New Japan dojo located in Santa Monica, California. I came to stay for a few weeks in March and maybe pick up a thing or two or a booking or two.

I didn't pick up much of either, truth be told.

The dojo was a large warehouse, with a ring, a weights area, showers, a kitchen, and a large padded area. We slept on old mattresses in the rat-infested attic. Fergal, being the incredible talent he is, had already made a name for himself in the short time he was there.

A couple of weeks into my stay at the dojo, Fergal got called to train in Tokyo, as what is called a young boy—essentially an apprentice wrestler.

When he left, I knew it would soon be over between us. The distance was too great and over the last few months I had simultaneously become demanding, clingy, and too scared of losing him. Whether that was a result of ego, or insecurity, or a combination of both, it didn't really matter; he was about to live out his dream, and I wasn't going to be part of it.

He would eventually go on to become one of New Japan's biggest stars and create one of wrestling's most talked-about factions—the Bullet Club.

But by the time he left we were barely talking.

I dropped him at the airport with one of our friends and fellow dojo roommate Chad Allegra (aka WWE's Karl Anderson), and we didn't as much as hug goodbye.

Chad comforted me as I sobbed my eyes out when Fergal left. Too embarrassed to tell Chad the truth, that I was devastated by my broken heart, knowing that this move meant me and Fergal would surely be over, I blamed my hysteria on an illness in the family.

On the phone, my cousin urged me to come back to Canada as I bawled, "I feel like a part of me just died."

I always did have a propensity for the dramatics. But this was my first real love and I had fucked it up. Now he was going away forever, leaving me behind. When he made it to Japan and called me a few days later, we agreed the relationship was over but that we would always remain friends. But to quote the famous song by the band The Script, "When a heart breaks, no, it don't break even"—and I was absolutely the more devastated one.

I came back to Canada, and like every heartbroken teenage girl, I set my sights on getting a better body. As if that would heal the pain and make him want me back.

I was offered to do custom matches in North Carolina by a company called Ring Angels, along with a lingerie photo shoot for $150, which sounded like a small fortune to me.

It was, of course, completely against anything I had set out to do. I wanted to prove that I should be looked at for my technical ability, and had never wanted to sexualize myself lest that take away from my credibility as a wrestler.

I did it anyway.

In my confusion, my heartbreak, my wanting to make it to the top and feel good about myself, I justified, *All the WWE girls do it; it's just part of the job.*

I hated it. I hated every second of it. Trying to fit into the mold that I had so vehemently set out to break felt like I was selling my soul for $150. I still cringe every time I see those photos—this fluffy, awkward nineteen-year-old trying to look sexy while so obviously feeling uncomfortable. It can be so confusing being a woman in wrestling. Doubly so when you're raised Catholic. You see what the women on TV are doing and think that's how to get ahead, but you also don't want it to come with the objectification, so you wonder if you should shun your femininity completely. It's a fine disorientating balance to be walked carefully when it should be easy. Just be you and do what you love well. But instead of realizing that I didn't need to sell myself as a hot little sex kitten, I put more emphasis on my body. As if that were the only thing that could lead me to greatness.

I cut my calories in half and pushed the intensity at the gym. It wasn't long until I started seeing big changes, in both my body, my mood (not for the better), and my pure obsession with the physical.

In the midst of my identity crisis, my Canadian visa was also coming to an end soon and if I didn't find a way to stay I would have to return to Ireland, where I promised my mom I would go back to college. The hourglass was running out and there was nothing I could do to stop the sand from falling.

I even had to drop my coveted SuperGirls title. At least it was to Lisa Moretti, formally known as Ivory in WWE.

I had grown up watching her on TV and was massively intimidated by the prospect of working with a future WWE Hall of Famer, but she couldn't have been nicer. Having left WWE a year previous, she felt like she was out of practice and listened to my ideas with no ego about her whatsoever. Unfortunately for both of us, my ideas sucked. Don't get me wrong, the match had its good moments . . . and a lot of bad ones too. When I came back, Starr looked at me with a wry, disappointed smile.

"What happened?" he asked.

"It wasn't good?" I responded, rhetorically really.

"Not like it usually is."

I tried too hard. Overcomplicated it. Overcompensated.

Lisa, however, was thrilled or at least feigned as though she was. She thanked me, complimented me, and pretended to hand the title back to me.

"This belongs to you." She laughed giddily.

Starr was right, though. I was capable of better. But on this night, as would be the case with many other upcoming nights, I tried to be something I wasn't.

I left Vancouver heavyhearted. A lot had happened in that one year. I had changed and grown in many ways. I had reached and achieved all my dreams in that first night in Japan and instantly began to spiral uncontrollably downhill afterwards, believing my own shit far too quickly.

I had done the things I said I wouldn't and with that found new insecurities that rapidly began eating me up as I floundered at home, looking, in a panic, for ways to make it to the big time before the summer was up.

Or certainly before I turned twenty. Because after that, I had decided, I was too old. I needed to be seen as the teenage protégée I was and get signed by one of the bigger companies, be it WWE or, more preferably at the time, TNA, where they put more emphasis on women's wrestling, while I was still nineteen, or, truthfully, before Fergal did, so that I could validate myself as being worthy and make him want me back.

Back to Ireland I went, now living under my mother's roof again, and considering my previous promise to her, she was pressuring me to have a plan.

I didn't have one, other than I planned to get signed. But that wasn't practical enough and she did not want me out there slinging pillows at another woman in a G-string.

THE FREE AGENT

Shima met me unexpectedly at the airport. He had heard that I had signed with the advertising agency and was piiiiiiiisssssed.

I tried to explain the situation, which was really just "Well, they offered me money and promised me fame and I was in."

I wasn't savvy enough to the politics or the proper chain of etiquette. I saw myself as a solo entity, talent for hire. Shima, however, felt like he had made me and thus he owned me.

But the agency was treating me like royalty, putting me up in the finest of hotels, feeding me the best of food. They didn't know much about wrestling, though.

The first day, they had arranged a photo shoot—another lingerie shoot, to be exact. Having decided I wanted to make it to the big leagues, I needed to figure out this sex appeal thing and, in turn, would continue to do what I said I wouldn't. On the flip side, I reasoned, Lita did, and she was still cool. *And I worked hard for my body, why wouldn't I show it off? I'm in better shape than the last time*, I told myself.

As a side note, I believe there is nothing wrong with showing off your body and feeling the power of your own femininity and sexuality. However, I also knew that if I wanted to be respected as an athlete and a wrestler I had to have more than sex appeal. In fact, I felt like I needed to reject it completely. . . . Not that it mattered, because in my confusion I went against it all anyway.

The people at the shoot were lovely, of course, and this shoot was much more professional and classier than the last one.

However, the magazines they ended up in? Not so much. I was horrified, but also too meek to stand up and say anything to the agency.

"Very popular magazine," they said.

Yeah . . . I can see why. . . .

It was the top porno magazine in Japan, and, as a result of my very Catholic upbringing and my intentions on how I wanted to be portrayed in general, I was mortified.

Meanwhile in wrestling . . . the agency had booked me on a show called *The Woman*, which included some of my idols. But I was facing a lady dressed like a bull.

The match was a blend of comedy and awful. I was out of my element. Between the language barrier and differing styles, it just didn't hit the mark. And I wasn't advertised or marketed in the same way Shima had done for me.

This was my one and only show on this trip and it sucked.

Shima met me after my match looking like the Godfather. I gave him a nervous smile, waiting for his disapproval.

"No good," he remarked, as my organs turned into pretzels in my stomach.

He was right.

I trundled back to Ireland, ashamed of myself.

With bookings in the summer months beginning to slow and my interest in my physique growing, I decided I would do a bodybuilding competition in September in Dublin. I thought if I could look flawless, maybe one of the big companies would want me. I could prove that I could be "fluff" too.

Who had I become?!

Of course, I had no idea how to go about getting in bodybuilding shape. But I knew someone who might. When I was growing up, there was a man in my neighborhood named Niall. He was a mountain of a human being, with biceps as big as curled-up toddlers, complete with veins as prominent as computer cords. He was a good sixteen years older than I was, and as a kid I was terrified of this brooding behemoth as he drove around in his muscle cars, gigantic arm covered in ink hanging out the window, sunglasses covering his pouting face.

Scariness and all, I sent him a message letting him know about my latest goal to compete. As fate would have it, he was doing the competition too! He even agreed to come to my house to help me with a plan.

He arrived at my house and got out of his vehicle, looking less scary than I remembered; there was even warmth in his eyes. How had I missed that as a kid? I must have been distracted by the fear he might eat me.

He wrote me up a diet detailing how many ounces of chicken I could consume, my water intake, how many grams of rice, and for the love of god no sugar. Maybe an apple after training if I went hard enough.

Immediately, my days began to revolve around food and training. I became consumed by what and when I could eat next.

I bailed on wrestling, partially to lift weights and eat, but mostly out of pure insecurity. Having felt like I was losing my step in the ring, instead of running towards getting better, I was running away completely. I felt like I would find salvation in a set of abs and that that was more important for WWE than what I could do in the ring.

With the clock ticking down in my head and in an attempt to be productive, get back to America, and also have that plan B that had been so highly recommended by my mother, I started researching personal-training courses across the pond.

That would tick all the boxes! Becoming a personal trainer would grant me a visa and a purpose to be in America while allowing me to take bookings on the weekend. . . . And I get a diploma at the end of it!

I found a four-month program in Orlando that accepted foreign students and began in September.

Orlando also happened to be the home of TNA, which had a thriving women's division. All things going to plan, this was going to be my in.

As my body fat decreased, the pain from wrestling increased. Hitting the mat and ropes with little padding to cushion the impact left me feeling tender for days. Not to mention I was wrestling infrequently now, so my body was losing its calloused shell that protected me from the pain of falling down for a living.

When the fat loss started to slow down, I cut my calories again to get to the next stage. Emaciation was the name of the game.

I was popping ephedrine like it was Skittles. When that stopped working, I was supplied with T_3, which is meant to speed up your thyroid function. But it can also be very dangerous and wreak havoc on your thyroid once you come off it.

Spoiler: it did.

I took another tour in Japan in my wilted state. But this time there would be no fancy hotels.

The advertising agency weren't seeing a return on their investment, so they decided to downscale. The only reason they saw me as a star was because Shima had presented me like one. On my own, I was just a poorly dressed teenage girl who liked exchanging holds in a wrestling ring.

I spent my free time scouring grocery stores, trying to figure out what I could eat, which was usually boiled cabbage and boiled egg whites.

My matches were awful, and everything hurt like hell.

Shima didn't even bother to come out and see me this time. I was a lost cause.

All I would do was fantasize about food I could eat when I was done. Like carrots, which were banned for their high sugar content. Fucking carrots!

I just wanted to go home. I lost sight of why I was doing any of this.

When I returned to Ireland, I still had another four weeks of this diet before the big bodybuilding show, which seemed like an eternity. I drank so much coffee and Diet Pepsi on top of my abundance of fat burners just to be able to get through a workout, and even then I would cry out of exhaustion.

My mother was panicking as I was dwindling away in front of her eyes. Sometimes she would catch me leering at cookbooks like a teenage boy who had discovered *Playboy* for the first time in his life.

As the days got more painful and my appearance became more frightful, I had enough. The competition was two more weeks away, but I couldn't make it. I needed a cheat meal; I needed sugar in my veins and in my brain. Now!

Niall thought it might actually help kick-start my metabolism, or leave me so disgusted with myself that I'd go full bore for the remaining fortnight.

"Your stomach has probably shrunk, so you won't be able to eat much," Niall warned me as we walked into Eddie Rocket's.

Niall was wrong. I could eat everything on my plate, his plate, everyone else in the restaurant's plate, and all the food in the kitchen too.

We didn't stop there, hitting up my favorite bakery for pastries I had been dreaming of for months. There was a panic in my eating. Like I was Cinderella and I had to stuff my face with as much sugar and fat as I could before the clock struck midnight and I'd turn into a pumpkin. There was a rush of adrenaline, or maybe that was sugar hitting. I was doing something I shouldn't, but being wrong felt so right.

The futility of standing up in a bikini on a stage and showing people my muscles dawned on me as I consumed my cream-filled buns. *What the hell am I doing?* It wasn't like I was going to win any money for my hard work. At best I would win a trophy, but by then I had just become a skinny girl with abs.

Like a pie to the face, it hit me that I was throwing everything away for this. But by then the eating disorder had already kicked in, and it was going to take years to shake.

The lack of food had a grave impact on my mood, hormones, and thyroid. Though I was once an upbeat, optimistic young girl with a clear road ahead of me, it all became murky as depression fogged everything around me.

In a power struggle to gain and lose control at the same time, I would binge eat, then purge, then diet as hard as I could, then repeat.

Cheat meals turned into cheat days, which turned into waiting till everyone was in bed and eating till I felt like I could puke and then making myself puke.

The narrative of "There's far too many blond beauties around here for anyone to be looking at you" still haunted me and left me with an inadequacy complex that felt damn near impossible to shake.

What I liked about wrestling was that I had given myself worth beyond how I looked. Now that was all I cared about.

THE FALSE FINISH

Italy had become a hot spot for wrestling, with some promotions drawing upwards of ten thousand people, so when I was invited for a tour, despite my existential crisis, I jumped at the opportunity.

I got off the plane into the muggy summer heat and was guided to the tour bus where two pleasant Canadian heads popped up from behind navy bus seat cushions.

"Hi! I'm Kevin!"

"Hi! I'm Rami!"

Kevin and Rami, aka Kevin Steen and El Generico, aka Kevin Owens and Sami Zayn, would go on to become two of the most beloved wrestlers in all of WWE, and WrestleMania main eventers.

But back then, they were just two best friends with a following on the independent circuit, bantering back and forth like a couple of old hens, and they were kind enough to let me join in their friend gang.

My opponent never showed up, leaving me as the only girl, meaning there was no other option but to put me in a match with Kevin and Rami. Two of the best wrestlers in the world, they carried me through some barn burners . . . even if there was no one there to see it.

The buildings had a capacity for about five to ten thousand people. Our best night drew one hundred people max. And even that's a stretch.

What the promoter failed to recognize was that advertising was a big part of getting people to come out to see a show, and having some big stars people would actually pay money to see. Not that we weren't big international draws at the time (we weren't). Yes, Kevin and Rami had big names on the indies, but to garner audiences in the thousands, wrestlers who had been on TV were preferable.

In between shows I binged on cereal and threw up constantly without trying to hide it, passing it off as drinking the dodgy tap water.

Even though I was struggling mentally and physically, Kevin and Rami offered reprieve for my broken soul. The two of them, who had traveled the world together for years, behaved like a comical old married couple, entertaining everyone on the roster with a 24/7 sitcom.

Though the tour hadn't been a success in how things are standardly measured and I was weak from wrestling and vomiting nonstop, I was sad to be leaving my newfound friends.

I still had one more weekend of bookings before I shipped off to Orlando.

Now slightly thicker than I had been recently, I rocked up to a venue in Germany and was greeted by one of the UK's most respected wrestlers, Doug Williams. "No more abs?" he asked as if I weren't a teenage girl with a complex. More tone-deaf than malicious.

"No, Doug. I have a fucking eating disorder and was killing myself" was what I wanted to say.

But instead, I just laughed and said, "Ha-ha, apparently not," and then cried in the bathroom.

My opponent was green as goose shit, but I wasn't in the business of toning it down for anyone anymore. I had wrestled internationally, had made a name for myself, had numerous tours of Japan under my belt, and was a regular main eventer.

I had the X factor. Someone on MySpace told me so.

We were having the match I wanted to have and it was going to be great. Whether my opponent liked it or not. Or whether she knew what she was doing or not. My previous goal of making everyone look good was now reduced to just trying to make myself look good.

But on this fateful night, I made no one look good!

She did not, in fact, know what she was doing.

The result being . . .

We went out there and stunk up every convoluted spot we attempted.

After one botch too many, the crowd started chanting, "Women's wrestling."

Nowadays, if the crowd chants, "Women's wrestling," it is meant as the highest of compliments. Back then, it was meant as the harshest of insults.

In a rage I grabbed the girl and attempted an impressive modified version of a German suplex. Terrified, not understanding what was happening, she clung on to me for dear life, landing right on my eye. The only thing impressive about my attempted move was the sheer volume of blood it caused to pour out from above my eye.

Almost immediately I couldn't see out of my left eye. It looked like the whole world was smeared with red paint.

I was furious at her for being so incompetent that she got me in this position, but it was my fault for trying too damn hard. Even at nineteen, I was the veteran and I should have known better.

I finished the match with blood pouring down my face and was brought to the hospital right after.

I had a concussion and the large gash above my eye needed stitches.

My biggest concern was how to hide the injury from my mom. She was already looking for me to get out of wrestling. If I came home looking like Frankenstein, she would lose her mind.

The next day, I arrived in Norwich to wrestle for a lady who was considered somewhat of a legend in British wrestling—Sweet Saraya. She only weighed about one hundred pounds but had a reputation for being a hard hitter in the ring. But then again, so did I. She was always great to me. And on this particular occasion she was an angel.

She met me at the airport and brought me back to her house to coddle me like a real British mammy, because she was one. She lit up as she introduced me to her kids, Zak, fourteen, and Saraya, thirteen. In one of those rare situations that can only happen in wrestling, she had bestowed her working name on her child.

Zach was a little more reserved, while Saraya was high-spirited and clearly excited about a new wrestler in their house.

"Saraya just started wrestling. She's really good; isn't she, Ricky?" mom Saraya said to her husband.

"Oh aye," says Ricky.

"She's gorgeous too, isn't she?" mom Saraya asked me. A rhetorical question, really.

"Stunning," I admitted.

"She's gonna be a star," mom Saraya cooed.

She was. Even from a simple "Hi" you could see it.

Years later, she became Paige in WWE. A true groundbreaker. Hell, before she even turned thirty they were making movies about her life.

Saraya (the mom) lathered my eye with aloe vera and gave me arnica tablets to take down the swelling.

"Will it be gone by tomorrow?" I inquired hopefully.

"Probably not."

"Shit."

Sweet Saraya took it supereasy on me that night, making sure to stay away from the face.

It was my last match for almost seven years.

I walked into my house, baseball hat dipped low, sunglasses on. *I am a master of disguise. No one will suspect a thing!* I thought.

Shockingly, neither the aloe vera nor the arnica had cured the bruising or dissolved the stitches overnight.

Like a cheetah, my mom pounced out from a corner and instantly began the interrogation: "What are you doing with those sunglasses on inside?"

"Wrestlers and rock stars, Ma. They wear sunglasses indoors. Don't worry about it."

"Take them off your head."

"No."

With one swift ninja-like snatch the sunglasses were in her hands and my scarred and swollen eye exposed. I of course blamed my slow reflexes on the concussion; on any normal day I'm quick as a cat.

"Jesus. What happened?" Mom gasped.

"Just a flesh wound, NBD."

"That looks awful! Are you okay?"

"I'm fine! A move just went a bit amiss. They took me to the hospital and stitched me up, though. All good," I reassured her.

"What are you doing? You need to stop this. You have no plan; you could have been severely injured. You could lose an eye or break your neck; you need to stop!"

The list of possible threats went on and on.

But I did have a plan now . . . kinda. I was going to Orlando. I was going to get my personal-training diploma. I was gonna wrestle . . . maybe. That part I actually wasn't sure of.

Dieting too hard had taken everything out of me, especially while trying to wrestle too. On my strict calorie-deficient diet, I wouldn't build muscle or look as ripped as I wanted to, so it's not like I would have gotten the attention of WWE as a body girl who could wrestle. And I didn't feel like I could add anything in my current state in terms of ability to the TNA roster. My plan had already failed.

I didn't know what I wanted. I didn't want the pressure. I didn't want the potential failure. I didn't want to be in pain. I didn't want to be so uncertain about what was happening next.

What I did know was I didn't have the balls to tell anyone I was suffering.

Like a coward, I used the injury as a way to step away while I tried to figure out my head, without having to admit that I simply couldn't hack it.

A doctor friend gave me a plausible excuse, something that sounded severe but that I could come back from if I changed my mind: "damage to the eighth cranial nerve," which is essentially tinnitus but sounds pretty gnarly.

At least this could buy me time to figure out the world, but my mind was so foggy that I had no idea what the right path was anymore. Only a year ago it had felt so simple and clear.

I left for Orlando all the same, an erratic mess.

I was connecting through New York when I felt like I had an awakening. Or a panic attack. Maybe something in between.

Wrestling was over. I was done. I needed to return home.

I was going to call my mom and let her know immediately. She'd be so happy to have me back and hear that I was going to leave wrestling and finally be the daughter she wanted me to be.

I found the nearest pay phone in the airport and dialed. Ready to get on the straight and narrow. Ready to finally make her happy with my decision.

"Mom, I don't want to do this. I want to come home."

"No." There was no hesitation in her voice.

Huh? That was the last thing I expected to hear.

She didn't want me wrestling. She didn't want me dieting and obsessively training. How could she say no to this? Especially since this was the first time she heard it. Had she anticipated I would back out?

The panic increased. *I just need her to know I'm genuine.*

"I know I've been all over the place. I'm sorry. I can't do this. I'll get a normal job. I'll go back to college. Please. I'll be normal. I promise I'll be normal. I just want to come home."

"You have dropped out of everything and you haven't seen anything through. You can't do that this time."

My heart sank. My stomach tightened; tears poured down my face; my voice strained.

"Please, Mom, please. I don't want to be like this anymore," I begged and pleaded.

"I'm sorry."

She hung up, leaving me in a cocoon of dread. Lost, alone, broken, and feeling like a complete failure. I had ruined my life for the sake of abs. For the sake of trying to fit into a mold so that I might be more worthy of my dreams. The dreams I had already been on the path to fulfilling.

As I made my way to the gate, face red, snot falling, passersby looked on with pity and concern.

I waddled onto my flight to Orlando with slumped shoulders and found my seat, starving, with only a big bag of raw oats to eat for some fucking reason.

After what seemed like an endless day of travel, I eventually pulled up to my new digs in Orlando. There were students everywhere, loud music playing, frat boys obnoxiously drunk dangling from the stairways. I pushed past them to find my apartment. Brown walls with brown furniture all resting on a brown carpet.

After I climbed into bed that night, under my sheet that provided about as much heat as a sleeve of newspaper, and rested my head on a flimsy pillow, I cycled between feelings of fear, sadness, and dread.

I called my mom the following day to let her know I had arrived safely.

She had a rage in her voice that was reserved for special occasions. On this special occasion, she had discovered the lingerie shoot I had done in North Carolina.

"You're acting like a porn star. You need to have respect for yourself. What are you going to do with your life? Are you going to be a forty-year-old wrestler living in a trailer park?"

I had no rebuttals, no more fire; I was defeated and ashamed of myself. And she had seen the lingerie shoot that *hadn't* ended up in a porno mag.

The brown walls were closing in; I couldn't see a better life ahead of me. All I had was the possibility of this personal-training diploma to try to get me on the right track, but it felt so wrong.

What I quickly learned in personal-training school was that as much as I loved training myself for my own purpose of vanity, I could not have cared less about training anyone else. Class was boring, the workouts basic. I had no motivation to do well and quickly learned to tell the difference between a real passion and a forced one.

I relied on my roommates for rides to school and back but was otherwise confined to the brown apartment and sitting on the brown couch, with only my meal prep and thoughts of better days to occupy my mind.

My golden years were behind me. At nineteen years old, I was a washed-up has-been.

THE
WANDER
YEARS

SEASON 2

THE HIGH FLYER

I returned home in February 2007 with my diploma, humbled, meek, and oozing insecurity. At least I had stuck it out.

With a forced smile on my face lest anyone know I was dying on the inside, I hit the Dublin pavements looking for employment. I was a long way from the main events of Korakuen Hall and being chased by hordes of fans.

My mother had been toiling over the decision to take a severance package from Aer Lingus, where she had worked for twenty-nine years.

Chris had taken a similar package two years earlier and she was torn between living a life of leisure with her now husband and continuing to do the job she still loved to do. And make no mistake about it, she loved it, the same way I once loved wrestling.

She was top of the food chain in flight attendant land, in both experience and position and as a cabin manager, i.e., the main eventer of flight attendants. She prided herself on creating a positive atmosphere for everyone she worked with.

"It trickles down from the top," she preached.

Ultimately, she chose her marriage and spending time with her husband.

As she had printed up her resignation, a thought dawned on her.

"Would you like me to hand in your résumé?"

"Sure, you might as well," I responded nonchalantly. Now bereft of my own dreams, I might as well follow hers.

I walked into my interview primped and primed, with my high heels, pearl earrings, and bright pink blazer.

Who was I?

A flight attendant, I guess. . . .

I got the job.

It was weird looking at myself in the same ugly green uniform I admired so much as a child when my mother wore it. When my mom donned that uniform, she was immaculate—makeup perfect, not a hair out of place, uniform fitted and crisply ironed.

My blazer was two sizes too big for me, my hair flew in several different directions, and I had never learned how to iron a damn shirt.

Despite the disheveled way in which I wore the uniform that Mom had taken such pride in, she beamed with delight, as if I were Kate Middleton about to marry the prince of England and soon we would all inherit the kingdom.

I was even trained up just in time to be on my mother's last flight. I saw firsthand that it was true, she created a joyful atmosphere and everyone loved her. She had presence, charisma, made everyone laugh and hang on her every word. She had authority but in a kind way, the type that meant you didn't want to let her down. It was different from how I knew her at home, as the woman I was terrified to piss off. Not because she'd be "disappointed" but because she'd be flat out scary as fuck.

I was Simba and she was the Mufasa of the flight attendant jungle, explaining, "Everything the light touches is ours." Only I didn't want to be king of the aviation land. I had always yearned to explore beyond the boundaries of the pride land. To "that shadowy place over there."

Giving up her career was immensely difficult for her. She was good at it, found purpose doing it, and was a star in her field. As I watched her struggle with the loss of her career and purpose, I couldn't help but see the similarities to how I was feeling walking away from my dreams. But I wasn't sure she could or would see those similarities between us. We both tried to believe that wrestling was simply something I was better without.

I could see why she wanted this life for me. Being a flight attendant afforded her the ability to look after both of her children, often as the sole breadwinner. It took her on trips around the world. When she began, the position had an air of glamour, and now that she had lasted so long, she ruled the roost.

I didn't inherit that same love of serving in the skies. It wasn't long before the novelty of staying in hotels and going on mindless shopping trips quickly wore off and the tediousness of 3:00 am wake-up calls and obnoxious overuse of call bells squashed me like a rhino sitting on a hornbill.

When my alarm went off in the morning, my first thought was *This is what's going to kill me.* I didn't know if I was referring to the exhaustion, flying thirty-five thousand feet in the air, or living a passionless life.

For someone with such a nomadic lifestyle, the transient nature of the relationships was unsettling to me, making me feel like an outcast. Every day was a new crew, meaning arduous small talk and a reminder that I was a bit strange.

My strangeness used to be my favorite thing about me, the thing I took pride in. Now I was ashamed of it and longing to fit in. My mother's advice to "just be normal" seemed so simple, yet damn near impossible.

I looked at everyone I worked with as a teacher on how to be normal. Everyone was privy to this knowledge and I just had to listen and act like them or think like them so that I too might become normal.

If I didn't make a connection with my coworkers, that was my fault. I was the asshole. I was the one who lacked the general day-to-day skill of normalcy.

Or if I was ever working with an uptight senior and was having trouble endearing myself to them, I would casually drop my mom's name and watch as they went from hostile to gushing over how wonderful my mom and Chris were, and the day got slightly easier.

One time someone had mentioned how I looked like my mother and in jest I quipped that I was "giving Aer Lingus the updated model."

"Oh, you will never compare to your mother; we all loved her," the woman barked back, stern faced.

Translation: "Know your role and shut your mouth, jabroni."

NEW SCHOOL

Desperately seeking a community akin to what I had found in wrestling, and in the pursuit of a new passion, I tried out jobs and hobbies like they were part of a wardrobe montage in a rom-com. I worked at a Pilates studio—too beige! Taught English as a foreign language—too detailed! Took capoeira classes—too many patterns! Took Muay Thai classes—too uncomfortable!

I actually did do a bodybuilding competition with only three weeks of prep time—too tight! Though I did come in third place, it was as vapid as I expected. My awkward posing routine to Shawn Michaels entrance music, in my cheap red bikini, while lathered in a chocolate-like subsidiary of fake tan is why I am happy iPhones were not in the hand of every human on earth in 2008. Additionally, the comment of "The third-place winner was too fat" that came from an audience member was scar-worthy. Especially considering I was already bulimic.

I had to find the right fit. Something comfy, but with a little flavor, maybe something elastic, allowing for growth. Then I saw it! A ten-week acting class at the Gaiety School of Acting! I would have the chance to express myself, perform, and maybe even rebuild some confidence. It was the perfect fit! I tried it on, twirled while all my friends clapped and cheered as I strutted around like a tiger. I could get into this shit.

One game of Zip Zap Zop and I was ready to give up my good, pensionable job, take out all my life savings, and go back to school with a bunch of theatre kids.

My mom, however, was not as enthused by my revelation.

"You're not going to give up a job in Aer Lingus to do that. We will lose all respect for you," she said in the most Irish mammy way of saying anything an Irish mammy ever says. "I'll tell you what you need to do. . . ."

Please tell, I thought, having lost faith in my inner compass and ability to determine what was right for me. Maybe I should just listen to my mom.

"You need to go see a guidance counsellor. I actually know one," Mom continued.

It didn't seem like a terrible idea. I didn't trust myself to make a decision anymore, and maybe a counsellor could help me with my unhealthy relationship to food as well as help me sort out my career.

Sitting in the front office of the counsellor's large and proper-looking home, it appeared as if she knew what she was doing. Certificates hung on the wall alongside pictures of her smiling children, while expensive-looking ornaments decorated the room. She sat with perfect posture in a pencil skirt, looking at me with faux sympathy from behind her desk.

I'm not sure this woman is going to get my conflict with wrestling, I thought, stereotyping her from the jump. Turns out she didn't get much of anything. After explaining my worrying relationship with food, she left the room and came back with a plate of cookies for me. As if that might solve my problem. I politely grazed the hard edges with my teeth, trying to guess the amount of carbs per serving and wondering if I'd have to do extra cardio that night for my sins. Dusting the crumbs off my fingertips, I explained my agony.

"I love wrestling. But there's no future in it. It's just not a realistic dream. I want to find something that I love as much, but that's a safer choice, you know what I mean?"

"Well, you can't do that anymore. But have you considered business studies?" she responded, deadpan.

Spending four years doing something so utterly boring felt like a prison sentence.

I left, barely able to see through my tears as I bawled my eyes out in my red Volkswagen Polo.

I drove across a suspended bridge and imagined myself veering to the left and plummeting into the water far below.

Just one flick of the steering wheel and it'll be over.

Hold on, ya bastard. It'll get better.

I was now white-knuckling the steering wheel.

Any move I make from here is better than this.

Fuck this, I thought. *You don't want to do business. You don't want to do sports management. You want to perform. Do that. Find a way. Find a fucking way, Rebecca.*

I crossed the bridge.

Immediately upon arriving home that night, I began researching acting schools.

American schools were first on my list. I hoped that if I could get over there, maybe I could be free to be whoever I wanted to be; I wouldn't have to be this unconfident weirdo wreck. Or more importantly, I wouldn't have to answer to my mom.

The benefit of being a flight attendant paid dividends as I set up my first audition to a New York school called the American Academy of Dramatic Arts on an overnight the very next week.

As soon as we landed, I discarded my uniform in a heap on my hotel room floor and rushed to the school, knees knocking together as I speed-walked down Madison Avenue. I arrived at the large red-brick building that had boasted an impressive list of alumni; everyone from Robert Redford to Paul Rudd had taken classes here. I tried vainly to fan the pit stains out of my shirt as I sat eagerly outside the audition room waiting to be called.

Either I take a step in the right direction to creating a life I want to live or I'm told I'm the shits and go back to my unfulfilled life. It was all riding on this one audition.

I had purposefully picked a monologue that would benefit from my unshakable nerves.

Afterwards, the judge sat there silent for the longest fifteen seconds of my life. It was like watching *The X Factor* and they're going to either be blown away or tell you you should never show your face in public again.

"That was wonderful," he said at last as my insides skipped like I was a schoolchild.

Holy fuck! Maybe not all is lost, I thought as I sighed relief and silently shouted out the magnificent playwright whose words managed to make me look decent at this crucial point in my life.

"Tell me, why do you want to act?"

I had never really thought about why I liked performing. It just brought something out of me.

"Well, at fifteen I became a professional wrestler, but I gave it up almost three years ago and I've felt a void ever since. I think that void is maybe artistic expression. I want to create. I want to perform. I want to live in another head and body that doesn't feel like my own."

He pondered my answer for a second before advising, "Don't tell yourself you can't do it. If it's not for you, other people will tell you."

(I'm aware that he meant this as a motivational tool against self-destruction. But people told me I wouldn't main event Wrestle-Mania and, well . . . we'll get to that.)

"I would like you to pursue this. I'm offering you a spot in the program and I'm willing to offer you our highest scholarship."

My eyes began to water.

"Thank you, thank you so much."

I left gobsmacked, flipping from wide-eyed wonderment to crying to joyously fist-pumping the air.

Maybe I could trust myself again. Walking through the streets of Manhattan, the place that held so much wonder to me as a six-year-old, I had a feeling I hadn't had in a long time. *Anything is possible*, I thought. *You just have to believe in yourself again.*

Returning to Ireland with an offer from a prestigious acting school gave my mother a different perspective on my unconventional dreams. Perhaps I wasn't pure dog shite. Maybe, by some great miracle, I actually had a spark of talent.

I had saved every penny I could while working in the airline for this exact type of opportunity.

Even so, and scholarship aside, living in New York City for the two-year duration of the course without having a visa to work was still far beyond my means, so ultimately I didn't enroll in the program. And while I would have to pivot with my plans, the biggest hurdle—my mother's disapproval—had been jumped, and it felt like I was open to a world of opportunities now.

Back at the drawing board, I found a course that seemed to be the best of all worlds. If I got in, I would get a theatre degree from the Dublin Institute of Technology, so my mother could be happy I was getting a college education. Plus, I would get to study what I wanted, and what's more, they had an exchange program with Columbia College in Chicago. So I could get over to America after all!

Of course this would all depend on whether I could finagle a spot from over one thousand applicants for one of twenty-five spots.

Finagle I did and promptly began wrapping things up with the airline. However, as the clock began to tick down, the thought that I would be stuck studying for the next three years began to terrify me.

Surely I should be out there, making something of myself. Doing more. Exploring the world.

Stop! The time will pass anyway, *you dope*, I reasoned with myself.

Only this time, no matter how hard things got, I could not quit. If an opportunity presented itself to me, I could take it, but I had resolved to not drop out of things anymore when they got tough. My mom was right about that.

The time had come for my final flight with Aer Lingus.

It was my favorite trip, the 105 to New York. After two and a half years working as a flight attendant, I finally had a pep in my step again knowing that this chapter would soon be over.

During a short work break, I sat down in the back on a crate as people asked me about what I was going to do next.

"Do you really think you're going to find a job better than this?" asked an arrogant lanky northerner.

"I just feel like I need to try something new," I responded, still meek as a little chipmunk.

"I think you're making a mistake. You're not going to get a better job than this."

"Yes, James, you wanker. I will find a better job than handing out peanuts in a metal tube" is what I wish I had said. What I really said was "Well, we'll see."

I didn't give a fuck what this prick thought, which was a new revelation in itself. I had spent the last few years caring about what everyone thought.

That further sealed the deal. I was finally gaining some confidence back.

I was going to have an exciting life. Even if it meant mistakes. Even if it meant falling flat on my face. Hell, I was craving a fuckup as much as anything else. This playing-it-safe, straddling-the-fence kind of existence felt like living in quicksand and I wanted out.

I waved goodbye to the life in the green uniform and the secure, pensionable job that had provided for me—not just in the last couple of years, but that fed me as a child, and I was aware of the new luxury it afforded me. My time at Aer Lingus gave me the chance to dream again and the confirmation that I would never be normal, no matter how many rules I followed.

And now it was time to hang out with some teenage theatre kids.

BROADWAY

My first day of school I walked in nervously, ready to take it all in.

There were a bunch of "theatre folk"—in touch with their feelings, open to emoting at any second, should the flicker of a sensation hit their being kinda folk—lining the hallways.

Having lived a quiet life of repression for the past few years, this was going to be quite the adjustment. On the flip side, no one was judgey and I liked that. It allowed me to try out this "being myself" thing from time to time.

The first year of the course was all about stripping back the layers and masks we wear in public or for other people. Some exercises were more peculiar than others; like watching chocolate melt and then becoming chocolate, which resulted in the class writhing on the floor and groaning like they were in some sort of weird chocolate orgy. Instructions like "drop into your anus" didn't help make this feel any less weird.

But then there were less peculiar classes. During one Meisner exercise where the objective was to simply look across from your partner and repeat what they say while they make observations about you, the professor admonished me for smiling too much.

"That's just how I am; I'm a smiler," I retorted.

"No, you're not" came the response from the rather determined teacher.

"But I am, really, just smiley; I'm always like this," I insisted.

"It's a learned habit. That's not who you are," he exposed me.

How the fuck did he know?!

I had been trying to mask how miserable I had been ever since I had given up on wrestling.

How could he so clearly see that I had plastered this fake yet authentic enough smile to my face for the past three years in the hopes that no one would know I was dying on the inside?

I was already getting more out of this course than I could have possibly anticipated, including being accepted to Columbia College for the semester abroad the following year. My master plan had worked and everything was going perfectly.

And when I thought it couldn't get more perfect, I was told that for our first-year play we were going to be doing an adaptation of my all-time favorite book, *Animal Farm* by George Orwell.

I ran a victory lap of the classroom before the teacher and now director, Susie, continued, "There won't be any auditions. You'll do that for your third-year play. I'm just going to cast this one."

Oh, great, I thought, aware that I wasn't one of her favorites.

The next day, she posted the cast list on the wall, sending everyone clamoring to see their position, some yelping with delight, some rolling their eyes.

When the mob had dissipated, I approached the list with bated breath and scrolled down to see my name:

REBECCA QUIN—COW NUMBER 2.

Not even Cow number 1. Cow number 2. "Number 2" being a euphemism for shit. I was cow shit.

I'm still salty about it.

Nevertheless, I put in an arduous amount of work on the background of this cow shit. I examined her likes, dislikes, family history, even naming her shitty ass.

And now that things had taken a U-turn from perfect to shit, ol' Susie kept on driving us down to Dumpsville. She announced that this particular play would in fact take place on an actual farm. Moreover, it was up to us to bring our friends and family in as the audience.

I told no one. I invited no one.

For the more-than-one-hour duration of the play, I knelt on the ground, avoiding actual cow shit and waiting to deliver my one big line.

"My udder is about to burst!"

Then it was back to staring at the ground and pretending to chew the cud.

Thoughts that I was once a regular main eventer in Japan or even that I gave up my well-paying job that brought me around the world swirled around my head.

We all have to pay our dues in any line of work. This was no different.

And even with this dues paying, I felt more on track than I had in four years if not longer. I was working towards something I wanted to be great at.

When summer hit and I had scraped the smell of goat piss from my pores, I set sail on my next adventure, bound for New York City on what was called a J-1 visa.

I still had cheap airfare, and a friend or two in the airline.

I booked myself into a grimy hostel beside Central Park that cost me thirty-five dollars per night for three nights. I had $2K in my bank account.

This should do me the summer, I thought. *Heck, I might not even need a job!*

After spending nearly six hundred dollars the first day on essentials like a phone and I'm not even sure what else, a slice of pizza, maybe, I realized I had underestimated how hard it would be to find accommodations or how expensive New York was. If I wanted out of this hostel, or to eat, I'd need a job yesterday.

I hounded every Irish bar in town, figuring they'd most likely have a soft spot for me.

A friend of mine from the airline had mentioned an Irish bar called Shades of Green down on 14th Street. She said they always looked after Irish people.

Résumé in hand, eyes wide with wonder, and as much pep in my voice as a semipro cheerleading squad, I asked, "Do you have any jobs going?"

"We don't at the moment, no. But here, where are you from?" the bartender asked with a heavy Kerry brogue, clearly detecting my accent.

It's a thing Irish people do, possibly more than any other nationality. When we hear an Irish twang anywhere else in the world, we want to know all about that person and if we have any relatives or friends in common. We usually do. There may be over 4 million of us, but we still feel like a tribe. And if one of us is lost in the wild, we try to take care of them.

"Dublin. I'm over for the summer on a J-1 and I gotta say, I underestimated how tough this city would be."

"Ah, 'tis, 'tis. Sure look it; won't you sit down here and have a drink now, won't you?"

"I will," I said, beginning to worry if I was going to have to pack up and go home within a week.

"Where are you staying?"

"Up at Central Park in a hostel."

"Ah, Jaysus. And how much are you paying up there?"

"Thirty-five dollars a night."

"Well now, we have a room upstairs. It's nothing fancy, but you could stay here while you search. I'll charge you five hundred dollars for the month. How does that sound?"

It sounded good. And much cheaper than anything I had looked at on Craigslist.

When he said it was nothing much, he really meant it was nothing much.

The room had a sink, a twin bed, and barely enough room to put a suitcase.

There was a communal shower and toilet down the hall.

The room next to mine housed a couple of drug addicts who had lived there for years under rent control and would return home at 7:00 am from god knows where and yell at each other for no less than an hour every morning. That was my wake-up call each day.

Although they were very nice to me, I'd never dare leave my door unlocked.

Running low on funds and in the midst of a mild panic attack, I got a call one afternoon from a bar called Hibernia up on 50th Street.

"Would you be willing to come in for a trial?" asked the manager.

The place had been dead when I went in there, so apprehensively I said, "Sure, when would you like me to come in?"

"Tonight? Around five?"

That's in two hours!

"Yeah, yeah, I'll be there!"

At five o'clock I rocked up, and much to my shock, the place was happening. The regulars were welcoming; the staff was awesome. The tips were flowing.

The place was like Cheers—the Boston basement bar of the iconic eighties sitcom—in that the same people were there every day and the staff made a conscious effort to get to know them.

I was their first experiment in hiring a waitress. I wasn't the best, but I could banter, so the customers liked me, tipped me, and it meant I kept my job.

One such customer who often came in for the chats went by the name of Ryan Callahan.

"Hey, what did you do before you did this?" he asked inquisitively.

"A lot of things, flight attendant, pro wrestler, perso—"

"Wait, you're not Rebecca Knox, are you?" he interrupted.

Taken aback, I thought no one knew who I was, nor would anyone remember me.

"Eh, yeah, that's me."

"Everyone wondered what happened to you!"

I don't think he was actually speaking about "everyone." Ryan was a dedicated wrestling fan, knowing the ins and outs of the whole business, including the indies. He would go on to become the lead writer of *Raw* and *SmackDown* less than a decade later.

Even when I had moved on from wrestling during those years, it would find little ways to pop up and say hi. And I would have to nod politely, give it a quick wave, put my head down, and keep moving as fast as I could.

Which, in a way, was a metaphor for living in NYC.

I was too cheap to get taxis home and too scared to take a subway after midnight, so I strolled the streets of Manhattan every night after my shift ended.

Contrasted to the hustle and bustle of the daytime, there was something beautiful about that late-night, hour-long walk. It was just me and the city that had been so overpopulated hours ago, now empty. The buildings were all shut down for the night, the bright lights still on. The bags of garbage on the street and smell of spilled beer and piss interacting at each corner and alley were somehow charming rather than repulsive. Realizing that I had come here with near nothing and had somehow made it through, built relationships, and was making enough money to survive was a reminder that sometimes you have to follow wherever that gut feeling leads you.

SIGN

Returning to Ireland after my blissful New York summer, I had gained a significant amount of confidence, which made my transition back to college easy. I knew I had Chicago just around the corner, but in the meantime I was going to immerse myself in Dublin life and getting better at this acting thing.

You know when you get caught cheating and the teacher says, "You're only cheating yourself"? That never resonated with me, because I didn't care if I was good at trigonometry or whatever. Acting, however, was different. I wanted to make sure it got all of my attention.

I even got myself a job in a little family-owned health food store across from the college. Learning about nutrition on my downtime from a health and wellness perspective as opposed to a physical perspective did wonders in rehabilitating my eating disorder. Of course it didn't cure it completely, but between finding a new interest in acting to fixate on and prioritizing how I felt over how I looked, I was making progress.

Five minutes from the college was my gym, though calling it a gym seems reductive. This was my safe haven, my hangout spot, my social scene. It may not have looked like much, a giant warehouse hidden in a back alley on the outskirts of the city. The cold white brick walls, fluorescent lights, and extremely basic equipment were all filthy but full of personality and grit, inviting only the most hard-core to train there.

Two such hard-core legends were Rachel Walker and Joey Cabray. I had known them from my wrestling days. Joey was a wrestler (one of those aforementioned IWW eejits) but was also a brilliant promoter. He had started a company called American Wrestling Rampage, which was selling out buildings all over Europe, bringing life to the Irish wrestling community. Rachel was his stunning girlfriend who had fallen into the business by association and was a natural in the ring. She was also the coolest woman I had ever met, and even though I was long since gone from wrestling, we quickly became the best of friends, training together daily, having sleepovers, baking healthy treats like a couple of old ladies.

I didn't know it at the time, but this friendship was going to change my life forever.

Two weeks before I had to go to Chicago, my grandmother felt desperately ill. She was taken into the hospital and was diagnosed with ovarian cancer.

I was in the room when the doctors offered her chemotherapy. "There's no point in prolonging the inevitable," she said. "I've had a good life." It was the most serene I had ever seen her.

As a child I remembered her being the fussy Catholic lady who would worry about everything and never let us do anything. On her deathbed, surrounded by her five children and thirteen grandchildren, she had found peace. And as she was a committed believer in a better life after this one, there was no fear.

Though never one to leave the party early, she didn't want to miss out on these last moments. So every time we thought she was about to pass on to the next realm, she'd open one eye to see who was still in the room.

At first, we all sat around crying at the thought of losing her.

Then we started laughing that she was here for the attention, cracking jokes to deal with the grief.

But someone had to shut this party down, so I had a decision to make: Do I go to Chicago or wait around for, well, the inevitable?

My family urged me to go, but I wanted to be there, for her, for my mom, for all of them.

I had always felt like the black sheep of the family. The problem child, the rebel, the renegade. I had caused my grandma so much heartache and disappointment in her life through my rebellious teenage years and unconventional career path in young adulthood. However, in the last few years, I had grown and matured, bringing us closer together, and I'd make sure to bring her out for coffee and chocolates whenever I could.

I held her hand, knowing that I'd never get to do this again. "I'm sorry for everything, Grandma. I know I was difficult. I'll try to be better."

"You were always very spirited; I hope all your dreams come true" were the last words she said to me before I left the hospital, a mess, about to take the next step in making those dreams come true, whatever they were now.

I landed in Chicago the following day. It was January 2011 and the Midwest winter cut through my bones. Life goes on.

When I woke up the next morning, my mom told me my grandmother had passed away peacefully that night.

Her last words were "I'm going to miss Becky."

I'd miss her too.

Columbia College was like something I had seen on an American TV show. A sprawling campus, spread out across downtown with film and TV students mingling among the theatre folk and everyone collaborating on different projects.

They actually ran plays during the year that you could audition for. *Audition for!!!!!* Fuck you, Cow number 2, I was gonna earn my roles.

The creativity, the trial and error, this was something I wanted to be a part of. Damn right I left my good, pensionable job for this. For the first time in my life I was getting straight A's.

With all this newfound tenacity, I decided to email one of the promotions I used to work for, SHIMMER in Chicago during my indie wrestling days. Not only did I work for them, but I had no-showed two events when I was in my darkest of times, five years previous.

I was possessed by an urge to make things right with everyone. Maybe it was the loss of my grandma; maybe it was my Catholic guilt; maybe it was a feeling of security in my current path without fear I'd be lured back to the wrestling ring.

Still, I wanted a sliding-doors moment, if you will, a chance to see what might have become of me if I had stayed, but I wasn't even sure if the promoter, Dave Prazak, would respond. I may have torched that bridge to the ground.

To my shock, he responded enthusiastically that he'd love to have me. One thing about the wrestling business is it has the tendency to forgive. For example, Madusa was inducted into the WWE Hall of Fame even after famously throwing her WWE women's title in the trash live on WCW television, WWE's greatest competition.

When I got to the Berwyn Eagles hall, the old stomping grounds for a young Rebecca Knox, the darkness of the interior gave me some solace as I crept in.

Maybe no one will notice me till showtime.

A younger me once walked into this musky old hall with the presence of a rock star. Twenty-four-year-old me was painfully aware I had become an outsider and was nervous how the other women would react to me. *Why did I think this would be a good idea?* I asked myself. As I was contemplating turning around and leaving before anyone saw me, no-showing for a third time, I ran straight into Sweet Saraya.

She jumped and yelled an octave higher than I would have liked, "What the fuck happened to you?" as she punched me on the arm with force. For such a skinny little thing, she was powerful.

I paused, not sure how to articulate the haze that had been my life over the past five years. She wasn't being hostile. There was even a smile on her face.

"We were all worried about you."

They cared. Shit. That stung even more than if they did hate me.

I felt ashamed and regretfully loved.

She grabbed me and gave me a big hug before her daughter, Saraya, came running up. She was all grown up from the last time I had seen her, an absolute stunner with an undeniable charisma about her. She was as friendly as she had been five years previous. It was obvious WWE was going to sign her as soon as they met her.

The locker room hosted a lot of familiar faces. Some had gotten jaded with wrestling and talked bitterly about the industry.

I liked talking to them the most. Their bitterness affirmed my choice to leave and reassured me that I had taken the right path, no matter how many years I had spent agonizing over it.

One of my strongest previous rivals had become almost skeletal; I had no idea how she could take a bump without dispersing into dust. I saw the pain of her eating disorder, but my fucked-up mind was envious of her abs.

The banter was strong among most of the girls, which made me feel like an imposter. I was the ghost of wrestling past, but like a really meek ghost who was too scared to say boo.

For the next two nights, I was the British girls' manager and got up to my usual shenanigans of taunting the crowd and making an ever-living show of myself. The crowd remembered me. They embraced me and were happy I returned. I enjoyed being back in front of them, but something was missing. They cheered me because of an old fondness for who I was, but I was no longer that person, and I wasn't doing what they came to see. I was putting on a show, but without committing my body, mind, and soul to the performance.

When the weekend was over, I felt like that was it. That I had gone back and had gotten a taste of what it was like. Only it didn't have the same flavor it once had.

After years of wondering what life would have been like if I had stayed, it seemed like I had my answer. I would have become one of the bitter ones.

Even though my time in the SHIMMER locker room felt like I was in Darren Aronofsky's 2008 movie, *The Wrestler*, by the time I returned to Dublin for my last year of college, along came that nagging feeling once again: *Maybe you should go back to wrestling. You have things you haven't done yet.*

I thought I was done with you! You saw what that locker room was like; you didn't belong there anymore.

You have unfinished business.

It's over, goddamn it.

Is it?

I don't know!!!!!

Why was this so damn confusing?!

A few weeks later, I cycled into town to meet Fergal, who was back from Japan for a few weeks. Though we had broken up many years ago and he had lived in Japan nearly the entire time after our relationship ended, we had remained close friends who were there for each other through thick and thin. He had become one of New Japan's biggest stars, but he was still the same grounded lad I met in that school gym a decade earlier.

We caught up on life; we walked around the shops; we sat down for lunch.

"You doing good?" he asked.

"Yeah, I'm doing great. I love college; only a few more months and I'm done. But can I be honest about something?"

"Yeah, of course."

"Part of me feels like I have unfinished business in wrestling. Like I've never been fully able to let it go."

"How old are you now?"

"Twenty-five."

"Jesus, is that all? Fuck. Well. Look. If you really feel like this is something you want to do, go back now, because I don't want to be sitting here with you in ten years' time and you say the same thing. Only then it'll be too late."

I let that sink in. Swooshed it around my skull and then let it go. Maybe he was right. But I didn't have time to think about it right now.

It was coming to the end of the school year and I had a lot of work to do. Between plays and thesis, I could hardly squeeze a workout in.

On a break from rehearsals one day at the gym, I ran into Rachel, who was on her way out. "Hey, can I talk to you a second?" she asked.

"Of course."

"I got a WWE tryout."

It whacked me like a heart punch. But not an entirely bad one. Just one that jars you and lets you know you're feeling things.

"Oh, wow! That's amazing." I was genuinely delighted for her, with only a twinge of envy.

"Would you have any advice for me?"

"Gosh, it's been a while, but what are you worried about?" I didn't know what I could really offer anymore.

"Character stuff, I suppose," she responded, making me feel a little more useful. Maybe I had picked up a thing or two in acting school that could help her.

"I'd love to sit down and chat, but I have to fly through this workout. Maybe we can get a coffee tomorrow?"

"That sounds great!"

During my workout I was filled with so many emotions. Excitement for her. Regret for what could have been. My brain spiraled with make-believe scenarios.

But I had my thing. I was acting. I had plans to move back to New York.

Rachel already had it in the bag. She was the total package. Beautiful, athletic, personable, a body that was ripped, jacked, and curvy in perfect balance. She didn't need my help.

We sat down and talked about ideas. I could feel myself lighting up talking about the business and all the possibilities that lay ahead for her. We went as far as picking new wrestling names for her. Why could I be so excited for her future in wrestling but was convinced mine would be so bleak?

She of course aced the tryout and earned herself a spot in NXT, as if there could be any doubt.

A few weeks later, I saw Joe working out like a madman.

"Looking swole, Joe," I encouraged him.

"I got a WWE tryout, so tryna get as lean as possible."

"Oh, man, that's so awesome." It really was. No one deserved it more than Joe. He loved it, worked his ass off for it, and had an amazing brain for it.

But there were those mixed feelings again.

Stop it! I'd tell myself. *You've got your plan. You get your degree. Then you'll go back to New York and you pursue acting. Like a goddamn adult. None of this kid wrestling shit.*

Ultimately, Joe landed a spot in NXT too.

This was great! I'd have friends to visit when I went to America. They'd be in Florida with NXT; I'd be in New York. They would be together.

Good for them. Good for me. Good for us.

I was happy for them. I wasn't jealous at all.

I lied to myself.

THE COMEBACK

Once college was over and I was out in the big bad world, auditions weren't exactly flowing and finding an agent was like mining for diamonds. Shockingly, no one wanted to take a chance on this perfectly average lady with zero experience beyond her college degree—somehow, I hadn't anticipated this. Still, I pounded the pavement delivering my résumé and headshot to every game and gig in town.

In the meantime, in a shitty turn of events, Rachel tore her ACL, which is about the worst knee injury one can have, mere weeks before she was to report to NXT.

I was devastated for her, but I think part of her was relieved to delay her departure to Florida. She wasn't looking forward to leaving her family, and the added time in Ireland made it more likely that she and Joe could start NXT at the same time. And in the meantime, we got plenty of time to hang, train, and talk about future plans.

With precisely zero acting work coming my way, I decided it was time to pull the trigger on my New York plans and booked my flights.

But as fate works, weeks before being New York–bound, I got a phone call from a new show that had started filming in Ireland called *Vikings*. It was one of the largest TV productions that Ireland had ever facilitated and they wanted *ME* to be a part of it!

Not in any role I was prepared for, however. I was called to be part of the stunt team. My résumé listed so much random physical experience I had amassed over the years in search of a hobby to replace wrestling—I listed my ability to horse ride, sword fight, snowboard, and scuba dive, plus my experience with Muay Thai and bodybuilding. They assumed this physical jack-of-all-trades was a stuntwoman.

"We might have a bit of work for you on set here," Paul Burke, the stunt coordinator, offered. "Would you be interested?"

"Absolutely I would be!" I accepted as the realization that I am not actually a stuntwoman came to me.

Sure, it wasn't acting. But it was acting adjacent and I could not afford to fuck this one up.

Okay, brain, think! How are you going to pull this one off? You were good at wrestling. Go down to Joe's school and brush up. Then apply that confidence to the stunt work! Bing bang boom! No one will notice a thing!

I showed up at a beginner's class, less nervous than I usually was in these situations. I was no longer wrestling and it was no longer the goal, so if I messed up, who cared?

Any remnants of nerves that I did have were put to rest by Joe's ease of coaching. He is a leader by nature, an alpha who is communicative, kind, and thoughtful, but you dare not cross him.

We began to lock up and move around, running drills with tackles and headlocks.

"You still got it," Joe started a mock chant for me.

I lit up like a New York Christmas tree.

After class Joe pulled me aside. "Would you ever think about going for a WWE tryout? You clearly still love it."

I felt transported to another dimension. My body screamed at me with an intuition so strong it couldn't be silenced. *YES!* I yelled in the confines of my own mind.

Externally, I still couldn't admit that was what I wanted to do. So after staring at him for what felt like several hours, I responded, "Ah, thanks, Joe, but I have my plan now; I'm going to

New York, visa's booked, so are flights, and I wanna pursue this acting thing. And I guess this stunt thing now."

"Well, think about it, 'cause I think you'd get it."

I didn't need to think about it. I knew this was right. After all the pushing I had done in the last six years, it finally felt like I was being pulled.

A few days later, after much self-talk, coming to Jesus, and finally being honest with myself, I knew I had to postpone all plans I had made for the future.

I called Joe. "I think I might take you up on getting that tryout."

"Excellent, I'll give Robbie Brookside a call."

Robbie Brookside?! I loved Robbie Brookside. I only met him one time, but he was someone you only need to meet once to feel like you've been friends forever. And now Robbie was part of WWE's recruiting team.

"Knoxy giiiiirl!" he called me with his thick Liverpool accent ringing like an angelic siren in my ear.

"Hey, Robbie! So good to hear from you!"

"I was wondering what 'appened to ya. I remember that young girl that was goin' toe-to-toe with Sweet Saraya. What have you been up to?"

"Oh, everything, Robbie, but I was never able to get wrestling out of my system."

"Well, I'd love you to come and give this a go. We're holding a three-day tryout in Birmingham in five weeks. If you can send me over some pictures and a résumé, I'll pass it on to the higher-ups."

"Absolutely! I'll send that over right away," I responded giddily.

Finally, I was determined I was going to get that contract.

With Rachel down with her injured ACL, I didn't want to be insensitive and act overly excited. But there was a strong possibility that if I got it, we might start at the same time, the three amigos, all off on an adventure to take over WWE!

My training picked up and my diet got tighter as I prepared for not just one big opportunity, but two.

I still had my stint on *Vikings*. With 4:00 am wake-up calls and twelve-hour days, long drives to and from set, and a stop at the gym on the way home, I was in my element.

The production was huge. The actors were cool and the stuntpeople were sound. If I wanted, I could keep doing this stunt thing. But I had to know what life was like in WWE, and if it really was my calling.

During a lunch break, one of the lead actors, Clive Standen, took a seat opposite me and struck up a conversation. Though it wasn't your usual small talk.

"What's your deal?" he dove straight in.

"Well, I just finished my acting degree, so I've been looking for work, but I also just got a WWE tryout!"

"A what?" His eyebrows rose.

"You know WWE? Hulk Hogan, The Rock. Wrestling."

"Yeah, yeah, of course."

"Well, I used to wrestle when I was younger, but I gave up six years ago, and I just got a tryout," I detailed.

"Wow, that's interesting. That's probably pretty all-encompassing, eh?"

"Yeah, it's a full-time gig."

"What about acting?" he pressed.

"Yeah, I'm a little torn on what to do, 'cause I love this, but I've never been able to let go of wrestling," I confessed.

"How old are you now?"

"Twenty-five."

"How long do you imagine you'd be wrestling for?"

"I don't know, really."

"You're at that prime age to make things happen in the acting world now; you wait much longer and it might not happen for you. I think you really need to consider that too," Clive advised.

He was making valid points in a valiant attempt to be helpful, and, if anything, he confirmed what I knew for certain: I would not be able to move ahead in any aspect of my life if I didn't give wrestling my best shot.

I spent the next few weeks training with whoever might be free to help scrape the ring rust off. Fergal, recommencing his role as coach, made sure my back bumps and lock-ups were snappier and tighter than ever, reminding me that "they're really just looking for the basics."

I made sure to avail myself of every contact in my Rolodex, and reached out to Sheamus, who had now become one of WWE's biggest stars.

"Work on your conditioning and your promo. The wrestling will be the easy part for you," Sheamus advised me as though I were still the eighteen-year-old who had once impressed him in a training session.

"Keep it simple" was the main message.

One thing that wasn't going to be simple, however, was the daunting task of telling my mother that I was getting back into wrestling.

"They heard about me and reached out and asked if I wanted a tryout. I'd like to at least give it a shot," I told her. It was more of a misdirection of the truth than a blatant lie, really.

She was shockingly not upset. The idea that I was being recruited by the biggest and most reputable wrestling organization in the world was more palatable than "Hey, Mom, I'm going to Luxembourg for the weekend to wrestle in a field for free."

Besides, I had proved to her that I could do the things I put my mind to. I got my college degree. Maybe I could show her that I could have an impact on the wrestling business. Change the way women's wrestling was viewed, usher in a new era. Sure, it was ambitious, but it wasn't impossible, and what is life if not for taking big, bold risks, especially when it can change the outlook of a generation?

I packed my bags, brought my nicest workout attire, got gear specifically made for the occasion, and showed up at Dublin Airport ready to earn my way into the world's biggest wrestling promotion.

I found the nearest ATM and took out a few euro to get me through the next few days. When I looked at my account, there was only thirty-five euro left. Welp. I had a little laugh to myself, because I really had nothing to lose and everything to gain. I better make this work.

THE TRYOUT

I landed in Birmingham all butterflies and enthusiasm.

I've always found, throughout all of my endeavors, that confidence is fleeting and largely circumstantial. However, waking up in this circumstance, I was confident. Everything had led me to this moment, every detour, every blunder, every head-scratching *What the fuck was I thinking?* incident, all led to this. And there was no way I was leaving without a contract.

I showed up in my most flattering workout gear, tanned up and makeup on best as I could do, which wasn't great, to be fair, but God loves a trier.

WWE had provided breakfast before the tryout. Everyone on their best behavior, elbows off the table, dabbing their faces politely with napkins, leaving the last piece of cantaloupe, all signs of people looking to impress.

We got to the tryout hall and were introduced to the people who would decide our fate: Canyon Ceman, who was the lead talent scout; the voice of my teen years, good ol' Jim Ross. There was Norman Smiley, a well-respected former WCW wrestler, and coach at NXT; Robbie Brookside; Gerry Brisco, a former wrestler and vastly underrated on-air stooge; and William Regal, who is nothing short of a wrestling legend and someone I was a huge fan of growing up. As they all stood in front of the ring with unreadable faces—the Mona Lisas of talent scouting—delivering their speeches, intended to be either motivational or sobering, I couldn't help but smile from ear to ear.

I was going to endure anything and everything.

I would pass out or die before I quit. That was the deal I made with myself.

It might sound silly, well, because it is, but when the drills got tough, I would sing "Lose Yourself" by Eminem to myself. "You better lose yourself in the music, the moment / You own it, you better never let it go," shuffle, sprawl, sprint. "You only get one shot, do not miss your chance to blow / This opportunity comes once in a lifetime," sprint, sprawl, sprint.

No matter how much I was hurting, I could never let it show. A smile was permanently plastered on my face, like I was going for a pleasant stroll through a meadow, even if it felt like my lungs might explode into a thousand pieces.

There were people who gave up when it got too hard or stopped mid-drill. It had been over a decade since my teenage self was yelling at the dropouts of *Tough Enough* on TV, and now I was witnessing it here, live in person, mind as boggled as it had been years before. When the possibility of achieving your dreams simply lies at the end of a round of burpees, do the fucking burpees.

By the time the physical part of the tryout was over, I knew I had outworked everyone. The coaches seemed to like me and I worked well within the group of thirty other hopefuls, even if I had mentally berated many of them for being little bitches.

Then it was time for my favorite part of wrestling—the promo. The part where you get to talk to the audience and tell them who you are and why they should care.

I put together a promo akin to my old indie character, Rebecca Knox, decorated with rhymes and puns and doused in energy. Rattling through it, I felt I was giving the Gettysburg Address, for the amount of confidence I had in my content.

However, I couldn't tell if it was the shits or maybe they just wanted to see something else when Regal spoke up, in his very Regal voice, distinct yet soft-spoken.

"Tell us your story."

Without the armor of my prerehearsed "masterpiece," I told the class my life story up until this moment. Opening up about my struggles with leaving wrestling and spending years trying to fill the void it left caused my voice to tremble and tears to fall from my eyes. I was on the brink of a whole new world.

Canyon pulled me aside afterwards.

"You did very well on this tryout and we liked you. We do want to offer you a contract, but I gotta be honest, we don't know what day your stuff is going to land on Vince or Hunter's desk. They could just be looking for models that day."

"Yeah, of course. Thank you so much; this has been the best experience of my life."

The other thing going against me was my age. They were looking for women aged eighteen to twenty-five and men aged eighteen to thirty. I was right at the cutoff point of being an old spinster.

Regardless, there's moments in life that feel like the whole universe is conspiring to make something happen. This was one of those times.

I walked away with only a slight twinge of doubt.

THE CONTRACT SIGNING

It was four weeks after the tryout when, en route to the gym, I got a call from an American number. "Hi, Rebecca, it's Canyon."

I pulled over to the side of the road, prepared to hear either the best news of my life or the worst.

"I'm glad I get to be the one to call you, because I know how much this will mean to you. We would like to offer you a developmental deal at NXT with a tentative date of beginning sometime in July 2013."

Floods of tears fell down my face. Butterflies did a complicated, synchronized dance number in my belly. My voice reached octaves it had never reached before as I squeaked out, "Thank you, thank you so much! I won't let you down!" I was filled with gratitude and wanted more than anything to make them proud that they trusted me.

By the time I reached the gym, I was too hyper to focus.

"Gah ma god!! You can't tell anyone, but I just got signed!" I beamed to one of my friends who happened to be there. "I wanna make women's wrestling the coolest thing on TV! I'm telling you now, man. I'm gonna main event WrestleMania!" I rejoiced as I jumped up and down and spun in circles.

"Ha-ha-ha. That's great! And it's nice and all to have dreams, Becky, but be realistic," he retorted in the most unoffensive way possible.

It might sound jarring to have a friend shit all over your dreams so flippantly, but it really wasn't. At that time, it did seem like a damn near impossibility to have women be the main event of WrestleMania. But the fact that he said I couldn't meant I absolutely had to.

Wanting to share my good news further, I made my way to Rachel's. But before I could fill her in, she let me in on her devastating news: she had retorn her ACL the night before.

It was a huge blowback and could possibly ruin her chances of ever actually getting to NXT. Certainly it meant all three of us weren't starting together after all.

Of course she was still happy for me when I told her. She's the best. But tearing your ACL twice within a year while on the verge of being in WWE is close to tragic.

For me, it was a warning sign that there was still plenty that could go wrong between now and the summer. I had to pass a medical exam, and though, as far as I knew, I was perfectly healthy, what if they found something? What if they changed their minds and they did only want models? Or what if I suffered the same fate as Rachel and got injured months before I was set to leave? These thoughts ravaged my brain daily; it was so close and yet I was scared it would somehow slip through my fingers again.

I was even petrified to go to wrestling training before I got there.

"What if I get hurt too?" I asked Fergal.

"They're going to have their own way of doing things, so there's no point in getting into bad habits. They'll want to train you up from scratch anyway," he counselled me from afar.

All I needed to do was cocoon myself in Bubble Wrap until July and I would get to start at a brand-new state-of-the-art training facility in Orlando that WWE was calling the Performance Center.

Joe had already left for Florida to begin training but was off to a rough start. A few days in and he had already suffered a concussion and was having a hard time adjusting to the new lifestyle.

There was a laundry list of etiquette and codes in the day-to-day life of a trainee. Joe made sure to give me the rundown lest I get off to a bad start.

"Shake everyone's hand. You have to ride with the girls. It looks bad if you ride with the guys. And do not get involved with any of the lads. They frown upon that sort of thing.

"They don't like people who've had experience. They think they're uncoachable. Be coachable.

"You have to always put your hands up when you're in the ring to protect yourself.

"Never talk back, even if they're wrong—just say, 'Yes, sir, won't happen again,' and move on."

The list went on and on and I clung to every word, wanting to make the best first impression I could and not offend anyone. I had also taken years away from wrestling and wanted to be seen as a blank canvas, but to have spent years and years perfecting your craft, to come in and be told you know nothing sounded like such a mind fuck. However, I had already decided, no matter how many tests they threw my way, I wouldn't let it break me.

I packed my bags and boarded my flight to Florida. This time was a lot different from the last ill-planned-out Orlando trip. This time, I knew what I was doing. I was going to change wrestling forever.

NXT

Grandma said, "I hope all your dreams come true," and it felt like she must have been shmoozing Jesus every day she was up there to make all of this happen, because after years of questioning, stressing, wondering, *What if . . . ?* I was finally in Orlando, ready to start at NXT and about to find out if I had what it takes.

The main thing for me was to not fuck it all up. Which was highly likely, as I do have a bright red self-destruct button illuminating at the front of my mind at all times.

Joe suggested I wear a "nice dress" for the big first day. Apparently all the girls wore "nice dresses." But I didn't have any nice dresses. I didn't have any dresses at all. And certainly not a surplus of money to spend on "nice dresses."

He brought me, appropriately, to Ross Dress for Less, where I bought three dresses for the grand sum of thirty dollars.

Not being well-versed in the art of nice-dress buying, I had acquired three frumpy bridesmaid-looking dresses. You know, the kind a bride buys her pals if she wants to be certain they don't upstage her.

I picked out the best one of the lot and hung it up ready for the morning. A fine, frilly beige fucker. *Who could resist me in this level of high fashion? They might send me to the main roster straightaway!* I thought.

I got up extra early, hardly being able to sleep from the excitement anyway, and spent hours meticulously straightening my hair and ensuring my makeup looked as good as I was capable of.

It was all for naught. By the time I had stepped into the humid Orlando air, my hair began to frizz and my makeup ran down my face. *Great.*

I was so nervous I could barely talk on the short ten-minute drive from our apartment. As we approached the warehouse, I looked out the window to see a giant sign on the building that read: "WWE PERFORMANCE CENTER."

This was exactly how I pictured a wrestling school would look all eleven years ago when I took my first class in that tiny school hall in Bray with six padded mats on the floor.

Joe and I entered the front door, polite office staff greeting us enthusiastically, ordaining us with official badges complete with lanyards. A bald man named Ryan Katz with a colorful suit and the world's biggest smile offered a guided tour through the building. He was part of the creative team and glowed as he led us through the building. "This is HHH's baby," he declared. HHH—aka Hunter Hearst Helmsley, aka Paul Levesque—was one of WWE's biggest stars, and the reason every child and teen in the late nineties was getting in trouble in school for yelling, "Suck it!" while gesturing at their crotch. Famed for his entertaining work with his popular group, or "faction" in wrestling terms—DX—he was also one of WWE's most versatile stars, going from comedy to badass in the blink of an eye and making it seem natural. He had recently been charged with heading talent development. The son-in-law to Vince McMahon, he was likely to one day run the whole company.

And his baby was immaculate. Freshly painted walls, unstained carpets, not a speck of dust in sight, it was like the whole place had been sprayed with new-car smell. Portraits of legends lined the walls: Dusty Rhodes, Vince McMahon Sr., Harley Race, Gorgeous George, Mae Young, Bruno Sammartino.

The facility boasted a state-of-the-art gym, a physio room, a practice area with seven wrestling rings, a promo room, a green-screen room, a kitchen, televisions, and the most beautiful locker rooms and bathrooms I had ever seen in a sporting facility.

After a long and winding pilgrimage, I had arrived at the Mecca of wrestling. The place you wanted to be if you wanted to be someone in this business.

And I felt totally out of place.

More so as I was about to get a side-by-side comparison with my direct competition. An all-talent meeting was about to happen on the gym floor led by the head coach, Bill DeMott, whom I had watched tear people to shreds on *Tough Enough* years earlier.

As I joined the congregation, any amount of pseudo-confidence I had had during my tryout had completely washed away. I began comparing my frumpy, awkward self against the other female newcomers, who happened to be the most beautiful and glamorous collection of women I had ever seen, coming complete with bubbly, captivating personalities.

The new influx of men were built like giant stone statues and had to turn sideways to fit through the doors.

When I was feeling like I couldn't get more insecure, the veteran trainees joined us. All equally as impressive and beaming as if their blood were made entirely of charisma.

If you looked around on that day in July 2013 and had to pick one person who 10 million percent was not going to make it, I would have been that person.

It didn't help that at the very introduction of the meeting DeMott kicked it off with an ominous warning.

"Look to the people beside you. It's very likely they won't make it."

It felt like the whole group just turned to look directly at the weirdo in the bridesmaid's dress.

When the group reverted their attention to the front, Bill, who was friendly in that "I will slit your throat and not think twice about it but also tell you a joke while I do it" kind of way, introduced us to the remainder of the coaching staff. To even regard these humans as my future coaches made my head want to explode in awe.

There was the legendary Dusty Rhodes, who would be our promo (promotional interview in wrestle-speak) coach. Himself a mold breaker and one of the greatest promos of all time, he now dressed like the sweet yet sassy old man he had become. He wore ill-fitting blue jeans tucked into work boots, a baseball cap, glasses, and a baggy T-shirt not quite long enough to cover his elbows, which sagged after years of bumping and elbowing people on the top of the head. I immediately wanted his approval.

There was the "Red Rooster" Terry Taylor, who informed me that before I quit, TNA (where he previously worked) thought about bringing me in. Which was a reassurance and made me question the last seven years as a whole.

There was Billy Gunn of the famed tag team The New Age Out-laws, who was even bigger in person. He shook my hand like he wanted to break it.

There was Joey Mercury, most notably known for being half of the tag team MNM or J&J Security, the underlings to a hot boy named Seth Rollins. Joey was also one of the best minds in wrestling. A savant almost. And he was as serious as a stroke. Despite being the smallest of the crew, he was the most intimidating. I was too scared to say hi.

There was Nick Dinsmore, formally known as Eugene—the intellectually stunted wrestling sensation. He was dry in tone and subtly welcoming.

There was Norman Smiley, whom I had already met at my try-out and already loved.

Then there was Sara Amato, the head coach for the women and the person I had been dreading seeing the most. *Fuck*. She was on the first tour of Japan I did. That time I was the main event, getting treated like royalty and still acting like a moany bitch. Hell, she was probably on both of the SHIMMER shows I no-showed.

What if she holds a grudge? What if she thinks I thought I was above learning from her? What if she hates me?

I imagined her inner monologue being a diatribe about how awful I am and wondering how I managed to slip through the cracks. *How the hell did this bitch even make it here? She hasn't wrestled in years and still gets to be in WWE? That's bullshit! She wasn't even that good back then!*

She would have been right to feel like that too.

I shook her hand, wary of acting too familiar with any of the coaches.

"Oh, hey, it's been a while," she said calmly with what I'm certain was a side eye.

It's official: she thinks I shouldn't be here.

The guilt was overwhelming. Who was I to leave the thing that afforded me so much for so long and waltz in here and get the keys to the kingdom when everyone else has suffered for years?

I was the Prodigal Son. And I fucking hate the Prodigal Son story. Bitch gets to blow all his money, live frivolously, do whatever the hell he wants, then struts back in like nothing happened while his brother stayed working and being loyal the whole time. And the dad is just, like, "No worries, fam—we good," and gives him whatever else he wants! Shit, if I'm that good brother, I'd be pissed. And if I'm those good wrestlers who stayed loyal and true to the grind, I'm superpissed.

The wrestling community really is a small village, so I already knew a lot of the people who had made it this far.

I first ran into my ol' pal Rami, whom I hadn't seen since Italy. I gave him the biggest, most enthusiastic hug, hoping he would be a temporary reprieve from my social discomfort. But his returning hug felt a little limp on the squeeze. *Does he hate me too?!*

I was sure I could feel his judgement. Or was it my judgement?

"Holy shit. What are *you* doing here?" he asked, less excited than I was hoping for.

I could ask myself the same dang thing, pal.

"I thought you left the business."

Yep. Judgement. That was definitely judgement.

I overexplained the many years of confusion: a potpourri of guilt, fear, approval seeking, and desperation.

As soon as I finished my spiel to Rami, I rounded a corner to meet another face from the past. This time, it so happened to be someone I went to college with in Chicago. He went by the wrestling name of Aiden English and was nothing but nice to me in the time we were in school, but now I feared he was also wondering how on earth I had managed to get here.

Ugh.

To break up the repetition of my perceived disapproval, Saraya, now known as Paige, ran up and hugged me. "I'm so happy you're here. I've told everyone how good you are," she practically sang in her musically British accent.

Oh no, no no no, why?! I'm not good. Not anymore. I haven't had a match in near seven years! I'm a blank canvas, remember? I don't know anything!

Fuck. The last thing I wanted was for people to have high expectations of me. It's one thing to prove people wrong. It's entirely another to have people think you're great and fail miserably. *Fuck.*

In an attempt to recalibrate, I slunk away to the locker room, closing my eyes and sighing in relief as I shut the door behind me.

Only when I opened my eyes, I noticed that the women's champion (or, as they so awfully named it, the divas champion) AJ Lee was standing to the left of me, typing furiously into her phone.

Without picking up on social cues, I enthusiastically greeted her—"Hello!"—four octaves higher than normal with the underlying desperation of *Please like me.* "I'm Rebecca." She looked up as I stretched out my hand to shake hers, grunted what may have been a "Hi" before going back to finger-punching her phone, leaving me with my arm outstretched, fondling the air.

This is going horribly, I thought as I sat in the bathroom stall, scared to pee too loudly lest I offend.

When I was done doing bathroom things, I washed my hands, not taking the time to dry them preventing I linger in the awkwardness any longer than I had to, I came out to find Big E sitting in a squishy armchair, looking blankly at his phone. The man had the physique of a well-chiseled cube, and if his current on-air persona was anything to go by, this was not a man who enjoyed things.

You cannot be deterred, Quin. You must shake everyone's hand!

So with the same gusto and desperation, I walked over chirpily. "Hello! I'm Rebecca!" *Here's my hand; please shake it.*

He looked up, a modicum of warmth on his stoic face. "Ettore," he said plainly, and unlike my last encounter went for the shake. However, just as he was about to engage in full clasp I realized, in my haste, that my hands were still wet! But by now, my arm had reached maximum extension.

Quickly and nervously I blurted out, "My hands are wet!!"

Too late to turn back now, he courteously shook my hand as his face curdled in disgust, the sound of moisture squelching between our skin.

Great. Now he hates me too. . . .

I walked down the stairs and back towards the practice area, anguished and embarrassed, when I noticed an old road-tripping buddy, TJ Wilson, sitting on the ring. TJ and I would road-trip from Vancouver to Seattle and Portland when we were both on the independent circuit. He had now deservedly made it to the main roster with his soon-to-be wife, Nattie Neidhart.

He was smiling and laughing in his unique TJ way, loud and charmingly obnoxious.

TJ is a special cat. For one, he is an absolute genius with a photographic memory and a charisma that draws people to him, with his ability to tell stories in a way that makes you lose track of time. As soon as you hear his signature voice and cackle, you want to find him so you don't miss out on the fun.

The other thing about TJ is he doesn't take shit from anyone. He's a straight shooter and will tell you, with no qualms, what he thinks about you or any given situation. He also has a deep love for the business and respects people based on the respect they show our industry.

Because of that, I was hesitant to approach him, figuring he'd hate me for giving up too.

He was polite yet apprehensive, or at least that's how I perceived, well, just about everyone I met that day.

After quick pleasantries, I worked up the courage to ask him, "Do you have any advice for me?"

"Yeah, listen to HHH's entrance music." He laughed.

Meaning, "It's all about the game and how you play it." Sure is, buddy.

PERCEPTION IS REALITY

The repetition of life in the Performance Center quickly set in. Not to say it was humdrum. Quite the opposite. It was a daily overdose of adrenaline. Looking at the WWE turnbuckle pads knowing what I was here for and what I was working towards motivated and terrified me in equal measure. With this combined with the crippling fear of failure, amplified by actual failure to deliver, I was an anxious mess.

Not only was it evident I did not look like a "superstar"; I didn't wrestle like one either. The years of ring rust were obvious, and my lack of natural athleticism seemed to reflect off the canvas.

Days began with four hours of wrestling training, a short break, followed by an hour and a half of strength and conditioning. If you were feeling spry, there was extra wrestling training in the afternoon.

Which all would have been fine and well if my body wasn't a little deteriorating bitch. It wasn't breaking down on me because I was taking brutal bumps or from the wear and tear of going hard five days a week and thoughts of impending doom keeping me up at night, but rather it was rolls, little tumbles. The stuff three-year-olds do and make look so fun and easy.

We started every class with a series of rolls, hundreds of the fuckers. But there was one little bastard that got me every time. The three-quarter roll. Roll across your shoulder, tuck your leg, stand up looking the opposite way. Sounds simple. Probably is. But for me, they were my mortal enemy. All the other girls were gliding angelically like elegant tumbleweeds while I dumped, clunked, and groaned across the ring. I'd get up embarrassed, dust myself off, and try again, my hip labrum taking an almighty beating.

"Try it again," Sara would coach, hoping that by some great miracle I'd get this simple maneuver down pat, the girls in the class sharing quiet secondhand embarrassment.

The inability to get these damn rolls felt like a fireable offense. And rather quickly became one, because after just a couple of weeks I was already sidelined with a sprained hip flexor. I was confined to watching practice from a folding chair and taking notes on how not to suck.

The mantra of the PC was "Perception is reality"—i.e., it didn't matter if you worked hard, as long as it looked like you worked hard. It didn't matter if you cared, as long as it looked like you cared. It didn't matter if you really had what it takes to make it, as long as you looked like you did.

I suppose that is essentially how the world operates, more so with the growth of social media, where everyone is attempting to create their own perceived reality.

The reality is the perception of me was awful. And the perception of this particular injury was "she's faking it" or "she can't hack it."

And while I certainly wasn't faking it, the thing I couldn't hack was being so close to my dream and having it ripped out from under me. Especially because of something as lame as a shoulder roll.

If things didn't turn around quickly, my days were numbered.

Girls with no experience at all were far and away surpassing me. Girls who had been there awhile were judging me. Or maybe they weren't, but that's what I perceived—there's layers to this perception shit. Onions.

I didn't feel that judgement from everyone, though. There were several girls I would turn to for a supportive smile or a mantra of encouragement. For the sake of avoiding confusion, I'll call them by their WWE names.

Charlotte Flair, daughter of Ric Flair, was warm and sweet, forever offering up reassurance from the side. She'd yell, "You got this, woman!" as I messed up time and again. One could assume that coming from such a prestigious family might make her stuck-up, but she was far from it. Perhaps the pressure she felt being the child of one of the greatest of all time made her sympathetic to the pressure I was putting myself under. She, however, was a natural. A former gymnast and volleyball player, she was taking to the wrestling ring like a duck to water. The ring also served as a safe haven for her, as she had recently suffered the tragic loss of her younger brother, Reid.

Then there was Sasha Banks. She was more reserved but equally as kind. She was fantastic in the ring and incredibly passionate. She was the only person I could never beat in being "the first person in the building in the morning," though I would try to always be the last to leave.

Hey, when you don't have much to remind them you're worth keeping around, you at least put in the time.

Sasha took me under her wing. Even though she was five years younger than me, she had a much better handle on the appearance aspect than I did.

She taught me that in show business, most of the hair is fake! Weaves, wigs, clip-ins, wefts—there's a whole string of tricks I had no idea about. Eyelashes too! It never dawned on me that this was what the women on TV did.

I know, I know, twenty-six and didn't know anything about anything. Judge me as you will.

She directed me to different cosmetics to buy, gave me eye shadow palettes to try out, and taught me about all of this new hair stuff.

At first, I was terrible at doing everything. When I put on eyelashes, they went closer to my eyebrow than my eyelash. My clip-ins were dangling out of my head. But hey, maybe perception could be that I was trying.

And oh boy was I trying. I was trying harder than anyone had ever tried. I spent hours in the gym, inside and outside the PC. I poured my heart and soul into rehabbing this damn hip flexor. When it finally got better and I finally figured out how to roll safely, I was able to rejoin the class and do everything I could to save my job.

I went to every extra ring-training session, I cut promos every single day. But I could not, for the life of me, get better in the ring.

What was also stopping me was the sheer abundance of restrictions put on the women in terms of how they could wrestle. The year was 2013 and women couldn't punch, couldn't throw uppercuts, and were encouraged to pull hair and slap each other. They couldn't use things like the ring posts or stairs or anything considered "too violent." The mandate came from the top and was commonly accepted as "just the way things are."

As if I weren't having a hard enough time with all of this, I was counselled by Bill to "move like a girl." What the fuck did that even mean? I was a girl, and I was moving—what more do you want? Wrists flailing wildly? Random enticing hair flips? To drop down into a split at any given moment? I was truly baffled by this weird stereotypical instruction.

I was so despaired of that one of the coaches told a girl in my class matter-of-factly, "She's never going to make it."

If even the coaches didn't believe in me, how the hell was I going to convince the biggest wrestling organization in the history of the world to put me on their TV shows?

My chances were next to zero. And that coach would have been right if I wasn't such a determined, largely lucky SOB.

I was eventually moved to the remedial class, while girls who had never wrestled a day in their lives were in the "advanced class."

"It's a test. Don't react," Joe would comfort me as I cried to him from the safety of our shitty apartment.

Luckily, my ol' pal Robbie Brookside was running the super-beginner class and he was an amazing coach. His classes were fun, and perhaps because I had been so desperate for Sara's approval, I was too in my head. With Robbie, I could relax; I knew I had his support. Hell, he was a big reason I was here. He made me feel like I was gonna be okay. And maybe that was all I needed.

It turned out to be a blessing. When I had to return to class with the rest of the girls, I had more pep in my step. I didn't doubt absolutely everything I did. Just most of the things.

One place I didn't doubt myself, however, was our weekly promo class with the one and only Dusty Rhodes.

Dusty was an original. One of wrestling's greats, but one who never fit the mold. He wasn't the most handsome, he wasn't in good shape, but he brought an energy and a passion that were unmatchable. His ability to cut a unique promo that was authentic yet entertaining with his lispy southern voice put him in a league of his own, and all because he was true to himself and had confidence in what he brought to the table.

With all of my battles with insecurity, I stood to learn the most from Dusty.

Promo class was how I could prove to them that I did actually have something. Anything. Some small beacon of light that was worth keeping. I'm pretty sure the Dusty Rhodes–Robbie Brookside support combo saved my job on more than one occasion.

Dusty was said to have loved his "broken toys." The ones with something off about them. The interesting ones.

Unlike the rest of the office, Dusty didn't care for the total package. Where there was no room for improvement, Dusty's work was surplus. But the damaged ones had room to grow and heal, and more to learn from him.

He was able to bring something special out of you so that you might reach superstar level. And usually that something was yourself. Even if you didn't know who you were just yet. He had an eye for a hidden gem.

It was as if he were the Performance Center grandpa, giving love and support to each of his grandkids as needed.

His support and encouragement every week at promo class was the boost of confidence I needed to get through the week. Joe's too.

Every night at home Joe and I would workshop ideas for that week's class, sometimes coming up with wacky characters and ridiculous scenarios. Over meals of slow-cooked chicken and rice, we momentarily left the stress of the daily grind of the PC behind as we prepared for our favorite class.

I was a mischievous old lady in disguise, a fortune-teller, an imp, a hippy, a disheveled maniac, a competitive Irish dancer. . . . Of course, none of these characters would translate to a wrestling ring. But that didn't matter just yet. What mattered was I was showing creativity, versatility, and that somewhere, buried deep beneath the dirt, there might be a diamond.

If nothing else, it eventually, after four months of training, gave me the confidence to ask to be put on a show.

Prior to that, I would go to each show, set up the ring, and hang out as all the other wrestlers put their matches together, and I tried to learn a thing or two. Then I would sit in the back and take notes as they executed. The women who were not wrestling would go out during intermission and dance rather awkwardly in our "nice dresses" to a song called "Let's Get Loud"—as we threw T-shirts to excited audience members. What was worse than this awkward dance number was that I wasn't even offended by it and was content to be any part of the show, regardless of its chauvinistic intentions.

But when women with no prior experience began getting matches on live events ahead of me, I knew it was time to speak up.

As bad as I was, if I could show them that I could connect with an audience, it might save my job.

"What should I do?" I asked Joe as we strolled through Walmart. "I can't seem to do anything right, but I've always felt good in front of a crowd."

"You should just ask Bill. What do you have to lose? You're already not on the shows," Joe responded directly.

I didn't know what I would do if I didn't have him to turn to.

I knocked on Bill's office door. He smiled as I walked in. As much as he despaired of me as a talent, I think he had a certain amount of affection for me as a person.

"Look, sir, I know I haven't exactly been killing it in training, but I do think I'm better in the moment. If you give me the chance to have a match on a show I believe I can show you that I have something." It was a ballsy suggestion, considering I hadn't had a proper match in front of a crowd in about seven years, but in front of a crowd, with the pressure turned up, is where I feel like I shine. And this was do-or-die.

I got my wish—that very weekend, I was going to make my debut on a live event!

All of a sudden, I realized that maybe I had been too hasty. I didn't even have proper ring gear. Or a character. Or a damn ring name! I needed to pick one ASAP! One that would be associated with me for the rest of my career.

Only every single name I submitted to the WWE office and decision-makers got rejected. So I sent in another list, which also got rejected. So I sent in another list and got some possibilities back. But none of these were names I had *actually* submitted.

There was Madeline, which reminds me of those French cakes, hardly the toughest things in the world. Then there was Becky Lynch. I wasn't sure about the Lynch part. There's a harshness to it that doesn't fall trippingly off the tongue, but I liked keeping part of my real name. Considering I was already pushing my luck by even having a job here, I didn't think I had the ability to ask for more options. Best not to highlight any more difficulties to my existence than the incompetence I was already bringing. So I went with Lynch. Regardless of my feelings of mild disdain towards it.

My debut was to take place in the old training center for NXT (formerly known as FCW) in Tampa.

The hall, painted black, had the energy of hundreds of lost souls. People had come to train here with the hopes of becoming WWE superstars only to have all of their dreams dashed, slashed, and destroyed, changing them forever. I had the ominous feeling that if tonight didn't go well, I could be joining them.

In the changing room, surrounded by the buzz of the other women, I prepared myself for my first match and, success depending, perhaps my last. I painted my lips and eyes with blue makeup in an attempt to stand out and look different. If everyone else was gorgeous, then it would behoove me to be weird. I didn't have the skill set for glamour, so no point in even trying to compete. There would always be too many blond beauties for anyone to be looking at me, right?

When I went out in front of that tiny crowd in Tampa, they responded as promised. Maybe it was a new face before them, or the innate ability that a fan has to detect passion in their wrestlers. It's an interesting sixth sense wrestling fans have. They can tell if you truly care for this business, and will respond favorably. They'll likely forgive your sloppiness or any mistakes because they sense your good wrestling love-energy and give it right back to you. Sure, I wasn't great, but I didn't stink up the joint and, like I told Bill, I could connect.

As I came back through the curtain, Bill's was the first face I saw. He tilted his head up and down with what I perceived to be a slight smile. It was the closest thing to a nod of approval and I basked in it.

Moreover, the friends I had begun to make during the daily grind of developmental were there to meet me with a round of applause, not because the match had been good, but because they knew how much it meant to me.

Finally, there was light at the end of the tunnel. And just as I was beginning to get hopeful, the light shut off as quickly as it had turned on.

THE HOPE SPOT

There was a term "black Friday" around the Performance Center. No, it wasn't cuts on merchandise prices; it was cuts on contracts.

Every so often, on a random Friday, those who had been on the chopping block got pulled into the office and told their dream was over. It never got less depressing. Not only would you lose the people who had become like family to you in this crazy circus, but it reminded you of the fragility of the dream. That it could be over in a second on the whim of someone else.

I was mid–training session Friday after my big live event debut when one of my friends, Frenchy, aka Tom La Ruffa, approached me.

"What are you going to do?" he said in his thick French accent

"About what?"

"I'm so sorry, Becky. You didn't hear? Joe's been released."

Joe had become a brother to me. He was my shoulder to cry on every night after training. He was the pick-me-up I needed when I was down; he was my reminder that at the end of the day, no matter how bad it is, if you have a friend to come home to who can make you smile it might all be all right.

He was also remarkably talented, with something special to offer. He'd stand up for what he believed in and what he thought was right. As a result, he pissed off the wrong people at the wrong time.

I came back to our dingy apartment to see him sitting in the brown recliner he had just bought a week previous. He smiled at me with his patent Joe smile, warm and mischievous at the same time.

"How are you feeling?"

"Relieved, to be honest."

At least that made one of us. I burst into tears as I hugged him.

It was a cruel end for foreigners like Joe and me. We had uprooted our lives, spent all of our earnings on setting up shop, paying off our visas to live here, and it could be all gone in an instant and you'd return home with the heaviness of rejection and no money in your pocket. It's the price you pay for the chance to live your dreams.

Now I was alone. I was broke. I had no idea how I would survive; I only knew that I would. Against all odds, I would make it.

In the quiet of the night I'd dream of better days ahead. Of days that felt easy and like my job wasn't on the line. Days when I got to the main roster. Days when I was the main event of WrestleMania. It did all seem so unrealistic, but I was the only one living in my head, and it was nice to give it some positivity between long bouts of self-doubt and loathing.

And then I'd return to work and be reminded of how far I had to go.

Norman Smiley, the nicest, most patient human on the planet, who had a hand in hiring my underachieving ass, pulled me aside in an attempt to motivate me: "You should be much better than you are. None of the other girls have been to Japan or wrestled the places you have."

I didn't need reminding that I was falling below everyone's expectations, and it was agonizing to hear coming from someone I respected as much as Norman. I knew he only had good intentions, but it wasn't motivation I was lacking. It was confidence. I was so scared of this slipping from my grasp that I couldn't get out of my own way.

I managed to get through that conversation without crying and it was perhaps my biggest accomplishment to date.

I even tried to reason that that was a test, like Joe had said, but really, it was just honest feedback from an honest man. I should have been better.

I was aware that I wasn't being primed to be a star for this company. And was reminded at every turn.

Bill would throw various tests my way, such as asking me, along with several others who were likely on the chopping block, to come in on our rare days off and "roll around." If you didn't respond to the invite, it was likely your days were numbered. If you did respond, you'd come in and do nonsensical drills that were borderline dangerous. Poor Frenchy even tore his ACL on one of these "tests."

Often I was the only one left out of photo shoots or video shoots or special events. It made me feel like the kid who wasn't invited to the party. All of the anxiety, being told I wasn't good enough, and not-so-subtle reminders like being left out led to Frenchy and me bonding over our shared anguish—his physical, mine mental. I broke down to him, crying from the bottom of my soul.

"I try so hard, and I just feel like I can't get anywhere! I'm so scared to lose this. I don't want to go back and be without it again. I can't!"

Frenchy comforted me, despite his own peril, wrapping an arm around me while my tears soaked his shirt.

In the midst of my distress, I had a strange realization: I wasn't a bad person; I was just a bad wrestler. It might sound silly, but differentiating between the two seemed to take the pressure off. I had been beating myself up so much for not getting the hang of things that I was starting to hate myself. But I didn't need to. I could be proud of myself for trying and forgive myself for messing up. And it could be worse; I could be out with a torn ACL for nine months.

Giving myself that leeway allowed me to start believing in myself. Finally, I was doubting myself less and changing my perspective as a whole. In a weird way, being left out and underestimated became my biggest blessing. Because I was given nothing, I was above nothing. Therefore, I could make the most of any morsel of an opportunity that came my way. Sure, I'd likely have to beg for said morsel of opportunity, but because I wasn't getting anything otherwise, who cared?!

But everything was changing in the wrestling business. WWE had just created its own network, in one of Vince McMahon's genius business moves, leading the charge in streaming apps. NXT's TV show became a huge part of its selling point. More so, NXT was becoming the cool, edgy thing in wrestling.

Historically, WWE has always thrived when opposed to a major competitor. In the late nineties it was WCW, nowadays it's AEW, but back then *NXT*, in a way, became WWE's own alternative to their main shows of *Raw* and *SmackDown*.

HHH was in charge, and he had turned NXT into what ECW was back in the midnineties. Not in terms of its gore and hard-core mindset but the fact that it was a subculture of the wrestling scene where the wrestlers didn't necessarily fit into the traditional pristine mold that the main roster had. The brand's goal was to accentuate the assets and hide the flaws.

NXT was the underground, where the craft and art of wrestling were revered more than biceps and triceps. While the main roster was the land of the giants, with most of its marquee names being over six feet and close to 250 pounds, in NXT it didn't matter if you were five-six, 140 pounds; if you could go in the ring, you could still be a huge star, and the audience responded in kind.

What was even more special was that it didn't even matter if you were a woman.

Women were getting time to tell stories and have the type of matches that men were. Whereas on the main roster the divas, as they were called, were getting three minutes for their matches. If a match was to lose time or get cut completely, the ladies would be first on the chopping block. Not in NXT, though.

Women being treated equally was groundbreaking. And I

wanted to be part of it. This was what I came for. This was what I felt called and compelled to do. This was my unfinished business.

Even though we were being told at the Performance Center women don't do this or can't do that, as an edict that likely came from an old-school view on how the audience wants to see their women. Hunter was different. He didn't enforce any of these outdated restrictions and he let women wrestle like the competitors we were.

Or rather the competitors the other girls were. I was still nowhere close to getting on TV.

But I saw an opportunity. One of the male wrestlers created a new character called Adam Rose. He was a rock-star type who had an entourage of wacky-looking groupies dressed in ridiculous costumes whom he called Rosebuds.

And I still couldn't even make the cut for that human bouquet!

With no shame, I once again went to Bill DeMott.

"Please, just let me be involved in some way; I promise, I'll be a great Rosebud!"

If I had to beg to be an extra, so be it. It wasn't like they were positioning me to be the future of the business, and it wasn't like I had any reason to expect that they ever would or should. But what I lacked in talent I made up for in enthusiasm.

My plea was granted.

I was going to rock the shit out of this extra role. I was going to parade on TV in a bright blue tutu with a light-up wig on my head and act like a complete psychopath like my life depended on it. In a weird way, it did.

I decided to take any opportunity as if it was my big break. When you are given so little you must make every moment count. I even had whims of becoming a lead Rosebud. Maybe turning it into a story line where they would put me on TV and I could actually wrestle!

As I stood backstage eagerly awaiting the tomfoolery I was about to bestow upon the world, I became befuddled as I listened to my fellow Rosebuds bitch about how they weren't being taken seriously as wrestlers and performers. Most had never even wrestled before getting signed to WWE and somehow felt entitled to a push, while I had to grovel to get this much.

I was taking nothing for granted. Happily, it paid off. I had done my job with such glee that when Adam Rose was called up to the main roster I was picked as one of the Rosebuds to go on the road and show future extras how it was done!

Important enough to be brought to television, yet not important enough to be flown, five of us misfit Rosebuds packed into a minivan and drove eight hours to Greenville, South Carolina, for an episode of *Raw*.

I was making progress with my nagging bulimic tendencies and sticking to a more well-rounded diet and bingeing less, which meant my nice dresses were getting tighter and shorter, all in good time to make a good impression in front of the bigwigs on the main roster. Because that is all I thought I was being judged on (which may or may not have been the case).

With my high heels that I couldn't properly walk in on and my dress that was so snug that one wrong move might mean I would moon all of Catering, I felt so unnatural and unlike myself as I stood around awkwardly making sure I introduced myself to everyone, with dry hands this time.

To my shock, someone actually came up to *me* and started a conversation.

And not just anyone: he was Seth Rollins (real name Colby Lopez), one of WWE's biggest stars, one-third of its hottest faction, The Shield, i.e., the Backstreet Boys of wrestling, along with Roman Reigns and Dean Ambrose.

Colby had a plate of food in one hand and a sheet of paper in another.

"Hey, I'm Colby."

"Nice to meet you, I'm Rebecca."

"What's your story? Why are you here?" he asked, genuinely interested.

An avalanche of words fell out of my mouth, and I divulged my whole life story up until that very moment, with my very short dress and my poorly done hair. By the time I was finished, his plate of food was gone.

He had an ease about him. A familiar feeling, like we had been friends for years. As if I could tell him anything and everything and he'd understand.

He was a megastar and held himself as such but was also personable and down-to-earth.

We talked for forty-five minutes until he was summoned to work.

"Good talk," he said calmly and coolly as he walked away.

"You too!" I yelled after him, nearly falling over in my high heels, not at all calm. Or cool.

I liked it up here. I had even just made a new friend.

With all this socializing and networking, the time to work snuck up on me. I donned my blue tutu and silly wig and made my way to gorilla (the position behind the curtain before you go in front of a crowd—so called after Gorilla Monsoon, the iconic backstage interviewer) with the rest of the Rosebuds. No one was going to be paying the slightest bit of attention to me, but that didn't stop me from getting nervous like this was my time to shine!

It was my first time experiencing a crowd of that magnitude.

Stepping through the curtain, I became intoxicated with the most potent, euphoric drug. It was invigorating, energizing, addictive, and I wanted more. I didn't know how anyone could want to do anything else.

THE DEBUT

All of that good wrestling energy was working in my favor, because as soon as we pulled up to Full Sail, the home of the NXT TV tapings, Sara met me with a big smile on her face.

"You're going to make your debut on *NXT* tonight!"

I looked behind to make sure she was talking to me and not one of my road-tripping partners.

"Huh?! Really? Me? Amazing!"

"Yeah, it's you and Summer Rae, one segment. Five minutes. You over. What do you think your finisher would be?"

"Let me think," I responded, dumbfounded.

Holy shit. Holy fucking shit. This is it. But. I didn't have a finishing move. I had never won a match since getting to NXT. I didn't even have a damn character.

As the excitement turned to nerves, I began to wonder if this was a shit-or-get-off-the-pot situation. But if we're using turd references here, in this particular match, with this particular debut, I went out there and took a dump all over the ring and smeared it all over the audience.

Remember when I said I wouldn't do a silly Irish jig on TV? Well, I lied. I lied right to your face.

I had been doing practice matches at the PC and in jest I had been doing a silly Irish jig, which delighted the crowd of other trainees with its absurdity and my utterly shameless humiliation. They even

sang a little song to go along with it, which went: "Diddledy diddledy diddledy dee diddledy dee diddledy dee," repeat.

*Of course that would be my gimmick! Who wouldn't love
an overly excited Irish dancing clown dressed in shiny emerald-
green spandex?*

Turns out I really do have no shame. As awful as it was, turns out
the crowd didn't care. And my god was it awful. It was possibly the
most shameful debut in the history of wrestling, with all due respect
to the 1993 WCW debut of The Shockmaster. If mine wasn't the all-
time most humiliating debut, it was at least a contender for top three.
And yet the crowd seemed to like this silly buffoon.

When we were done and the awfulness was over, oblivious to the
shame I had brought upon myself, my family, my country, the company, and humankind in general, I was beside myself with happiness.

I had done it! I had wrestled on TV. I had made it!

Fellow trainees flooded gorilla, meeting me with hugs and congratulatory messages as if I were Shawn Michaels having just wrestled The Undertaker at WrestleMania 26.

Miraculously, it felt like I had earned my fellow wrestlers' respect,
clearly not through my jigging capabilities or even wrestling abilities
yet, but through the work I put in and maybe the attitude I kept.

As I was leaving the building high on life and adrenaline, I ran
into our big boss man, HHH.

Perfect time to talk to him and find out how great he thought I was.

"What did you think?!" I asked excitedly.

He looked at me kindly, though I'm sure scratching his head, thinking, *What the fuck are you and how did you get on my TV show?*

"Well, you could tell you were excited. . . . Excitement crack, I
call it. You were nervous. That's okay; it's all new to you. You just
have to slow down and, when you think you're going too slow, slow
down some more."

"Okay, yeah. Yeah! Thank you, sir!" I answered, barely taking in
the words and ready to do shuttle sprints in the parking lot.

I was too excited to sleep that night. Too proud of myself for getting there, for surviving.

It wasn't until a week later when I sat straight up out of bed at 4:00 am, hair standing vertically on my head like a troll doll, that I broke into a cold sweat as I realized the embarrassment I had just brought upon myself. Everyone I had ever known, or will ever know, and the world in general, was going to witness my uncoordinated ass Irish jigging in bright green spandex and there was nothing I could do to stop it. I sent a prayer to Grandma that they wouldn't air my segment. Maybe they'd find a package to fill up the allotted time segment. Maybe I wouldn't have to face the humiliation of this living on for eternity on the WWE Network.

Granny must have been busy making up for lost time with Grandpa. My prayers went unanswered. It aired, to much public scrutiny.

Welp, I thought, *I guess I can wave goodbye to that dream of main eventing WrestleMania*. No one could rebound from such a low point. But maybe I could still make a living wrestling. Maybe they could keep me on to put women with more potential over.

Over the course of several weeks, I worked with Ryan Katz and Dusty Rhodes to try to find a more suitable character—one that had a shot at not getting fired.

Ultimately, we ventured into generic babyface territory, replacing Irish jigs with equally enthusiastic head banging. My new tactic was simply screaming at the top of my lungs at random increments or whenever I would feel the discomfort of a silent crowd, along with other nervous twitches. It was not good. Not good at all. And I quickly fell into the role of jobber, i.e., the person there to take the fall; i.e., the loser.

Despite my obvious shortcomings, the audience still somehow liked me, cheered for me, and wanted me to succeed. They were my saving grace.

That, and NXT had a supply-and-demand issue. Considering

there weren't many female wrestlers serviceable enough to be put on TV, I had the benefit of being flexible and dispensable. Certainly no one was worried about how I should be booked or protected, nor should they have been.

Even so, this "jobber" role was rather short-lived on account of the fact that they needed more heels, and I was paired with Sasha Banks, who was killing it as her newfound "The Boss" character. And, well, every boss needs a lackey. So lackey me up, honey britches!

I was going to turn on my pal and beloved babyface, Bayley. There was no one more sympathetic to the audience than sweet superfan Bayley. Bayley wasn't your typical cookie-cutter lady either. She was an actual megafan and played her character to reflect the overwhelm of love she felt for wrestling. The audience related to her because they were her. And they hated me for betraying her.

Sure, I was relegated to the "other guy" role, but I didn't care. I was getting television time and the opportunity to get better at the thing I loved.

Sasha and I were chalk and cheese together. She was all flash and diamonds. I was all grunge and plaid. But somehow, it worked. We gave ourselves the arrogant name of Team BAE—Best At Everything. And we were racking up wins and accomplishments promptly.

Nowadays *NXT* is a live two-hour show, but back then we filmed four episodes in one night. Thankfully, they were only one-hour episodes, but it meant multiple appearances, several matches a night, and pure chaos. But unlike the main roster, where shows can change the day of and even moments before, in NXT story lines had to be thought out weeks in advance. This longer lead time gave us the beautiful opportunity to develop a character, have a clear story arc, and familiarize ourselves with the audience.

I was learning and progressing rapidly and developing self-reliance along the way. I was hardly able to believe my own luck, that every twist and turn had brought me to this point. I was finally able to do what I love, with equally passionate women with the same goal. Even the fact that the food I ate, the car I drove, the roof over my head, were all paid for by wrestling felt like a dream.

WOMEN'S WRESTLING

"You see those three over there. Those three are the future! They're going to change things here. But three come in, three go out." HHH was introducing us to his latest recruits after a series of TV tapings and also warning that if you didn't step up, you'd step out. These three lads were going to take your spot.

As someone who had spent time on the chopping block, I'd hate these guys. Well, I would if two out of the three weren't my good friends.

He was talking about Fergal, Kevin Owens, and a Japanese phenomenon named Kenta.

With the popularity of NXT growing at an exponential rate, it had turned into its own brand under the WWE umbrella. No longer was it looked at as "developmental." Now it had its own following and was akin to Raw and SmackDown.

Now HHH was going to great lengths to bring in wrestlers from the independent circuit or Japanese promotions that could bring more eyes to the brand and increase the work rate.

The whole auditorium turned to look at the three infiltrators, a wave of telepathic disdain flooding the room.

I sent them an ardent smile and a thumbs-up. Content that I had finally secured my spot in NXT and happy my friends had joined me, Kevin and I picked right back up where we left off almost a decade ago, bantering and joking and catching up on life. He was now a husband and a father, but nothing else had changed; he was my friend for life. As was Ferg. No matter what had happened in the past or how complicated our relationship with each other had been, we had a deep-set bond that would never break.

Turns out HHH was lying, though. The next day, they didn't fire three people. They fired five!

Thankfully, I was safe now. I was becoming an integral part of the show as Sasha's sidekick, but I was also improving in the ring, building steam and getting the rub from the great work she was doing.

By the end of 2014, the world was catching on. Women in NXT were being booked better than the main roster and for the first time seen as equal. They had character development, significant story lines, and matches that were given time and consideration.

Emma and Paige lit the torch in NXT—competing for the first women's title. Then, once Paige was called up to the main roster, Natalya came down and fought Charlotte Flair for the championship in a barn burner, with Charlotte ultimately coming out as champion. The match reminded the world how talented Nattie is and when given more than two minutes of match time on TV she could put on a classic.

Then it was Sasha and Charlotte who upped the ante again. Each big match was like adding another brick to what would one day turn into a palace.

And at last, it was time for me to put my own brick on the foundation as I prepared for the biggest test of my life. We were going to a fatal four-way for the title between what had become the pillars of the NXT women's division: Bayley, Sasha, Charlotte, and miraculously me.

Despite my awful start at NXT, I was turning this car around and making something of myself, mixing it up with the three best opponents I could ask for.

We were the four women who were telling interesting stories, putting on good matches, and getting the audience invested.

But more than anyone else, this was my opportunity. The other girls had had their moments in the spotlight and proved themselves. This was my time to be able to show the world, the company, and myself that I could step up and contend with the best of them.

I stood backstage in the brightly lit, confined grey hallway, pacing and going over the match, the most nervous I had ever been.

I've never had a prematch ritual, so to speak. I just pace like a motherfucker, nudge myself to take deep breaths, and if I'm feeling spry I'll count to ten to chill my ass out.

Come on, Becky. Get it together. If you can't do this in front of four hundred people, how do you think you'll ever be able to wrestle at WrestleMania? I told myself.

This was big. But it wasn't *Mania* big. All I had to do was not stink up the joint and I could move forward and find out what real nerves were all about.

You belong here. Everything in your life has led you to this moment, I reassured myself, or tried to convince myself; I'm not entirely sure which.

My music hit. I strutted out. I had gone from generic babyface to generic heel. Snarky, cocky, mouthy. I stood in the ring barely knowing what do with myself. *Do I move? Do I stand still? What's natural? Maybe I'll touch these ropes? No, you look awkward! Stop looking awkward, idiot!* I thought as I tried to figure out how to exist in that moment as millions watched at home.

Once the bell rang, I settled in. I felt proud of myself as I didn't botch anything or ruin the match.

I had finally entered the conversation as one of the women who would change the game.

The wrestling community was abuzz about the Four Horse-women, as we became known, who would change the landscape of women's wrestling forever. It felt like wrestling's version of the Spice Girls, each different, but that was what was great. We could each appeal to a particular demographic.

All of us brought something different to the table.

Charlotte, her legacy, her athleticism.

Bayley, her passion, her technicality.

Sasha, her star presence, her finesse.

Becky, that Rocky Balboa–like heart.

THE UPPERCUT

NXT had just begun to expand outside the state of Florida for shows, and the first "road show" was at the Arnold Classic in Columbus, Ohio. I wasn't invited. It was back to feeling like an outcast no matter how much ground I had been breaking lately.

"Why am I not on this?" I asked Bill DeMott.

"It's either that or WrestleMania Axxess, and I know which one I'd prefer to be on," he said with a smirk.

Okay, that was some relief . . . but wait, why couldn't I do both? The other Four Horsewomen were on both. Fergal and Kevin, who just got there, were on both. I had proved myself. Was I still secretly on the chopping block again? I had so many questions. People who hadn't done anything on TV were going. It was a reminder that I was still the Performance Center's redheaded stepchild. I was a weedy flower that had broken through the cracks to see the light, but it felt like I was never going to get watered so I could fully bloom.

I couldn't look at social media that weekend, feeling like the ugly duckling that never got invited to join the flock.

But while everyone was away having the time of their lives like the stars they might become, news came in that would change the dynamic of the PC forever—a slew of bullying and abuse allegations came out about Bill DeMott. He firmly denied the allegations and a WWE investigation found no wrongdoing, but he resigned from WWE.

The entire energy at the PC shifted. Whether it was by accident or design, everyone felt like they were walking on eggshells with DeMott, and once he was gone there was a newfound sense of safety and freedom in the air. Bill had an almost stereotypical drill sergeant roughness to him and was a throwback to harsher times, throwing obstacles in our direction. In a way, though, if you got through it, it made you tougher.

Regardless, I was going to WrestleMania 31 in San Jose. My first experience of the "showcase of the immortals" and I was going to get to wrestle in the thick of it.

I wasn't actually wrestling at Mania, but at their annual convention that surrounded the event called Axxess, which had everything from merchandise to memorabilia, autograph signings, and wrestling matches. Starting as early as 8:00 am.

That's where I came in. We were having matches all day long in front of the excitable foreign audience. And for the first time since I got to NXT I realized that wrestling could be fun. With Bill gone, we could let loose and experiment in our matches, see what worked and what didn't.

What I learned was that when you're having fun the audience is too.

When Mania day arrived, we got dressed up to the nines and arrived at the arena early. All the wrestlers were abuzz with nervous energy, wearing their best new ring gear.

Sasha and I snuck away and got a prime spot on the floor that gave us an amazing view of the ring and I got to witness my first WrestleMania live among the tens of thousands of rambunctious fans, all of whom were losing their minds as the people I knew came to the ring. Friends like Nattie, TJ, and Paige. Colby having the biggest night of his life. Having a banger of a match at the beginning of the show and cashing in his Money in the Bank contract at the end, leaving as WWE champion. I was there to witness it all.

I vowed that by next year I would be performing in that very ring. And it reaffirmed, stronger than ever, that, come hell or high water, I would main event WrestleMania.

I came back to the PC with a new fire in my belly. I was determined to get my own spotlight and time to shine.

Sasha was now NXT women's champion, and I would be her first opponent. I naturally shifted into the role of babyface, what with being a big ol' underdog and all.

At long last I got the chance to cut promos and tell the world how much this business meant to me and let the world know who I was. Even if I was still figuring it out. I really hadn't nailed down any character per se. But I felt like I needed a definable look. Something people could look at and say, "That's Becky Lynch!" Something kids might want to dress up as for Halloween. But what?

I came across a picture on a Pinterest board of a lady in steampunk attire. Bright orange hair, quirky clothes, and welding goggles. Something about the quirkiness of the attire matched the quirkiness of my personality. I sat down with Dusty and Katz and showed them what I was thinking. We were all in agreement: this look, a new attitude, it would make me stand out.

Becky Lynch 2.0 was incoming, complete with a supercool trench coat. But the thing I loved about this more than just feeling like I had a cool look was that I could be whoever I wanted behind it. It didn't require me to be "badass" or "crazy" or "mean"—I could just be me, without the doubt and insecurity, and turn it up to 11. In turn, it gave me more self-assurance in the ring as a whole.

The build had been working. The wrestling world was talking and I wanted them to keep talking.

In fact, my hero Mick Foley was so invested in the story that he promised to drive twelve hours to come watch the match, which, like the legend he is, he did. I had met Mick briefly at a small house show in Florida several months earlier and told him how much his career meant to me. Whoever said "Never meet your heroes 'cause you'll only be disappointed" never met Mick. Or idolized Mick.

My point is, just a year earlier I was desperately clinging to my job. Now the person who made me want to do this in the first place was driving half a day to come see me wrestle. Life had done a 180.

I rocked up to Full Sail in my brand-new look, feeling like I was about to unleash something special. Only the message that I was changing my appearance never reached HHH and word got back to me that he was less than enthused.

"She's not winning. She comes out with this new look, which is cool, but just to lose? She should lose and then come back with this."

It was too late, though. I was committed. Win or lose, it didn't matter. This was my opportunity to claim my spot as a top player. Better to beg for forgiveness than ask for permission.

I went from feeling like I was king shit to being back on the edge. Taking a risk like this, I had to pull through. If I fell flat, I might not get another chance. I'd prove that I couldn't be trusted. Everything had to be perfect.

When I walked into the arena, one of the stagehands grabbed me. "We're going to give you steam on your entrance," he said.

"Are you serious?" I responded in awe.

"Sure am. Come on, let's go test it out."

I was trying to remain calm, but inside I was freaking out.

I still wasn't cool, but I looked cool and my entrance was cool, so it was only a matter of time before it permeated the rest of me, right? Or until HHH fired me for changing my look without asking. Either way, if I was going down, at least I was going down in a blaze of glory.

When the time came for the match, nervous as I was, I was full of fortitude. I looked different, I had a brand-new entrance with steam, and it was all, sigh, full steam ahead.

As I ran through the billows of vaporized water, my illuminous orange hair beaming in the black arena, I could feel a shift in the energy. There was an "oooooh, ahhhhhh" factor, a certain je ne sais quoi about me. A statement of sorts had been made. And I hadn't even done anything yet. Wait until they saw this fantastic match that we had concocted and all the new maneuvers I was about to pull out.

Except, of course, in the first minute I fucked up a pin that Norman Smiley had shown me. No one else might have noticed except me—and Norman.

For the rest of the match, I proceeded to mentally berate myself for being a big ol' classical fuckup. Imagining Norman backstage, shaking his head from side to side. Probably letting out a "tsk tsk tsk" for good measure.

I could hear chants in the crowd, but I was too in my own head to make out what they were. Was it "This is awesome"? Or "This is awful"?

At one stage Sasha had me in a hold and whispered, "I'm having so much fun."

Oh, goooooood for you, I thought in my best Christian Bale voice.

I was not having any fun. I was trying for the life of me to get through this and keep my damn job.

In my mind I could vividly see Norman and HHH having a proper bitching session about me in the back.

"You know that's not how I taught her how to do that pin," Norman would say.

"You know I never approved that new look," HHH would chime in.

At last, the match was over and I tapped out to Sasha, relieved. Ready for the misery to be over. As I'm sure the crowd was.

I sat back on the ropes overcome with emotion. This was my biggest opportunity to show that I could be a player and I failed.

When all of a sudden the crowd broke into song, singing my music. As I looked around they all stood up and started chanting my name in what I assumed to be appreciation. Surely it wasn't irony?

But for what?

What was wrong with these people? Were they being facetious? Didn't they know I'd messed up a pin at second 56 in the match?

I slumped back through the curtain, bewildered to find Sasha smiling and hugging Hunter. Wrestlers and producers were all standing around, clapping in appreciation.

I was so confused.

"Was that okay?" I asked Hunter nervously.

"That was awesome," he said as he gave me a big warm hug. "I'm so proud of you," he added.

I started weeping uncontrollably. When I got signed, I wanted to make them proud they took a chance on me.

One of the writers approached me and said, "I think that's one of the best women's matches we've ever had in WWE." I wasn't sure I believed him, but me and "best" in the same sentence felt like we were off to a good start.

Just then, Norman turned the corner, approaching with a big smile on his face.

"That was great," he said as he shook my hand.

"*Phew.*"

"But you messed up the pin at the beginning!"

I laughed. I knew he'd be fixated on that.

"I know!! I was worried about that the whole damn match!"

"The leg goes to the inside, not the outside," he continued.

"Yeah, yeah, I know, I know."

"Well, good job anyway."

I'd take it. It was my biggest win to date.

PEACOCKING

Now that NXT was touring the country, as the "third brand" behind Raw and SmackDown, Sasha and I were having our match outside the borders of Florida.

We had arrived in Pittsburgh and were having lunch at the hotel before the show when one of the referees came running up to us.

"Did you hear?" he asked.

"Hear what?" I said.

"Dusty died."

It was like the air had been sucked out of the building. Everyone became silent, unsure of how to react or how to process it. We didn't have any indication he wasn't doing well. He had been shuffling around the school every day like normal, in his uniform of boots and blue jeans, teaching the kids and telling jokes. Maybe he had lost a few pounds, but it's the wrestling business; everyone's weight fluctuates.

He was the soul of the Performance Center, and without him there would be a little less magic.

His last words to me were "Shut up, Becky" as I was following him around, pestering him about different ideas I had. Truthfully, I couldn't imagine better last words.

He was the one who believed in me. The one who saw something in me before anyone else did, myself included.

Even his last tweet was: "Lynch, @NXT Star Time she be great, top 5 of the last 5 years! Max #1."

I still didn't have as much belief in myself, but I hoped one day I could prove him right.

That night, we all vowed to put on a show that Dusty would have been proud of. We dried our faces, pulled back our shoulders, and gave the people of Pittsburgh their money's worth.

Sasha and I went out and did our thing, beating the hell out of each other in a championship match with her ultimately winning. But as I began to walk up the ramp after the match, my leg seized up and I began to limp. It was that damn hip flexor again—the one that had plagued me at the beginning of my NXT journey.

Sasha and Bayley got a wheelchair to push me around in and tucked me into bed like I was their little baby.

It was going to be at least six weeks before I could get back in the ring. And here I was after finally gaining momentum.

Sitting at home with nothing but my thoughts, I was becoming increasingly anxious, wondering if I had lost my spot.

However, simultaneously, there was an outcry from the online audience about the treatment of the women on *Raw* and *SmackDown*. They saw what we could do in NXT when given stories and time. While on the main roster, Nikki Bella and Paige, two huge female stars, had a match that was relegated to just thirty seconds.

The audience let their voices be heard by starting a hashtag: #GiveDivasAChance. It trended for three days straight and forced the higher-ups and decision-makers to start thinking about, well, giving "divas" a chance.

With all my newfound free time, I continuously sent pitches for the Four Horsewomen to be called up to the main roster. But it seemed like the creative team had something brewing for us anyway. Rumors of invasion angles were circulating in the PC and on the internet, but it never seemed to be all four of us; it was either three out of four or two out of four. I was convinced my name wasn't going to be mentioned now that I was hurt, and the other three had been there longer and were seen as bigger prospects than me anyway.

BECKY LYNCH: THE MAN

To take my mind off of the guessing and wondering, I decided to take a boat tour around a local lake in Orlando with a friend of mine.

As we took our nautical adventure on this gorgeous day, I was shocked to discover that Orlando was more than just strip malls and theme parks as our guide regaled us with the substantial history of the area.

Most impressively, he explained as we drifted by a gorgeous mansion where the original owner had purchased three hundred peacocks to protect his house and wife while he was gone! He could have bought a guard dog, an Alsatian; a wolf; a tiger, but no, he went for three hundred peacocks. Genius. I leaned over to my friend and whispered, "That's what I'm going to buy when I get that main roster money! Peacocks!"*

Not a minute after I uttered those words, a "203" number popped up on my phone, 203 being the area code for Connecticut, the home base of WWE. Whenever I got a call from an unknown 203 number, something big was happening.

I answered the call with an apprehensive "Hello?"

My friend, seeing the suspicious look on my face, mouthed, *What's going on?* as I gestured for them to hold on a damn second.

A familiar voice came on the phone.

"Hi, Rebecca, it's Mark Carrano, from Talent Relations. I'm calling because you're needed on the road this weekend. I'm not saying you're debuting. They're still not certain on the creative, but they'd like you to be in Atlanta for Monday."

I was smiling like a lunatic as I got off the phone.

"Well?" my friend asked.

"It's happening!!!" I squealed.

....

* Spoiler: As I write this, it has been eight years, and I am yet to acquire a single peacock.

WELCOME TO THE BIG TIME

SEASON 3

THIS IS AWESOME

The internet was abuzz with rumors. There was going to be a female invasion from NXT on *Monday Night Raw*.

Everyone had their different opinions on who the invaders were.

"It's the Four Horsewomen."

"It's Charlotte, Sasha, and Bayley."

Realistically, it should have been Bayley. Her character was more established, while mine was still being workshopped. But they didn't want to deplete the NXT roster completely, and considering they'd need someone reliable, they left Bayley in NXT to lead the new troops like the phenomenal talent she is. I was slowly proving my worth, but I was still a risk.

Charlotte and Sasha, however, were pegged for greatness.

On this particular adventure, however, as the email advisory came from WWE's travel department, Charlotte and I would be riding in a car together and sharing a room. As we were independent contractors, it was up to us to get our rental cars and hotel rooms, but for the first few months of our being called up WWE covered the expense.

We met up at the gym the day before, hanging off StairMasters discussing future plans and creative pitches with stars in our eyes. Best of all, we were going to get to do it together.

At the airport as Charlotte and I waited to board our flight, giggling with anticipation, we saw Sasha, who kept to herself. I figured she, understandably, felt that she should be debuting on her own. She was already a star, and she deserved an isolated spotlight.

Our debut was Monday, July 13, 2015, just over two years since I had arrived at the Performance Center. Charlotte and I mentally prepared ourselves to be berated by the established members of the female locker room. Having heard horror stories of the hostility new call-ups would endure, such as having their clothes destroyed or bags thrown into the hallways or shower, or being bullied out of the makeup chairs, and other general sabotage, we felt ready for anything.

To our shock, we received warm welcomes and hugs. Everyone seemed excited to have us there and kept asking, "What are you guys doing tonight?"—to which we had absolutely no answer.

Keep in mind, this is a live TV show. A live TV show that goes into the homes of millions of people worldwide. We were going to go live on TV, in front of millions of people, and likely perform wrestling moves, and as the hours ticked down we remained completely in the dark. The whole thing was a giant secret, even to us, the people involved in the secret.

At one stage one of the makeup ladies dragged me into her chair.

"That's okay! I don't even know if I'm doing anything!" I responded, not wanting to skip ahead of any of the more tenured women and genuinely not knowing if I was actually doing anything. But she insisted that if I waited any longer it would be too late.

Eventually, after the doors had opened and the show that was live in front of millions of people had gone on air, we were told that we would, in fact, be making our debut tonight.

The plan was that we would be broken into teams, decided by Stephanie McMahon. Stephanie, the daughter of Vince and the chief brand officer for WWE, played a powerhouse of a woman on TV, but behind the scenes she was even more impressive. She's a grounded, down-to-earth woman who can do it all: businessperson, on-air legend, mom to three girls, ambassador, wife, writer. She's smart, personable, and despite being one of the busiest people in the world makes time to talk to everyone on all rungs of the ladder like they're the only person in the world, with eye contact that is both comforting and at times intimidating. There was no better endorsement than being introduced by the most authoritative woman in all of WWE.

But storywise we were fighting for . . . eh, honor? Turf, maybe? But we didn't like the other teams, because, eh, we were the best. Or something. I'm still not really sure on that one.

On one team was myself, Charlotte, and Paige.

The other was Tamina Snuka, Sasha, and Naomi.

The third was Nikki and Brie Bella and Alicia Fox.

We went over the segment in an empty hallway in the back lest anyone see the mastery that was about to play out in a matter of minutes.

They wanted the Three Horsewomen looking strong at the end, with each of our submissions on a member of Team Bella.

It was all a bit of a clusterfuck.

I wasn't even sure if I should wear my really cool trench coat and goggles. Was I allowed to? Was now the time? Would it be awkward and clunky? What would I do with it once we started fighting? Practicing how this would go down would have been really nice.

I stood in gorilla waiting for my name to be called, without my entrance gear, when someone asked where it was.

I didn't know what the fuck I was doing. I was trying not to mess anything up and was inadvertently messing everything up. Classic Rebecca.

I watched fervently as Paige, now in the ring, bickered with the heel tag team—The Bella Twins. Stephanie joined her to also admonish the heel team of the Bella Twins for being too prissy or whatever. When the bickering had culminated into its crescendo of bickeryness, Stephanie announced that there was going to be a revolution!

A revolution, you say? Yes, ma'am. A goddamn women's revolution, and it would be televised! But this revolution was different from, say, the French Revolution. This revolution came with gal-pal teams, and Stephanie was about to make the big announcement. . . .

Meanwhile, in the back, I tried to calm myself. *Holy shit, this was it. I was making my debut, as a character that was meeeee. Not an extra, a featured player. I was a featured player. And I didn't even have my goddamn cool-ass trench coat.*

Stephanie had selected a teammate for Paige and announced "the Lasskicker *Beeeeecccckkkkkyyyyyy Lyyyyynnnnnnch*."

I ran out of gorilla and the crowd popped as if they knew who the hell I was. The giant black-and-yellow NXT logo filled the 'Tron behind me.

They were excited to see *me*?

I improvised, to quote HHH on my NXT debut, an "excitement crack" entrance, then bolted to the ring as fast as my shaky legs would carry me. Then stood there trying to look calm, cool, and collected. God, I was so uncool.

Stephanie continued her friend assignment. Charlotte would also be on our revolutionary friend team. She was much more composed than I was. Walking down the ramp like a regal queen as if she was bred for this since birth, which in a way she had been.

So, okay, good. This was my new team of friends whom I was friends with for reasons unknown.

Which brings us to the other set of friends! Naomi came out with Tamina also wanting to be part of the revolution. But luckily for them, Stephanie had recruited a friend for them too! NXT women's champion Sasha Banks!

"The floor is now yours, but it is up to you what you do with it," came Stephanie's parting words.

I still wasn't entirely sure what that meant, but allegedly the crowd was, because once the teams broke into a brawl the audience serenaded us in delight with chants of "This is awesome" and "NXT, NXT!"

It was as good as you could hope for with a debut when you didn't have your very cool trench coat that made you look cool. (I'm still maybe just a little irked by it).

We went back to a standing ovation in gorilla. Charlotte and Sasha were crying, while I was in stunned awe of what the hell just happened.

Strangely, though, I felt far more comfortable up here than I ever did in NXT. Maybe it was the thought that I survived, or that my job had just become a little more secure.

I don't think that anyone in that room then, or even in the arena, would have predicted that I would one day be the first woman to win the main event of WrestleMania.

But maybe they would if I had had my trench coat. Okay, okay, I'll let it go.

(I won't.)

THE ROAD WARRIOR

I loved life on the road—the big arenas, massive crowds, getting in rental cars and road-tripping across America. It didn't matter that we worked fifty-two weeks a year, on the road four or five days a week, a different city every night. I had energy for all of it and no one waiting for me at home.

It felt like a full-time scavenger hunt, looking for the healthiest places to eat, the best place to get coffee, gyms, even the little things like finding a well-priced hotel in the towns we went to or good deals on rental cars. Stopping in gas stations and loading up on snacks still felt like a thrill.

Every week was a mini-adventure that nourished my wanderlust soul, even better because I was doing it with my best friend, Charlotte. Rocking out on car rides to Adele with her, sharing updates on our love lives and often lack thereof, and fantasy booking the shows, we were living the high life.

I had heard a lot of people who got called up to the main roster had a hard time adjusting and preferred the lifestyle NXT offered. There you had the stability of sleeping in your own bed every night, having more time in between big matches to prepare, plan them out, and practice in advance. Story lines were thought out at least four weeks ahead of time.

Life on the main roster was much more chaotic. The show is in creative flux, ever-changing. The direction may change multiple times over the course of the day. Sometimes it is even being rewritten while the show is live on TV.

Because of the live nature, you have to learn how to adjust matches to the times you're given so that you can hit commercial breaks while getting beat up, performing high-risk moves, finding the right camera angles, and looking like you're not flustered by any of this. It is a wild circus unlike anything else and I love that about it. And sometimes I hate that about it.

The communication channels can be hard to navigate. There's you, then there's a team of writers, producers, creative consultants, and then there's Vince. Sometimes things get lost in translation or never make it up the chain.

I had my first experience with this kind of miscommunication when we needed a name for our new gal-pal group.

Sasha, Naomi, and Tamina came up with the cool name of Team B.A.D.

The Bellas and Alicia Fox were Team Bella, for mostly obvious reasons. . . .

We were asked to submit name ideas, so each one of us made list upon list of possible group names. Our lists were ignored completely and WWE gave us the random name of The Submission Sorority. Something about Paige's gothiness and my steampunkiness didn't exactly scream "sorority," but there we were. We voiced our concerns but were quickly shut down.

Whoever came up with this genius name and cleared it through all the channels seemingly missed the rather arduous task of "quick Google search," however, and as soon as our group name was mentioned on TV, it sent people right to the ol' interweb, where they swiftly came upon a rather prolific adult website.

The shout-out on TV drove their traffic numbers through the roof. But it was maybe not the most wholesome name association for the leaders in this women's revolution. Alas, we could no longer be The Submission Sorority. However, the owner of the site was so grateful for the soar in website views that he sent a nice fruit basket to Vince as a thank-you. I think everyone won, really.

In the end, and after much deliberation, creative insight, and concentration, they came up with the very original name of Team PCB, i.e., Paige, Charlotte, and Becky. But you got that already, didn't you?

The first order of business in this turf war was the upcoming pay-per-view *Backlash*. A member from each team was assigned to represent in a triple threat to determine, em, greatness.

My first WWE PPV on the main roster. I had made it.

Well, sort of. The other girls would wrestle. I'd watch, standing ringside, cheering on my teammate Charlotte.

The upside of not wrestling on my first PPV was that I got to be out there and experience the environment without any of the stress. I could actually take it all in. And so I did . . . to a certain point.

I looked out on the giant sea of humans and was gobsmacked to see there were signs for me in the crowd already! I hadn't even done anything sign-worthy.

While I was standing ringside, slapping the mat, twinging with jealousy, there was even a small "We want Becky" chant.

I didn't know what to do. Selfishly, I loved it. I wanted it to grow, and if I had turned to embrace it, it would have. But I had a conflicting internal monologue.

I don't want to take away from their match. That's going into business for myself. But they dig me.

So I gave them a quick head nod of acknowledgment and went back to being invisible lest anyone notice me and I get in trouble for it.

The end came. Charlotte won. Team PCB was claiming this turf for the right of PCBers everywhere!

We did it! We were on the main roster and making PPVs and getting Ws.

Even though I was essentially a valet on most occasions, I was happy to get out of NXT. It always felt like anxiety to me. I associated it with the fear of not being good enough, or that my dreams could be taken away on any given Friday. It had broken me down and built me back up again, and maybe I could walk into this new life on the main roster with a new level of confidence, be seen as a big deal, show them that I'm not a fuckup . . . except it wasn't going to be that easy, was it?

BOTCHFEST

There is a long-standing tradition at WWE of showing respect for those with more tenure than you. Whether that be not taking up too much space in the locker room, shaking everyone's hand, being the last one to leave and tidy up, or making sure you watch everyone's match on the monitor backstage, it was important to convey that you were paying homage to those who had been there longer.

Some of these traditions have fallen off in recent years, but I like the idea of paying your dues. Though at times I was a bit too timid. I wasn't even sure if I should speak up when planning matches and stayed quiet unless asked. I was afraid to look bossy, afraid to look stupid, so instead, I stayed meek but safe.

Being sure-footed enough to speak up was one thing that I did miss about how I had grown during the end of my run in NXT. I eventually got to a comfort level where I felt like my voice mattered and I had good ideas.

I would, however, get a chance to use my voice again, as I was asked to be part of a fatal four-way match on NXT TV. This particular show was going to be taped before NXT's first huge PPV show in Brooklyn.

It was to take place the night before *SummerSlam*. One of WWE's biggest PPVs of the year.

SummerSlam was going to be the first PPV I would actually get to wrestle on on the main roster, and it would be the culmination of months of turf wars. Once and for all, we would find out who the dominant team would be.

My mom and Chris were coming over for this huge weekend too, as part of WWE's documentary series *WWE 24: Women's Revolution.*

They had never seen me wrestle live before. I was going to finally show my mom how good I was at this. How all the sacrifices had been worth it.

I saw my parents for the first time backstage at Barclays Center. Between nerves and excitement, I was yabbering on a mile a minute. Trying to make sure they were taken care of, fed, comfortable, I guided them through the backstage area into the catering area, showing off the dessert section as if I had hand-baked the cakes myself. I felt a certain kind of poise as I introduced them to colleagues. Sure, it meant nothing to them who had never watched wrestling—but being able to introduce Randy Orton and The Undertaker to them as my coworkers felt pretty badass.

I had put my mother through so much while she was raising me, but she was going to see how worth it it all was. How good I was in front of a crowd and how I was going to prove my worth to the company and the world.

We put together the four-way, which included Charlotte, Dana Brooke, and Emma, and from what we had planned, it sounded like it was going to be awesome. Charlotte was ultimately meant to come out victorious, and as we were technically teammates, there would be no hard feelings and it would all be civil and lovely.

We went out in front of the fifteen thousand fans in sold-out Barclays Center. The building was electric with energy from the fans, my mom and stepdad sitting front row full of anticipation. I locked eyes with my mom as I made my entrance. She smiled warmly, though I could tell she was worried. The idea of me getting hurt still gnaws at her. I smiled back with the undertone of *I'm okay, Mom. I got this!*

We got into the match and all was going great. The crowd was roaring; the false finishes were biting.

That was, until I got hit with a move by Emma in the corner, enough to jar me for a second.

As I lay there thinking, *Is this where Dana comes to break it up? Where is she?* I heard the referee count to three. *Wait; three?* I had forgotten to kick out. By the time I realized it was the wrong spot, the match was unceremoniously over. There was an audible "Eh, what?" from the audience as they realized they had witnessed a giant fuckup. *No no no! Redo! Redo!* I thought as I sat up, confused, but it was too late. It was over, and it was my fault. I had ruined the match with the mother of all botches. I saw Charlotte looking furious from the other side of the ring. I had also stolen her victory.

Emma looked confused as she got her hand raised.

I looked up at the full arena—fifteen thousand strong had seen me fall flat on my face—and then I saw my mom, still an encouraging shy smile on her face, but pained with sympathy. She didn't understand wrestling but understood enough to know I did something wrong.

I wanted to crawl into a hole and die.

There would be no redos. My family was there to witness my failure and I had no one to blame but me.

When I got to the back, I was certain I'd be handed my separation papers: "Thanks for coming, you're the shits. Now please never show your face in this company again."

Charlotte couldn't hide her frustration as I apologized profusely. I walked over to the desk where Vince was sitting, headset on, ready to be told he wouldn't need me the next day for SummerSlam.

To my shock, however, he was simply worried about me.

"Are you okay?" he asked genuinely and kindly, fearing I had lost consciousness from the knock in the corner.

Stephanie, being the sweet angel that she is, did her best to comfort me with tales of her own fuckups. It didn't help; I was too far down the well of self-loathing.

My mom and Chris were led to the back to meet me. I didn't want to face them.

I had wanted so badly to prove to them that I had followed my own path and become a success. Instead, I was wondering if I'd be flying back to Ireland with them at the end of the weekend, unemployed.

It didn't help that the other half of the Four Horsewomen, Sasha and Bayley, went out that night a few hours later and tore the house down in the best match I had seen two women have. It told a story; it was gripping. They pulled out moves I'd never seen before, and I watched from the back, extremely inspired as the crowd lost their minds at every pin and submission attempt but also downright jealous and full of shame.

When it was over, Bayley had now become the new NXT women's champion and Sasha shook her hand in respect. HHH sent Charlotte and me out there for a curtain call. *"The Four Horsewomen who changed the business."*

I have never felt like more of a fraud in my life. Standing in their glory, crippled with humiliation.

Charlotte, whom I had been sharing a room with, didn't come back that night. She slept in her sister's room, probably needing a good vent.

I didn't sleep at all. Lying there in the small Sheraton hotel room in Brooklyn, thinking my career was over, my life was over, and that no matter my best efforts, I felt I was, and always would be, a giant fuckup.

The next day, I showed up to SummerSlam exhausted, hoping I would blend into the walls. The first person I saw was Charlotte, who had cooled off overnight and seemingly accepted my apology.

Now as long as I didn't fuck anything up tonight we should be good.

Our producer, Fit Finlay, came and found all nine of us women at ringside in the middle of the afternoon to give us the direction of the match. We were going to do this elimination-style, with Team B.A.D. being outed first. I cocked my head to the side, confused by this seemingly tone-deaf decision, considering the night Sasha had had before.

My confusion multiplied as Fit continued. The person who would be standing tall at the end of this match, the finale of this portion of the "women's revolution" . . . *me?*

Eh, excuse me, what? No no no, you must be mistaken? You see, I'm a fraud, and now I have proved it. My career should be over, starting at about seven fifteen pm last night, and I should be punished by a public lashing.

Which would have been much less painful than this. It didn't make me feel better that I was winning. In fact, it made me feel worse. Clearly, whoever had made this decision had made it before the world saw me fall flat on my face and watched Sasha have a historically fantastic match.

I didn't deserve to be there. Not in that spot, not after last night. To make matters worse, as I expected, when Team B.A.D. was eliminated, the crowd erupted in chants of "*We want Sasha*" for the duration of the match.

Team Bella and Team PCB powered through, and I won by pinning Brie, in a highly uneventful end to the story.

The trend kept going. . . . The following night at Monday Night Raw in Barclays Center after two long PPVs, it was Team PCB versus Team Bella for three segments.

And the crowd let us know how much they hated it. They did the wave, they threw beach balls, all the while yelling at the top of their lungs, "*We want Sasha!*" Only a couple of months after the famed hashtag of #GiveDivasAChance had broken out online, igniting all of this, the crowd was letting us know how little they cared about the rest of us.

And my mom was there to see all of it.

THE SELL

"Let's promise to never let wrestling come between us." Charlotte and I vowed to be friends forever en route from Raw to SmackDown. We discussed the future, food, fitness, and world domination from the inside of our rental cars.

We shared our hotel rooms, our passions, everything. We were as close as sisters. Her dad even dubbed us Thelma and Louise. And I suppose we were, except without the handsome man in the back.

Having a good road partner can make a huge difference. Wrestling can be the most adventurous, exciting whirlwind romance that you've ever had. It can also be an infuriating, soul-crushing, heartbreaking relationship too. But as with all relationships, so much of it is how you react.

That is why no-selling, i.e., showing no reaction, is so strongly encouraged. You have to be above it, not let them know they're getting to you. It's a constant power struggle.

I ain't wired that way. I'm a firecracker of emotion. I feel things deeply, passionately, and with little to no ability to corral and rein in these wild feelings. Disclosure: being so reactive is terrible from a mental health standpoint and I'd do well to meditate and take a stoic stance on a few things. But life is for living, and living to me is feeling.

But that is why, in wrestling, it is so important to have someone you trust, and someone who can rein you in when things get too crazy. Charlotte and I were that for each other.

We were viewed in two very different lights: her, with her natural ability, radiating stardom and regality, having been bred for this. She was being positioned early to be the top star, being given media opportunities and highlighted on TV.

I was the exact opposite: scruffy, scrappy, there against all odds, but with a certain intangible charm and spark that few could see. It was the ember at the campsite fire, flickering while everyone slept, waiting for the right gust of wind so that it could be carried to a new lease on life and set the whole place on fire.

But that gust wasn't coming today.

Paige, who had been doing remarkably well on her own before her assigned buddies came along, had pitched to turn on Charlotte and me. There was a story people could get behind—the betrayal by one friend of another would be much more impactful than random turf wars.

The only problem was, Charlotte and I weren't nearly established enough for the audience to care very much, so when Paige turned on us and started beating both of us up simultaneously, we didn't get sympathy. She just looked like a badass and we looked like weak little bitches.

I tried to explain this to a writer who nodded along sympathetically, but ultimately, nothing would change.

What I've learned along the way, and this is not meant to disrespect the writers, is that bringing up gripes to them can be futile. Not because they don't care: they care deeply about us; they even become friends and in many ways like family. But they don't have the power to change things; that resides with Vince or Hunter.

And the writers' jobs are already immensely difficult. They work endless hours on a show that when they get there will often get completely thrown out, torn up, and have to be rewritten. They are on call to be thinking about the show 24/7. Then, should the talent say something that the boss doesn't like, they'll get yelled at or, worst-case scenario, could even lose their jobs. And so for them, like all of us, they are trying to get out of *Raw* and *SmackDown* with their careers intact. We all have the same goal, of making the best show possible, but talent tend to be more protective of their respective characters, having birthed them, and spend all of their time worrying about our characters' life spans. In turn, we can wrongly direct our frustration over certain stories and promo lines at these hardworking writers, who are just doing their best.

In this scenario, it all came to a head in one particular promo in Corpus Christi.

Paige was in the ring with us, running down all the other women in the division to massive cheers, the exact opposite you want for a heel.

Then she turned her attention to me.

"And Becky, the least relevant woman in the divas revolution."

Oof. I didn't know that was coming, and it stung to the core because it was true. But also, she made a great point!

In a strange turn of events, however, the crowd actually booed.

To everyone's amazement, it was clear that, despite her badassery and the little focus I had gotten on TV, people liked my irrelevant self.

However, to make things worse and make me feel a bit more losery, as I went to step in Paige's face, Charlotte, of her own accord, pushed me out of the way as if I weren't able to defend myself, and, well, Charlotte has the natural strength of twelve bulls, so I had to move the hell out of the way. *Welp.*

Sure, it was all story-line shenanigans, but at the time, being as insecure as a house built on quicksand, I felt like the world now knew that I didn't matter, and my own best friend accidentally told them I was a little wuss too.

When we got to the back, Paige gave me a big, excited hug. "Did you hear how much they booed? They love you!"

"Yeah," I responded, despondent, before turning to Charlotte. "You pushed me back, as if I wasn't able to stand up for myself. It just makes me look like I'm weak."

"I'm sorry, woman! I didn't think about it! I just got so mad in the moment."

"That's okay. In the future, if that happens again, just let me fight my own fight."

"I will; I promise," she said as we hugged, resolving this very not serious yet serious matter.

I walked off and found a quiet hallway where I could sob my real-life weak little bitch eyes out.

I knew, deep down, that there was something I could bring to this world. I knew that I could connect with the audience. But I had no idea how I would ever get the world, or more appropriately the company, to see it. How could I run with the ball if I never got it?

Still riddled with self-loathing from the take-over incident, I was irrelevant because I couldn't be trusted, and I couldn't be relevant until I could prove I could be trusted. It was a catch-22.

A writer I was friendly with happened upon me as I was mid-sobs. "Becky, what's wrong?" he asked.

It took me a few minutes to pull it together to feel like I could speak coherently.

"She's right. I *am* irrelevant. Why even bring me up?" I sobbed.

He had such a kind and sympathetic demeanor: "I know it can be so tough up here. I don't think anyone thinks you're irrelevant. You heard the crowd; that was the only time they booed! Vince sees something in you. He told me so at Backlash. He was putting you over."

In my head I was thinking, *That was before I proved that I was a huge fuckup at NXT.* But I didn't want to speak of it ever again.

The writer did a good job of talking me off the ledge that day, which complements my earlier point about our writers from earlier. Sometimes their jobs go well beyond writing, and it's something they may never get credit for. Well, until now.

Eight-year-old me dressed as a wolf for Halloween. I got second place in the costume contest. Which I think we can all agree is robbery.

....

Ten-year-old me dressed as a hippy for Halloween. I did not place in the costume contest. Which I think we can all agree is fair.

....

My uncle Walter, my mother, and a young Becky on a boat. I am practicing my "leg sell"—which came in rather handy on the run-up to WrestleMania 35.

My uncle Sheamus's wedding reception. My mother is in the background in the obnoxiously large hat. I'm with my cousins John (left) and David (right). The wedding cake was delicious.

Richy and me dressed up in our school uniforms looking like we're about to enroll in Hogwarts.
....

To this day, Ventry in County Kerry remains my favorite place to vacation. My family went every year when I was a child. One year Richy and I found a kitten.
....

Mom and me before my first day of school.

On my first transatlantic flight as a flight attendant, and my mother's last.

Before going to the Debs—Ireland's version of prom. In my hand-me-down tiger-print dress with my two friends Kev (left) and Brian (right).

. . . .

Christmas 2018 with my dad and aunt Judy.

My final college play, *The Beggar's Opera*, in which I played Mrs. Peachum.

....

Katie Lea Burchill, Natalya, me, and Sarah Stock on my first trip to Japan.

....

A grand entrance for Rebecca Knox somewhere in the Northeast.

....

The SuperGirls champion Rebecca Knox in Vancouver, 2005.

....

Group photo of the NWA Ireland crew in Saint Brendan's College, circa 2003.

Richy and me before I took my flight to Orlando to start with NXT.

Chugging beers live on TV with "Stone Cold" Steve Austin, March 16, 2020.

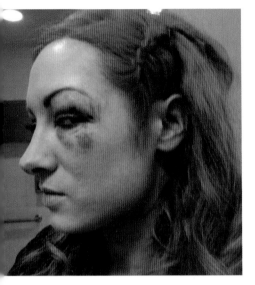

Post-match profile—
WrestleMania 32.
. . . .

SmackDown crew at
the end of a European
tour, November 2017.
. . . .

Bianca, Natalya, me,
and Sasha before a
show in Saudi Arabia,
2021.
. . . .

You knew this photo had to exist, didn't you?
....

When Mick Foley stopped by Colby's wrestling school in Davenport, Iowa, for a seminar.
....

Babymoon in
Wyoming with Colby.
. . . .

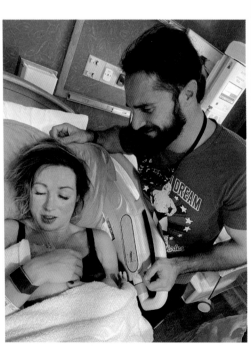

Minutes after Roux
was born.

. . . .

Me and my little angel.
. . . .

At the gym. I was
mid-workout, but
Roux needed a nap.
. . . .

Flower girl Roux at our wedding, June 29, 2021.

Take Your Baby to Work Day.

Marrying the love of my life.

The entire wedding party and guest list in Kauai, 2021.

I am The Man.

DUSTY FINISH

While Paige went on to feud with Charlotte, I was relegated to the sidekick role, cheering my buddy on from the edge of a ring.

Paige, being more familiar to the audience, with more relatability, was favored even if she was supposed to be a heel. Charlotte, despite being a sweet human being, isn't the most sympathetic of characters. As she is the daughter of one of the greatest heels of all time, heeldom comes naturally to her.

And so, instead of fighting the tide, the creative team decided to make Charlotte the bad guy. But there was only one irrelevant babyface who would be endearing enough to garner the sympathy of the crowd.

You bet your sweet ass it was me! So with an odd stroke of luck and a lack of bodies, the story was changed on a random Monday in Nashville.

Paige stirred the pot between the two real-life, well-known best friends and encouraged us to have a wrestling match.

During this friendly competition, Charlotte landed weirdly on her leg, acting as though it was injured. As a good buddy, of course I was massively concerned. With me distracted by worry, she took advantage and rolled me up!

The audacity! She was faking the whole thing!

She got the cheeky win. As I looked on, flabbergasted that my friend was a real-life cheater, it planted the seeds for her to do a full heel turn. While I would be the scrappy underdog trying to take down the glorious queen.

Her dad even began accompanying her for extra arrogance as a reminder that she had that second-generation privilege.

It was just what this "revolution" needed: a likable babyface the audience could get behind, an entitled heel champion who would do anything to keep her title, and a relatable rift between friends.

I was starting to understand this storytelling thing. Despite how much emphasis I had put on how I looked or the moves I did in the ring, it was beginning to dawn on me that at the end of the day, story, and how you tell it, really is all that matters. With so much content out there today, and great wrestling content at that, matches are easily forgotten, but how people feel is not.

A good guy. A bad guy. Conflict that is engaging. It is that simple.

And in wrestling, we get to tell a story in the most engaging way possible. Through consensual violence!

We as people are so drawn to conflict—that is undeniable. You see it in the news. On social media. Or even a more appropriate example is if you went to see a concert. Say it was your favorite band. We'll use mine here. You're at a Pearl Jam concert, and Eddie Vedder is singing his heart out with "Black," and it's touching your heart as you hear the pain in his deep, gravelly voice as he sings every lyric. When all of a sudden two lads start slinging haymakers right in front of you.

I don't care how much of a die-hard Pearl Jam fan you are or how you've been saving your whole life to come see them, once that happens, all your attention is on the fight in front of you.

As wrestlers, we get to do that in a very controlled manner. But when there's even a hint of realism to it, people lose their minds.

The following week Charlotte and I were given another match, where we wrestled our little hearts out again. Only this time I thwarted a cheat attempt from the Flairs and managed a quick roll-up of my own.

Charlotte went berserk, big booting my head off (not literally: I am still with head) and pummeling the soul out of my body. The crowd lost their mind with abject hatred and the dawning of a new era had begun.

It was beautiful thing. We both played our parts and knew our roles.

Everyone could relate to having that one friend for whom everything seemed to come easy, while we struggle and try our best at every turn but are met with obstacle after obstacle. That friend you have a very conditional friendship with, who must be the star of the show, and you must be the one on the back burner.

This is what the crowd was talking about when they said, "Hashtag GiveDivasAChance," and after six months of concerted effort to highlight women and give them more screen time, we were delivering.

All of the hype would culminate in the biggest opportunity of my career and a step in the right direction for women in wrestling. It would be *Becky Lynch versus Charlotte Flair at the Royal Rumble*, PPV, January 29, 2016, for the divas championship.

It was the first time the divas championship had been defended at the Royal Rumble in years. And more than that, this match was given time and a well-executed story build.

The Royal Rumble has always been my favorite PPV. In this namesake of the most exciting match in all of wrestling, thirty competitors come out at ninety-second intervals, the guessing game of who's going to be next keeping you on your feet. Will it be someone from the past? Someone new? Your fave about to punch their ticket to WrestleMania? Anything can happen! *The Royal Rumble* was the PPV that kept me up till 4:00 am on a school night watching because it was so damn exciting, and I was here.

I knew I wasn't going to win. The plan had always been Charlotte versus Sasha for WrestleMania, but it didn't stop the fans from wanting me to win, and it sure as hell didn't stop me from trying to prove that I deserved to be in the mix.

That even though I had been the afterthought of the division, I brought heart and soul to the table.

When I showed up at the Amway arena that fine Sunday, I had an extra bit of bounce in my step. When given the chance, I could show that I could tell a story, and tonight they were going to be taken on one hell of a ride.

Only I had no idea that I would be too.

Charlotte and I got together with our producers and came up with what, in hindsight, was a real wacky match. But we were trying to make moments here. After all, that is what our business is about.

Oh, boy, did we make moments. After much deliberation and racking our brains, it was decided that to assist the cutoff (where the heel takes over the match, thwarting the efforts of the baby-face) Charlotte's dad would plant a big auld smoocher on me.

Of course, now we can admonish someone for the idea of an elderly father violating his daughter's young friend without consent live on pay-per-view.

But after all, he wasn't any old dad. He was Ric Flair, the Rolex-wearing, limousine-riding, jet-flying, wheelin', dealin', kiss-stealing son of a gun.

Woooooo.

Not only that, but the way that Charlotte would win was that I would have her in my patented arm bar and Ric would throw his coat over my head so I couldn't see and would let go.

So very silly, but also so very wrestling.

I felt good about all of this malarkey. If nothing else, it was fun. And even though I wasn't winning, I was in a much more prominent position than I had been previously and we were on our way to WrestleMania season.

When all of a sudden, Lita, who was my producer that day, got word about a change to the match. Sasha, who had been out with an injury, was going to be coming back after I lost. Which was great:

she's fantastic and the fans love her. But her direction was to physically kick me out of the ring before beating up Charlotte.

It felt, in that moment, like a betrayal. I was getting kicked to the curb like I didn't matter after building hype and giving the audience a proper underdog to root for, so that they could go to the two girls they actually wanted to concentrate on.

I was devastated but wasn't even sure I had the right to be—I had exceeded all expectations by even making it this far. I was going to get to wrestle at my favorite PPV for a title. Maybe that should be enough.

Sure, maybe they didn't have a match for me in the cards at WrestleMania. But Sasha and Charlotte was always the plan. And besides, none of this is real, right? So does it even matter? It mattered to me, damn it!

We went out and had our match. It wasn't very good. It certainly didn't live up to the hype that preceded it.

I don't watch any of my matches back, so I couldn't tell you all the things that I didn't like. But I do know that Vince absolutely lost his mind in gorilla over Ric Flair kissing me. It has since been erased from history. Probably for the best.

When the match was done and I sat there dejected for long enough, Sasha's music hit to a huge pop, i.e., ovation. She was always so damn over.

She sauntered down to the ring at what felt like a snail's pace and kicked me out of the ring like the jabroni I was, to another huge pop. *Thanks, guys.*

Then, when it looked like Charlotte and Sasha had an alliance, Sasha stabbed Charlotte in the back, literally (well, kind of; her move was called the backstabber, but no actual stabbing was involved) to the biggest pop.

I sat on the outside, leaning against the announce desk, as the audience erupted in cheers and the tears streamed down my face.

I worried I was never going to get anywhere in this business. I just wasn't The Man and I was never going to be.

"All the girls are always crying; you be the one that doesn't do that." Kevin Owens pulled me aside on Monday after a picture of me in tears at Royal Rumble had circulated on the internet.

"Yeah, you're right. I just couldn't help it."

"You just don't want to be that guy. Be the badass. Why were you crying anyway?"

"I told everyone that I was just so happy, that I had wrestled at the Royal Rumble and it meant so much to me. But the truth is I felt like a worthless piece of crap. Like I can only ever get so far before being reminded, 'We don't think you're worth shit.' And maybe I'm not worth shit. I dunno, man; that one just stung."

"I get that. But it'll pay off. I promise you that. You hear those people. They love you."

"Thanks, Kev."

Kev is the best, and always the man to go to if you needed cheering up. Or to have a chin wag in general.

Later that afternoon, while I was wandering around aimlessly, exhausted from not sleeping the night before, feeling like I was about to sink into irrelevancy again, it being my twenty-ninth birthday and feeling like I had reached my peak and it was downhill from here, Brie Bella interrupted my woe cycle.

"What's their plan for you for WrestleMania?" she asked.

"I guess nothing."

"You should be in that title match. It should be a triple threat," Brie said confidently.

"I think they planned on Charlotte versus Sasha all along. I was just a stopgap."

"Yeah, I know, but the crowd is into you. And it ties up the story. You three all came up together. It should be a triple threat. I think you need to talk to Vince."

"What would I even say?" I asked.

"Well, always start with being grateful for the opportunity. But let him know you feel strongly about this and are passionate."

"Okay. Okay. I can do that," I responded, not sure I could do that.

"Go do it now; I think he's free."

"Now? You mean *now* now?"

"Yeah! Go!"

Oh, fuck. I wasn't prepared for this. I had never knocked on his door to ask for anything. I never really had much of a conversation with him at all. I had, of course, witnessed other talent waiting outside Vince's office for hours and hours at a time to try to pitch their stories and ideas to the most powerful and most iconic force in the history of the business. The guy who created Hulkamania. The guy who invented WrestleMania. The guy who had recently started his own goddamn wrestling network.

And I was about to knock on his door and ask to be given a match at the biggest WrestleMania yet.

This year the event was to take place at the Cowboys' stadium in Dallas, which held over one hundred thousand people.

After my disgraceful performance both before SummerSlam and in the wacky way my Royal Rumble match went down, was he really going to trust me to perform at the biggest event of the year in front of a historically huge crowd?

Only one way to find out.

I stood outside his door, knees weak, arms heavy; there's vomit on my sweater already, Mom's spaghetti. . . . Okay, it hadn't gone that far and my mom was two thousand miles away, but you get the picture.

The eccentric billionaire Vince McMahon, who was now in his seventies, was as intimidating and jacked as ever. But part of me thought that if I could get past the nerves to be able to talk to him, Vince might like me. For no other reason than I'm Irish and he's a proud descendant himself.

I let that thought marinate in my brain for a minute as I lingered in the hallway, envisioning how this conversation might go and working up the nerve to go in.

You hear so many things about how to talk to Vince. There's a *Ulysses*-length list of dos and don'ts. "Be grateful, but assertive. Be direct, and tell him how you feel, but don't show any weakness."

After working up the courage, I knocked on the door at an acceptable tone.

"Come in."

Ah, fuck. Here we go.

"Hi, sir."

"Hello." That signature gravelly Vince McMahon voice that was very professional with a bit of "What the fuck do you want?" thrown in.

"So, first of all I just wanted to thank you for all the opportunities. It's meant the world to me and I really appreciate it."

"You're welcome," he replied, with a hint of *Stop sucking up.*

"And I just wanted to pitch having a triple threat at WrestleMania. I think I've proved that the fans really like me, and I think it completes the story of Sasha, Charlotte, and myself all coming up together."

I have no idea how he managed to understand me because I truly was talking one hundred miles an hour out of sheer nervousness. I guess he really was Irish.

"I'll take that into consideration. Thank you."

"Thank you."

And I walked out of there quick as a cat, filled with adrenaline as if I had just dived out of a plane.

But if you don't ask, you don't get.

THE TRIPLE THREAT

There's a phrase that goes "Shoot for the moon. Even if you miss, you'll land among the stars."

I landed among two stars. Charlotte and Sasha were unquestionably the ones primed to be the top and future of the women's division. I just happened to be in the right place at the right time with enough grit, heart, and determination to make it work for me.

Plus, I looked at my life and career as a Rocky movie, and without downswings there are no comebacks. There is no heroic overcoming of the odds. And if there's one thing I love, it's overcoming the odds.

As it turned out, the talk with Vince worked (or management were veering in that direction anyway). They decided that it really would be the best match to have at WrestleMania.

I wasn't going to get my hopes up, not until I actually got to Dallas. Not until I was out in front of 110,000 fans, which, by the way, is the population of Cork, the second-biggest city in Ireland! And even then, I had a mental image of one of those giant circus hooks wrapping around my neck and pulling me back through the curtain as soon as I stepped onstage.

I had already wrestled at my favorite PPV, the Royal Rumble. I was about to wrestle at the biggest WrestleMania yet, and there was one other goal that was about to be ticked off the list.

Mark Carrano gathered the women's roster in a room for a big announcement from HHH and Stephanie. We were surrounded by camera crews and a podium was placed off to the left with a mystery item covered in a black cloth. The roster waited impatiently to see what was about to be unveiled until, with one swift flick of his wrist, Hunter removed the cloth, exposing the most beautiful thing I had ever seen. A new women's championship belt. A stunning collection of white leather and diamonds shimmering against a red backplate.

No longer would we be fighting over a dainty butterfly belt, but a proper, legitimate-looking women's championship belt. They were changing the ladies' title from the awfully named "divas championship" to the much more progressive title of "women's championship."

I hated the term "diva." The very definition of "diva" is "a self-important person who is temperamental and difficult to please"—a connotation I would rather not be associated with. Since the moment I got signed, it was a goal of mine to change the term back to "women's." And we were doing it on the grandest stage of them all.

I felt bad for anyone not fighting to win this gorgeous bit of hardware. Every woman on that roster had a hand in getting us to this point. But only three of us would be involved in making history.

Charlotte and I arrived in Dallas and hopped in Ric's service car. This was old hat for him, but for us, this was the most exciting week of our lives and the most important match of our careers so far.

The energy in the city matched ours. Fans were camped outside of our hotel hoping to get a glimpse of us. Doing anything that involved leaving your room required meticulous planning based on the extra time that would need to be carved out for autograph signing and picture taking.

But if anyone asked me for something, I couldn't say no. It was the fans who had supported me and carried me to this moment. Waves of gratitude followed me wherever I went. I found myself tearing up in the soup aisle of Whole Foods, thinking about how far I had come. Even the fact that I could now *afford* Whole Foods! My once-upon-a-time idols were now friends and mentors and I was getting to create history with two women I respected and adored. It was monumental. Thank god no one noticed me as I wiped the snot from my face and bawled over the kelp chips in my basket.

But there was just this one thing that bothered me. It may seem petty, well, I suppose 'cause it is. Everywhere I turned on the streets of Dallas there were pictures of superstars slated for big matches.

Only one person's face was missing. Mine.

It gave me that chip on my shoulder that had helped propel me thus far. The race wasn't over and there was still much ground to cover. I wasn't meant to be in this spot. But here. I. Was.

Fuck you, motherfuckers. I'll prove how great I am. Whether you want to attach a rocket to me or not, I telepathically berated the company that I had dreamed of being in, who were now paying my wages and putting me in their biggest show of the year.

I love a good shoulder chip. Sometimes I think I just invent them to keep me on my toes. Again, horrible way to live in terms of happiness but works great in wrestling.

Even if I wasn't meant to be there, even if I wasn't on the posters or banners, even if I was never pegged to be a "top guy," I was proving I could hang with the best of them.

I walked into WrestleMania looking like a traffic cone: freshly dyed orange hair, orange-tinted spray tan, and, to keep with the theme, a bright orange jumpsuit.

We had already put the bones of the match together, but it needed a little more oomph, a little chutzpah. We still didn't know who was going to win, and were dragged in a million different directions.

This was a historic WrestleMania for women. It was rare that the women's title would actually be defended at WrestleMania, and more than that, there were two women's matches on the card! Only a few years previous, the women had been standing in gorilla ready for their match when it got cut completely for time purposes. We had come a long way and we were setting the ground for generations to come.

I sat in the stands looking at the colossal stadium, imagining how this place was going to look in just a few hours as my opponents practiced their entrances on the ramp. Charlotte was being led to the ring by her legendary father while Snoop Dogg, who just so happened to be Sasha's cousin, was going to serenade her to the ring. At the intersection of pop culture crossovers there was me. Becky from the block who needed no rehearsal but probably several punches in the arm, because what the hell was this life?

When the stars had finished rehearsal, we gathered in a practice ring in the back to iron out the kinks of the match, trying not to be distracted by the passing of megastars such as The Rock, "Stone Cold" Steve Austin, Hulk Hogan. This match was the jumping-off point to one day be placed in the same category.

After much deliberation, it was decided that Charlotte was going to win by tapping me out in the middle of the ring. I knew my chances of winning were slim, but getting to put my friend over in the biggest way possible at WrestleMania was the next-best thing.

Besides, I didn't need to win. I was going to do a suicide dive, i.e., torpedo through the top and middle rope onto Ric Flair at ringside in retaliation for Rumble, and that was as big a victory as anything.

And then, there was nothing left to do but do it.

I stood behind the curtain in gorilla, feeling the energy of the 110,000 excited fans in attendance. (Yes, there's discourse about this number, but hey, shut up.)

The fans were ready to witness the dawn of a new era. We had the opportunity to set the table, change how women were presented in the industry, and steal the freaking show.

And as all of this swirled around my head, a feeling of calm came over my entire body. I was ready. I was prepared. I was shockingly not nervous. How could this be? I got nervous for every match I had ever had. And yet here I was, the biggest match of my career, and I was cool as a cucumber.

My music hit and I walked out, head down—as was my thing at the time. *Hell yeah, Becky. Let's freaking go. You're so cool!* I thought in my calmed state, feeling like an absolute rock star.

Only when I popped my head up and saw all those fans crowding the giant stadium, I peed myself a little. Not metaphorically, I literally peed just a wee (ha-ha) bit. I hypothesize that I was, in fact, actually so nervous that my body wouldn't let me know it lest I die. Lest I just curl up in gorilla and cease to exist. *Thanks, body, you're a real pal.*

I stood in the ring taking in the size of the place while the others made their grand entrances. Occasionally, I glanced down to see if I had any exposed pee on my shorts.

My brain couldn't really comprehend what was happening as we went through the match, narrating, *Yeah, fuck yeah, we are killing this shit!* But also not being able to hear the audience reacting.

Are they in stunned awe of our greatness?

I remembered a warning that Sheamus had given me weeks before: "It takes a while for the sound to reach you in these big stadiums. You may have done a move a minute ago, and you hear them react to it when you're seemingly doing nothing. Sometimes the sound just escapes and you can't hear anything." I felt like I couldn't hear a damn thing as we went through our collection of moves and sequences. At one point Charlotte landed on my head from a suplex and I could feel my eyelid being cut, waiting for the blood to gush and inevitably stop the match and ruin this history maker. But it never came. I was wearing so much dang makeup it acted like a clog, saving my ass as we carried on—I dove on Ric, Charlotte moonsaulted from the top turnbuckle to the outside, there were frog splashes and dropkicks; me oh my, we were cooking. All leading to a crescendo of Charlotte getting me in her signature finisher and Ric holding Sasha back from making the save on the floor. I tapped out as Charlotte thanked me: "We did it, woman."

I took the side ramp back to gorilla, adrenaline being shed with every step as the fans slapped my hand in excitement.

Sasha followed close behind and collapsed in floods of tears as we reached the back. Lita was there to hug me: "You did it, kid; that was fucking great."

Great, now I was crying. Everyone in gorilla gave us a standing ovation. *Follow that, fuckers*—all three of us had the same communal thought. We had made history.

THE BRAND SPLIT

After the high of WrestleMania, I spent several months meandering. Such is the nature of the business. Nothing remains in a homeostatic state. You heat up, you cool down, you heat up again.

The wrestling business and community is always changing. It's transient by design. People coming, people going. Wrestlers become like family. We see them more than our own family, and then one day they can be gone from the roster, fired, quit, injured. And you're sad for a little while and you hope you'll stay in touch, but then you get on with the grind and the never-ending cycle continues. Same wheel, different cogs. Life on the road can be all-encompassing. And when you're really trying to make sure you get to the tippy top of the tippy top in sports entertainment, you give it your all.

But it can be lonely and hard to meet people because of your insane schedule.

I had begun to date someone as a distraction; I was 99.9 percent positive he wasn't the dude for me. He was a nice lad, and we had somewhat similar interests—he was a UFC fighter; I was a WWE wrestler—but there was no real deep connection, no commonalities, and our conversations felt forced and labored. But I thought I needed something else in my life other than wrestling, so I forced myself into a relationship I had no business being in. And so when work life felt so very meh and uninspiring there was some more meh waiting for me on the other side, but it seemed better than nothing.

As I've matured in the business, I realize it's all just waves; you catch the big one when you can and ride it till the end; then it's time to wait for the next one. But you can't be constantly on top of a wave, 'cause, well, that's not how surfing or this metaphor works. Work is never actually meh or uninspiring—one can simply become disillusioned by how things are and wish that they were different, or we just become downright impatient. But it's all about mindset.

And so my time and attention were split between being in a relationship that constantly felt like a struggle and struggling with accepting my current position at work. Like my life was being mirrored with constant effort.

But the year was 2016, and there was a shift a-coming.

Rumblings of what was called a "brand split"—i.e., the two shows, *Raw* and *SmackDown*, would now have their own individual rosters and operate as distinct brands. Additionally, *SmackDown*, which had standardly been a prerecorded show, was now going to be live on Tuesday nights.

This was something that had been done years previous, going back as far as when I was a fan at home in Ireland. Admittedly, as a fan I hated it! I wanted to see all my favorites on whatever show was available to me.

However, the talent loved it because essentially it was a lighter schedule. You would tour with your specific show, which meant a schedule of live events on Friday, Saturday, Sunday, and television on Monday for the *Raw* crew. Or live events Saturday, Sunday, Monday, and television (which would be newly live) on Tuesday.

It's hard for anything to stay a secret in WWE. There are always rumors and rumblings. Be it in the locker room or on the dirt sheets, one way or another, everything always seems to get out.

I had heard I was going to *SmackDown*, which was a big deal for me dating all the way back to watching it on the weekends in Ireland when I was a fan. But as happy as I was to be going to *SmackDown*, I was going to be separated from my best friend and travel buddy, Charlotte. My road wife. The woman who stayed off the loneliness of endless travel and gave me a shoulder to cry on. Plus, driving through all parts of America in the middle of the night after shows can be intimidating to a young foreign lady, so being with her was always such a comfort.

To add to that, Mick Foley had now been assigned to the role of commissioner for Raw. I had been pitching a story line for the two of us for at least six months. In it, he would be the Mick to my side persona Becky Balboa as a play on the Rocky movies.

The other part of being drafted to SmackDown meant that we had live events on Monday, and considering we got paid based on how many people attended a show, the paydays were lower, as not too many people were going to live events on a Monday night. Most of the time, there was no show at all on Monday, so we had to pay for an extra day on the road, including rental cars and hotels, without getting paid for that show. Oftentimes meaning it cost us money to go to work.

The draft happened in real time on the first live episode of *SmackDown* with the whole roster in the back to watch and comment as we were being drafted.

Charlotte was the first woman to be drafted to Raw. I grabbed her hand excitedly, hoping that the rumors would be wrong. That we would be kept together after all.

Alas, I wouldn't have to wait long. The rumors were true. I was the first woman to be drafted to the blue brand.

Charlotte and I held it together until the draft and TV taping were over, before crying and hugging each other like we were being separated by war, never to see each other again. As if we didn't have access to cellular phones or live in the same city. We were now islands unto ourselves.

I only knew life on the road with Charlotte; how would I survive on my own?! As I took inventory throughout the night as to who was going where, it seemed like most of my close friends were all on *Raw*, Sheamus, Colby, Fergal, Charlotte, Big E (it turned out that, post–wet handshake incident, Big E is a giant teddy bear of love).

Who would I even hang out with on *SmackDown*? I imagined myself sitting lonely at tables in Catering while everyone laughed and joked around me. Maybe writing insults about my belly shape on planks of wood.

But the roster, which included some of the biggest stars and best wrestling minds in the world, such as John Cena, Daniel Bryan, Randy Orton, Bray Wyatt, and AJ Styles, made for a special atmosphere.

Once the dust settled and the sadness of being separated from Charlotte passed, I could see that being put on *SmackDown* was a chance to stand out on my own and find out who I was as a wrestler and as a woman. I even found new travel partners in Luke Harper from The Wyatt Family and Viktor from the Ascension, who became like road brothers to me.

I had only been on the main roster for a year, and though I didn't have the most experience, after being highlighted at Royal Rumble and WrestleMania, I had established more equity in recent months than the rest of the women's roster. Thus, I felt it was my responsibility to create a supportive working environment. The wrestling business can be stressful enough, but I wanted everyone to feel excited when we went to work. Like my mom had said when she was ruling the skies, it trickles from the top down. My theory was when people work together and help one another, that's when the best stuff happens. Even if we're in the (pretend) conflict business.

A couple of months after the brand split, and the SmackDown women having nothing to fight for, considering the only women's title was being held by Charlotte over on *Raw*, a new title was about to be debuted. It was exactly like the Raw one, only with a blue background instead of red. It was perfect, and I wanted it.

Turns out, the crowd wanted me to have it too.

The moment it was revealed and the diamonds sparkled throughout the arena like beams of light, the crowd erupted in chants of "Becky, Becky," going against the company's original plans of who they wanted to be their champion.

Nikki Bella, a tried-and-true champion and global star, had just returned from a potential career-ending neck injury and had been penciled in as the inaugural champion, set to be crowned at Backlash in a six-way elimination match, but judging by the audience reaction, if they wanted Nikki to remain a babyface, that wasn't going to fly. Me and the audience, we were buds, and they were ready to slap some gold on my waist.

As the six of us competitors gathered around the ring before the PPV, each practicing our "I won't be sad if they don't choose me" faces, Fit found us and bestowed the news. It was official: the crowd's chorus of "Becky" had been too loud to be ignored. They were carrying me to my first title in WWE.

Everyone slapped me on the back and hugged me, smiles on their faces with accents of disappointment.

I tried to play off my jubilee, *I'm cool; it's, like, whatever. No big deal. It's all fake anyway*, while my heart pounded with delight inside my chest cavity.

On the other hand, I had an immense amount of guilt for being the one chosen. I wanted everyone to win. *Maybe we just take turns. Share custody?*

I looked around and wondered, *Are they fake smiles? I think they look like fake smiles. They don't think I deserve it. Do I deserve it? Maybe I don't look like a champion. Or dress like one. What did a champion look and dress like anyway? Other than "not like you"?* And by the way, all of these things are true. I did not carry myself like the champion of the world's biggest wrestling promotion. I still bought my clothes from Ross Dress for Less. I afforded myself the ability to splurge on food, but that was it. I had to save as much as I could, still not comfortable that this might all be gone tomorrow.

One often meets their greatest insecurities when they achieve their highest dreams, especially if they care about the criticisms of others. And that was me! No matter how hard you work or how deserving you might be, there will always be people there to negate and dispute your worthiness. The real trick is to let yourself believe in you and silence the negativity in your own mind. It would just take me a few more years to understand that.

We all worked putting the match together. But even putting the match together I was too insecure. I worried about looking greedy if I suggested doing *any* of my moves or being in the ring longer than a hiccup, knowing that I was going to be the winner at the end of the night anyway. Plus, I wanted everyone to succeed with the old undercurrent of *Hey, guys, don't hate me.*

The end of the match came down to me and Carmella. Crowd on their feet chanting my name—with many thanks due to the hard work the other girls had put in during the match and Carmella being a reliably unlikable heel. The audience made me feel like the most special girl in the world. In my many moments of insecurity, they offered me reprieve.

After Carmella and I traded moves briefly I locked in my arm bar before she tapped out. The girlhood dream had come true! I had just become a WWE champion and didn't know whether to laugh or cry, so I think I did something in between.

The crowd chanted, "You deserve it," and my blood tingled like I had been doused in fairy dust as one of the interviewers rushed the ring to get a firsthand account of how I was feeling. It had been a while since I'd held one of these title belts, and I couldn't yet gracefully hold it. Being brand-new, it felt more like a replica than a real one. The strap was still stiff and unworn. I stood there awkwardly trying to put this rigid belt on my shoulder while trying to take everything in, looking very not like a champion.

I spent much of the night walking around in a haze, feeling like I was dreaming.

It wasn't until the next morning that it hit me after breakfast at Denny's. Real champ shit. As I made a bathroom stop on my way out, I caught a glimpse of myself in the mirror and realized

I was looking at a WWE women's champion. That same face I had looked at for twenty-nine years, with its poorly plucked eyebrows, had now achieved the highest honor in the world's largest wrestling promotion. I jumped and twirled and did a little dance number next to the stalls, until another patron walked in and I awkwardly adjusted myself as I exited the restroom.

I got to the building that night for a live event when Randy Orton walked past me.

"What's up, champ?" he said.

Oh, shit! That's me he's talking to! I laughed nervously. Not sure how to respond, I answered, "Oh, hey! Hey there. Eh. Good! Good. I'm good. How are you?"

He clearly sensed my nerves, as he responded kindly, "I remember when an old-timer called me champ for the first time," as he imitated himself being chuffed with himself, then trying to brush it off as if he was cool. "I thought it was cool anyway."

Even Randy Orton had felt like this. The same Randy Orton I fangirled over when I was seventeen at a show when I was convinced he made eye contact with me. Now we were peers, feeling a common insecurity.

Maybe this was normal after all and I wasn't so undeserving, even if I was more scared than ever.

WE WANT TABLES

It wasn't long after my momentous title victory that the audience was already getting sick of me. Or rather I was getting sick of me. Probably a combination of both.

It can be tough being a babyface champion. More so if you've been an underdog on the way to the top. Because if you've garnered popularity by overcoming the odds, what happens when you become the odds to overcome? Then it's all just odd.

It didn't help that my first title defense would be against Alexa Bliss, a tiny, sassy newcomer to the main roster who cosplayed different superheroes and pop culture icons. She was easy for the fans to get behind.

The noticeable size discrepancy didn't help either, her standing at a mere five feet tall, making it difficult to put matches together. If I beat her up too much, I looked like a bully. She couldn't overpower me because that would be silly.

It's also hard for heels to do anything underhanded these days. We've become so sophisticated with our wrestling that we analyze (often overanalyze) everything and don't want our referees to look like the bad guy/stupid, leading to an encyclopedia-sized list of rules we must adhere to, often resulting in cool bad guys who outsmart or outwrestle naive good guys.

It was stressing me out. I was already feeling the adrenaline dump of achieving my goals, but the realization that this was only the beginning of the hard work was daunting. I wanted to be not only a great champion but one who helped build people along the way. I just didn't have a clue how to do it, and had no idea how to make these matches with Alexa any good. I wasn't the best at "getting my shit in."

Struggling, I asked the one person I knew who could come out of every situation looking great: Superman.

Aka John Cena.

"I'm having trouble trying to structure this match. I want us both to look good, but it's hard when she's so small."

In his straight-to-the-point, wise Cena manner he answered immediately with no hesitation, "This is your time; make sure you take it. The young gymnast's time will come."

It was great advice. Cena has that Tibetan monk sage–type quality to him. But I had absolutely no idea how to put it into practice.

To make matters slightly more complicated, for several weeks I had been putting off attending to a large lump that had been growing on my right side. Feeling the pressure of being a brand-new champ, I didn't want to get checked out lest I have to come off television, and hoped it would just go away on its own.

However, the week of my first big title defense on PPV I landed in Nashville after a loop and was going to see the nice boy I was forcing the connection with—only the lump had grown so big and so painful that I had to go straight to the ER.

It turned out to be a cyst that had abscessed and had to be cut out immediately.

I was put under local anesthesia and given additional pain medicine, neither of which seemed to help at all, resulting in the most pain I have ever experienced as I was cut open.

The drugs didn't kick in till after. But, oh, when they did, I felt marvelous.

"Can I wrestle?" I asked, drugged out of my mind. "Wrestle" is a real slurry word when you're fucked-up.

"Sorry, what?"

"Wressstttlllleeee." It felt like my mouth was filled with bubble gum and dish soap.

"Can I wres-uuuullll this weekend?"

"Wrestle? Absolutely not," the doctor responded, decoding my word soup.

Well, shit. My first title defense and I would miss it. If I weren't so high, I might feel like a failure.

When I sobered up, I felt like my body had let me down, or that I had energetically brought this on myself. I didn't own being the champ the way I should have and got what I deserved. I was letting everyone down: the crowd, the company, and especially myself.

If nothing else, though, the nice boy looked after me and took care of me. So what if we couldn't talk about much beyond food and training? He was sweet. And after he drove me to the ER, I decided I would make the risky choice to move out of Orlando and up to Nashville to be with him once my lease was up in a few weeks.

What's the worst that can happen? I thought.

When I returned to work after taking a week off, they used the ailment in the story line in the most detrimental way possible, saying I was a chicken with a "yellow spine" who was just trying to get out of a fight I knew I couldn't win. That might be all fine and well for a heel to say if they didn't back it up in the booking. Alexa beat me down and literally sprayed a yellow streak down my spine. This whole story line was killing me as a babyface and I couldn't wait to get out of it.

To this day I still go, "Lads. What were you thinking?"

And they'd probably go, "You try writing two live TV wrestling shows every week for fifty-two weeks a year with no vacations and little thanks and see how you like it!"

To which I would retort, "Fair point."

At least I was going to win my first title defense when it did happen in a tables match at the TLC PPV. As icing on the cake, this was a historical match in some ways. There had never been a singles tables match for ladies in WWE. Finally, after an underwhelming run, this would be how I would turn this whole shitty championship reign around.

Then the call came in.

It was 12:06 pm on a Friday and I was in the Performance Center training—I was a bundle of anxiety thinking about this move to Nashville. My gut was kicking in to let me know I was making a giant mistake; this relationship was never going to work out. We were completely different people. Everything that could go wrong in the moving process was going wrong. I couldn't get ahold of the movers, I wasn't going to be able to get anything out of my apartment in time, and they had already rented my place to other people. But instead of canceling the whole thing, I barreled right on through, constantly repeating to myself, *What's the worst that can happen? It's all an adventure, like Dad says!*

Work-wise, I felt like I was failing miserably.

This call cemented it.

"We're going to put Alexa over at TLC, but don't worry; you'll win it back at Royal Rumble."

You won't put the title back on me at Rumble was my first thought. I was never championship material. This was a one-and-done situation, I was convinced of it, and I had messed it all up by doubting myself. *And now I'm moving somewhere I don't want to with someone not right for me. It's all going wrong.*

"But why?" I asked, riddled with fear, guilt, and sadness.

"We don't think anyone will expect it."

Well, yeah, sure, they wouldn't expect that you would have given me the shittiest title run possible, but here we are! I thought in my anger but thankfully didn't vocalize. I wanted to escape my body and all the anger, the anxiety, the feelings of failure, the feelings of being trapped. But where could I go? There wasn't another body I could hop into. And if there was, my same stupid mind would be there to tell me how awful I am anyway.

If this all sounds very dramatic for fake losing a fake title that I fake won, that's because it is. But in a world that depends on suspending disbelief, sometimes we suspend our own. And though nothing is life-or-death, it feels like life-or-death for the character you have birthed. A bad creative or an unexpected loss feels like it could kill them.

Or, more simply, this fake scenario was making me feel like a real-life loser. I had built up being a champion to almost something ethereal. Something that felt unrealistic for me to hold.

Alexa was being given the media time and the interview time in advance of the PPV. I was the champ in name only.

Nevertheless, despite losing, I wanted to give my all.

But I had no idea how to have a tables match. I didn't even know how to set up a damn table.

Thankfully, Bray Wyatt, the charismatic cult-like leader of the faction The Wyatt Family and all-around gem of a human, pulled me aside to show me how to pick up tables and how to structure the match, and he and I put most of the match together.

I spent hours with him, flipping the tables, working with the wood and steel, trying to make it look as if I had been doing it my whole life. Sucking splinters out of my fingers and no-selling my bruised and cut shins from flipping the heavy tables.

Meanwhile Alexa was talking to ESPN, premonitioning her inevitable win.

Despite the advanced effort I'd put in, because we hadn't had much time to practice together, the match ended up being clunky and quite frankly shite.

We had our match in Dallas, the same place where I had had my big WrestleMania match. At WrestleMania I felt like I had won, even in my defeat. But this loss felt so much more hopeless. I crashed through the table, which felt strangely poetic, considering how I was feeling in life at that moment.

GET YOUR SHIT IN

"Holy shit! That could have killed us!" I gasped to Charlotte, who was sitting in the passenger seat as a car sped by us near the exit to 8 Mile in Detroit.

Wham!

Another car whizzed by and we were hit from the side.

Our car swerved as I tried to control the steering wheel. My mind was having a hard time registering what was happening, but I was 99 percent sure we were going to die as I prayed I wasn't veering into any passing semitrucks.

We jolted from side to side, possibly hitting cars. Possibly hitting walls. It was too much of a blur.

We finally crashed hard against the center wall in the highway.

The windscreen was completely smashed, the airbags inflated.

I couldn't see out the window or where we landed. We could still be in danger.

I looked over at Charlotte and saw a stream of bright red falling down her forehead.

My heart was in my mouth as I feared the worst.

"Are you okay?"

Three seconds felt like an eternity until she responded.

"Yeah, are you?" she said as she picked the red line off her head and looked at it, disgusted.

It was a red pepper from a prepackaged meal in the back that had gone flying.

Phew. She had just moved from Raw to SmackDown and this was a horrible way to begin the Thelma and Louise reunion tour.

We cautiously got out of the car, which had now turned into a mound of smoke. Stepping out onto the grassy patch in between an exit and the highway, we quickly moved away from the vehicle, terrified it could explode at any minute.

After trying to wave down passersby to help us, with no luck whatsoever, I apprehensively approached the wreck, climbing inside to retrieve our phones to call for help.

The police came quickly. We hadn't been the only ones who got hit, though the other wrecks were nowhere to be seen. You could only see flares shimmering in the dark smokey night some distance away. We really had gone adrift.

We rejected being checked out by paramedics, though I was almost certainly concussed, and my wrist had been jacked up by being jammed in the steering wheel. Charlotte is akin to the Terminator: you can't injure that woman.

The police offered to drive us to our hotel, so I got to ride in the back of a police car for the first time in my life. Sitting on the hard plastic, which had clearly not been designed for comfort, I thought of how close that could have been to the end. That could have been my last breath, my last show, and would I be happy with how I had lived?

I waited for some sort of beaming light to come down from the heavens, telling me that I was doing it all wrong and needed to denounce my life and go live in an ashram in India. Certainly get out of the dead-end relationship I was in. It never came.

Charlotte and I still made it to the rest of the shows that weekend, though we were certainly traumatized.

For the next little while, I was terrified to drive anywhere, suspicious of every driver who passed me, sure I was only moments away from certain death anytime I was behind the wheel.

I called my dad, the best driver I knew, as if he could give me some reassurance. But there was nothing he could do. Getting anywhere was going to be tough for the next while, both physically and metaphorically.

I had been with the nice boy for over a year now and I would lie awake with a sense of dread that I was wasting my prime years with someone I knew wasn't right for me. We had even moved into a new apartment in Los Angeles, as if that would help things. It only seemed to make things worse.

With Charlotte back on *SmackDown*, she was now the priority and I was moved to the back burner. Obviously it wasn't her fault, and I never held any resentment towards her in real life for that. But I felt like my career had come to a standstill. I was even left off SummerSlam that year.

But I was still brought to New York for the odd appearance and would have to watch the event as a fan.

The night before the big PPV, I went down to collect some shoes that my friend and trainer, Joshy G, had given Colby to give me.

I knocked on the door of Colby's Holiday Inn hotel room. He opened the door looking sleepy, box in hand.

"Thanks, Colby."

"No problem."

"Are you ready for tomorrow?" I asked.

"Yeah, I guess so. How are you doing?"

"I'm okay," I lied as the tears built up in my eyes.

"What's wrong?" he said, startled by this emotional outburst over such a benign question.

The tears were now streaming down my face, impossible to stop.

"Come in, come in, you can't be crying in the hallway." He ushered me into his cramped hotel room, quickly clearing off the clothes on his bed to make space for me.

"Sit down here," he said kindly as he stood, not wanting to crowd me. "What's going on?"

"It's everything," I blubbered as I went into the problems in my relationship. "I like the guy as a friend, but I'm not happy. But I'm also not brave enough to end it 'cause I'm an insecure coward."

He listened, knowing there wasn't really any advice he could give if I wasn't ready to end it.

"And I just don't know what to do with work. I feel like every time I gain momentum, it just gets shut down. They'll either take me off TV, or I'm pushed aside for whoever else they want. I don't know what to do," I continued through sobs.

This was his area of expertise. What with being the world's best wrestler and all.

"Man, it's tough. How are you at getting your shit in?"

"Not good," I admitted.

"You gotta get your shit in, dawg," he said in the cool way he says things.

"I don't know how."

"You know who you should look at?"

"Who?" I asked.

"Daniel Bryan."

"Does he always get his shit in?"

"So when I say that, I mean moments. It's not that he has to do a shit ton of moves or anything, but he carves out moments for himself. Or will have a way of selling that gets him more over; look for those opportunities," he advised.

I had stopped blubbering.

"It's all gonna be okay," he reassured me.

"How do you know?"

" 'Cause it always is in the end. And if it's not okay, that's okay too."

"Thanks, buddy. You're the best."

He gave me a big, comforting hug before I went back to my room, feeling a bit more uplifted and grateful I had a friend like him.

That was the kind of guy I needed to date. I just didn't think there were too many Colbys in the world, so I stayed stuck in my rutty relationship.

THE HEARTBREAK KID

I was about to get a break away from wrestling, which felt very needed. Not because my body was hurting, but in a world that's so competitive without being an actual competition, a bit of space to garner perspective can be very helpful.

At the same time, it wasn't lost on me how much the business had changed since we got here. That was what I wanted to do, right? Create a more equal space?

In a matter of years we had made sure women were positioned in a favorable spot. I had already made history more times than I could count.

I had been involved in the first-ever women's ladder match, and the first time women had main evented SmackDown in a cage match. I'd been in the first-ever tables match for a women's title. I had competed in the first intergender match in a decade. Anytime I got the chance to tell a story I could make the people care. Wasn't that victory in itself?

It was. But I wanted all the superficial shit that equated success, not that internal satisfaction or fulfillment that comes from knowing you were doing a good job and creating change.

No! I wanted to be on the posters, the DVDs, the billboards. I wanted to main event WrestleMania and it looked no closer in sight than trying to get a glimpse of the ancient pyramids from the Emerald Isle. Impossible.

My brain was going to get to focus on something else for a month.

I had been cast in one of WWE's franchise films, *The Marine 6*. They are low-budget, cheesy action movies, but I was elated to get a chance to show off my acting chops, take a few steps away from the ring, and garner a new approach.

It helped that I was starring alongside the legend that is Shawn Michaels, one of the greatest to ever lace up a pair of boots. As we drove to and from the set together, I took every second to pick his brain, wishing for red lights and traffic jams so I might pick up a thing or two. His raspy voice detailed his trials and tribulations and lessons he learned along the way. He told me about how he had found the character of the "Heartbreak Kid," admitting he didn't always feel confident but could live vicariously through the character. I listened, my mind boggled that even Shawn Michaels didn't always feel confident. To me he was the living embodiment of confidence. Maybe everyone feels like this? Maybe I wasn't so out of place. Maybe we're all battling those demons that tell us we're not good enough.

"But what about wrestling? Did you ever struggle with anything in the ring?" I asked, hopeful we could find more common ground.

"Nothing really. It always came quite easy for me."

Ah, fuck, I thought. *Well, that I can't relate to*. It had always been a struggle for me. So maybe I wasn't going to be the next Shawn Michaels in the ring. But I didn't have to be.

I just needed to be able to tell a story and connect with the crowd.

"How do I change things, though? I feel like I'm in such a rut. What can I do when I go back?" I implored as we pulled up to our London hotel room.

"Go back with a different air about you. A different aura. Hold yourself like a star. I think Miz did that when he came back after shooting his first movie. He repackaged himself and everyone looked at him differently," he said as he got out of the car.

"I can do that," I said unconfidently, already wondering if anyone would buy it.

LET'S GET READY TO RUMBLE

While WWE may not have felt like I was the one yet, the lad I was seeing certainly did. When I got back to LA, he planned an evening out with me, taking me to the arcade on Santa Monica Pier.

"Let's go on the Ferris wheel!" he suggested.

"I'm not really feeling it today," I responded without admitting I'm a scared little baby when it comes to heights.

"Oh, come on! It'll be fun!" he insisted, pulling me towards the rickety ride.

I climbed in reluctantly, terrified, clutching the edges with a death grip. When we reached the top, the Ferris wheel stopped.

"Oh no! It's broken!" I yelled, fearing this would be the end of Rebecca Quin.

Just then he started to get up, shaking our capsule, petrifying me further, which only amplified as he got down on one knee and produced a small black box.

Oh no, I thought, *how could we have such wildly different views of this relationship?*

"Will you marry me?" he asked, opening the box and producing a pear-shaped diamond ring. Or, as I saw it, a teardrop.

"Yes," I said, like a fucking coward. What's one to do? Unless you're ready to break up there and then, you say yes like the good person you are and then break their heart at a much more suitable, convenient time . . . for you.

As we embraced and I wondered how the hell I was going to get out of this one, the Ferris wheel started to move again.

I was ambushed by a photographer and a man popping a bottle of champagne and a giant bouquet of flowers as we stepped off.

At least I had said yes; otherwise this would have been purely mortifying.

I hid the ring from the public eye, embarrassed to wear it. I would ask my happily married friends ad nauseam, "How did you know they were the one?"

"I just knew," they'd all inevitably respond like the clichés they were.

Surely that's bullshit. Surely you go through the same painful doubt every single day of your life wondering how the hell you're going to get out of this. Surely?

Surely it's perfectly normal not to want to tell anyone about your engagement, especially not your mother. It's not unusual to hide rings in photographs, or not to think for a single second that you will ever actually go through with it?

The few friends I admitted my condition to were all very nice about it. Realizing I would probably come to my own conclusions eventually, they gave me the standard "as long as you're happy" spiel.

Colby was not one such friend and when he found out immediately texted me: "What the fuck are you doing? You were just in my room crying about this motherfucker a few months ago."

Jeez, man. Don't yell at me, I thought.

"I know, I know. Look, I'll be honest. I don't think I'll go through with it. But if you're not ready to break up, how are you supposed to respond?"

"Fair, fair."

At least he understood. Unlike my mother, who wouldn't talk to me for three weeks after I finally told her.

"I'm not going to marry him," I insisted.

"You're ruining your life. You just told me at Christmas he's not right for you!" she scolded.

It was the worst when she was right.

The weight of all the guilt was crippling, making it hard to keep that "I'm a star" aura Shawn Michaels talked about.

But I would need to get my act together quickly. The dynamic of the women's division was about to change due to two things.

Number one, for the first time in history, and from now on, there would also be a thirty-woman Royal Rumble at the namesake PPV. The winner would go on to get a championship match at WrestleMania.

As a person whose favorite PPV was *The Royal Rumble*, it was already monumental to compete at it, never mind competing in an actual Royal Rumble. Additionally, I was one of the first two people in the match, along with Sasha Banks.

I knew there was no hope of me winning—that was reserved for Asuka this year—but what really got the world talking brings me to:

Number two, the signing of MMA sensation and former UFC champion Ronda Rousey to WWE. Ronda, the catalyst for change in women's MMA and the reason women were allowed to compete in UFC, had transcended the sport to become one of the most widely recognized names in popular culture, being on the cover of magazines, on TV shows, in movies. And now she was one of us.

The champions of each brand (now Charlotte for SmackDown and Alexa for Raw) entered the ring after Asuka won to give her a choice. Before anything else could happen and while the remainder of the fallen Royal Rumble participants were in gorilla watching, Ronda Rousey was ushered through the group of sweaty wrestlers as her signature entrance music, "Bad Reputation" by Joan Jett, blasted in the arena to the sheer delight of everyone in attendance. She stormed down to the ring and pointed at the WrestleMania sign.

But what did this mean? Was she going to get a title shot? Did she even know how to wrestle?

The whole world was abuzz with the same questions.

The monumental signing of one of the world's biggest sports stars to WWE eclipsed the Royal Rumble.

But how did the women who had been grinding it out for years and years feel about this?

Personally, it made me both excited and nervous. It was an incredible show of how far we had come that someone of Ronda Rousey's caliber wanted to be involved in our division.

Had we still been relegated to thirty-second matches and bikini contests, I highly doubt it would have been an intriguing proposition for her. Rousey signing with WWE had the potential to shine a light on women's wrestling like never before and I loved that for all of us who worked so hard to be seen as equal stars to the men. But I was nervous, because in the last year I hadn't been highlighted much. With the addition of this global star, I wasn't sure if I'd be highlighted ever again.

We would be on different brands, but I was hopeful one day we might meet in the ring should she decide to stick with it.

Despite the title of her entrance music and several rumors I had heard about her temperament, she was lovely. She was excited to be there, smiling and introducing all of us to the giant entourage that surrounded her.

She also wasn't used to the "competition" being so friendly and supportive. But this ain't real, and it takes two to make money. And Ronda was money.

She wouldn't be making her in-ring debut until WrestleMania, two months from now. Which was a wise decision. With so much content, it's hard to reserve matches and make people or stories feel important. But Ronda was an anomaly, and someone who needed to be handled carefully.

Meanwhile, on *SmackDown*, I was doing . . . nothing. Okay, so maybe this whole coming-back-as-a-star thing was overrated. Or maybe not even, but it might take a second.

The build was on for WrestleMania, and I was in none of the conversations for big matches. Or any matches, really. While Asuka chose to challenge Charlotte for her title, I was relegated to the battle royal on the kickoff show. That's where all the wrestlers who don't get matches are sent. It serves mostly as a reward to the wrestlers who work their asses off every year that they'll still get a spot on the card and a decent payday, even if it's a token gesture and a match no one cares about.

I confided my disappointment to Sami.

"I feel like I work so hard, but I can't seem to break through."

"You know, man, enjoy it. WrestleMania feels like such pressure every year. But last year I was in the battle royal and it gives you a chance to really soak it in and look around. Try and do that."

"That's a really good way to look at it," I admitted. And he was right.

I took his advice to heart. But my god, all I wanted to do was main event that show. It's the ultimate goal of every wrestler, and it had never been done by a female. But hell, I could barely get on TV; how did I think I could main event?

I was trying to take Sami's advice, but hanging out with Charlotte and hearing her talk about her match and the ideas they had, I would be lying if I said I wasn't jealous. Which I felt horrible about. I should have felt happy for her. I should have felt inspired. That if it could happen for her, maybe one day it could happen for me. But darn it, at this point, after years of being the bridesmaid, I wanted to be the bride. But not actually *the* bride, 'cause that homelife situation was the shits.

When Mania came and I went out for the preshow battle royal, Sami was right: I could soak it in more. I got to look around at the stadium and watch everyone being so happy to be there and experience it.

There really is nothing like being in front of a crowd like that. And when you allow yourself to soak it in, you never want it to end.

Ultimately, however, I was thrown out so unceremoniously and with such little focus, most people had no idea I was no longer in the running.

I got to the back and cleaned up to watch the rest of the show.

Ronda's match was excellent. She was in there with the greatest leaders she could have asked for in HHH, Kurt Angle, and Stephanie McMahon and they had gone over every part meticulously.

Charlotte and Asuka also had a barn burner.

My friend texted me: "How great were Ronda and Charlotte's performances this year? It has to be them in the main event next year!"

I will be that main event, my gut insisted.

I was on the preshow, eliminated with no one giving a shit whatsoever. I had absolutely zero reason to ever believe that I could be the main event, but there was a teeny tiny voice that said I could, and I was mildly annoyed that this friend hadn't recognized it.

But in the meantime I drowned my sorrows in copious amounts of free champagne at the after-party, annoying Colby with my drunkenness and crying about my tear-shaped engagement ring that I now dubbed my "ring of sadness."

MONEY IN THE BANK

I awoke suddenly one night, must have been 3:00 am, lying next to my fiancé, when a little voice in my head said, *All your dreams are at the other side of this relationship.* I wanted to excel in my career and main event WrestleMania, but in my personal life, I *did* want to get married and become a mother one day. Just not with him by my side.

After four months of being engaged it had become inevitable this needed to end.

For several weeks I said to myself, *Next time we fight, it will be over.* So I'm not proud to say that when that fight did happen, with me out of town and over a text message, I broke it off.

He moved out while I was away in Europe for a two-week tour. I did feel bad, I liked him, but I knew it would never work. I knew it from the first day we met; I just wanted the company in this often isolating industry. And that was so very wrong and selfish of me.

Once I had cleared up my personal life from the hole I had buried myself in, my professional life suddenly started to bloom.

I felt like a magnet of good energy. I felt free, alive, and utterly invincible.

Suddenly I was more engaged in work, more invested in my friendships, and more creative.

We were approaching the *Money in the Bank* PPV. And I would be part of this year's ladder match. Maybe, just maybe, I thought, they might give me the briefcase.

I'd been working so hard and the people still liked me, mostly based on my underdog status and online presence. Whenever I wasn't featured on TV, I would always go to WWE's digital team and film something, anything. An interview, a silly pun video. Or make my own (what I found) funny videos or stories for social media. But it would at least give the internet audience a chance to get to know me when I wasn't being showcased on TV.

Charlotte was also going to be out of the picture after this match, as she had to get surgery, so who better than me to win?

Alexa Bliss! That's who.

Oh, well, there's always next year, I comforted myself.

"Who should be the last person on the ladder before Alexa wins?" our producer TJ asked the group.

"I think Becky would get the most sympathy," Nattie chimed in.

We were the first match on the main card that night and Chicago was a rowdy bunch as always.

I went through the curtain not fully knowing what to expect. We thought it was a good match, but was it? We thought they would sympathize with me the most, but would they?

I took the ring in the beginning while the rest of the girls scattered looking for ladders. The crowd immediately started chanting my name. *Oh, cool, they like me!*

Whether it was a semi-Irish connection between the natives and myself or if it was that they genuinely hoped I'd finally pull one out, they rallied behind me like I was their hometown gal. As soon as I would put my foot on the bottom rung of the ladder, the applause and cheers got audibly louder.

I finally made it to the top of the ladder. The briefcase was in my hands. But where was Alexa? Fuck. She was late. I was fumbling, trying to not take the briefcase off and accidentally win but also trying not to look like a complete incompetent idiot. Finally, what felt like ten minutes later she showed up to tip me off to a chorus of boos.

I crashed onto a ladder below before bouncing out of the ring. I watched as Alexa climbed to the top and unhooked the case. A mix of cheers and boos cascaded through the arena.

Well, I thought as I rubbed the goose egg on my head, *I think that went all right.*

We all dragged our broken bodies back to gorilla, where we were met with a standing ovation.

"It was the right call to have you up there last," TJ remarked. "I think they liked you," he said as he smiled like a Cheshire cat.

The next day, the crowd's favorable reaction to me became the talk of the town. It's not very often that someone catches fire with little momentum, so when it happened podcasts and online outlets alike were urging the WWE decision-makers to take notice.

Which they did—and pushed me to become the number one contender for the SmackDown women's championship against Carmella at SummerSlam that year.

After two years of failing to capture any gold, and for the first time ever, I was getting a one-on-one title match at a major PPV. It felt like me and the audience were all on a tandem surfboard, riding this WWE wave together.

Could I be the confident, unapologetic champion that I was not in 2016 but wished I was? Only time would tell.

Or would it?! *Heavens no!* This is wrestling! We need friction; we need controversy; we need . . . betrayal! Kind of . . .

Charlotte, who had been out for surgery, rushed back from her time off. You could rip an arm off that woman and it would grow back a week later. Nothing kept her down and just about nothing kept her out.

In an act of heroism, she ran out to save me from a merciless beating I was receiving at the hands of the dastardly champ.

When Charlotte had done her duty and chased Carmella away, she offered me a hand up.

I would have rather taken the beating with honor than be spared a whupping but show weakness. I wanted to stand on my own two feet, be it success or failure.

Her interference won her a spot in our match. Now it would be a triple threat for the title and the crowd was not happy about it.

Charlotte had been so prominently featured since we were called up three years ago, and the crowd felt that this was my time to shine and she had bogarted it.

Ultimately, this was the plan of Creative. Charlotte was going to win at SummerSlam, and I was going to turn (heel) on her. And somehow, someway, the creative team could not see how I would be the babyface in this story.

Not only would Charlotte win in the triple threat—on the night that, in the fans' eyes, was meant to be a monumental coming-out party for me and my return to the top—but she would pin me to do it while I had Carmella on the verge of tapping.

"The turn needs to be justified" was a note that came from the production office.

Justified? But I was the bad guy? They were about to turn me into a badass megababyface.

When the day came, SummerSlam 2018, I asked one of the writers, "Are we really doing this?"

"Yes, the understanding is that you'll likely get a babyface reaction here in Brooklyn, but that's just 'cause they're a heel crowd."

There was a certain amount of tone deafness from the creative team. Or maybe they genuinely thought that Charlotte was a strong enough babyface. As good as she is, she's a natural heel. But this was setting her up for failure.

She knew this wasn't going to work and was visibly upset by it. "They're going to turn you into Stone Cold."

Meaning I would be a complete badass. She was right. I didn't have anything else to say about it except to shrug. Being booked like WWE's biggest draw in history was nothing I was going to object to.

If done right, this was going to catapult my career like never before. After years of taking a backseat, I wasn't going to let this opportunity slip through my fingers.

That night, before going out, I was warned of several things.

"Because this is a heel crowd, they'll likely cheer you when you turn."

I mean, it's not 'cause they're a heel crowd, but cool.

"Don't look at them in recognition."

"No problemo."

At the end, I had Carmella in my finisher and as her hand raised up to tap the mat in submission, the crowd on their feet cheering, *bam!* Charlotte hit me from behind with her finisher "natural selection."

One. Two. Three.

"Annnnnnndddddd neeeeeeewwwwwww SmackDown women's champion Charlotte Flair."

A mixture of cheers and boos while I sat there looking heartbroken. Internally, I was happy as can be, knowing that this would be the biggest moment of my career.

Charlotte stood over me, title in hand, face apologetic as the tension in the building rose. She prospered from my despair and everyone knew it. I got up and went to her, the audience unsure of what was about to happen. I hugged her, and they erupted in a chorus of boos. They hated that I didn't stand up for myself, that I was just going to accept passing the baton yet again.

As Charlotte hugged me she whispered to me, "This is your moment. Give it all you got."

So I did. I slapped her so hard it was felt by the PE teacher who failed me all the way back in Ireland and back in time. The crowd let out their biggest pop of the night.

As I steadied my focus on her, trying to summon venom and hatred in my eyes, I couldn't help but think, *This is foooooooking cool!*

The audience was chanting "Becky" and "You deserve it," which could be interpreted in two ways: Either it was directed at her and she deserved a beating. Or they knew this was the start of a new journey for me. A new push, and that I deserved it.

I did what I was told and never looked up at the crowd. Though I so badly wanted to take them in. We had been on such a journey together.

I walked back towards gorilla, only looking back at the damage one more time before getting through the curtain.

Charlotte soon followed me through and we hugged and thanked each other.

"Are you okay?" I asked.

"Oh, yeah, woman, I'm good," she responded unconvincingly and a little standoffishly.

I knew she was upset. I'm not sure if she was hurt physically or mentally.

"Are you sure? I whacked you pretty good."

"I'm all good, seriously," she insisted, the tears building in her eyes.

You would think she is untouchable by watching her on TV, but she's an emotional and sensitive lady who wants to be liked.

In the story, she was supposed to be the good guy. But everyone could identify with *my* story. The one who always tried their hardest. Was never the best, or the strongest, or the most naturally gifted, but who had heart and fire and fight. They knew what it was like to be passed over for that promotion or not asked to that dance. Charlotte's story was much less common. Most people aren't born into fame, or a multitime champ, or built like a goddess. The storytelling was all wrong. I knew it, and she knew it. But it worked in my favor.

THE PROMO

By the time SmackDown rolled around two days later, it was official. The turn was a success. But in reality, I hadn't turned into a heel; I had transformed into a bigger babyface.

"You're going to need to turn on the audience," I was told by writers.

"What would I say? It's obvious that they were the ones that supported me the whole way. To say they didn't is foolish."

"It's the only way they'll boo you."

"Look, if we do this, we have to play the long game. They're not going to boo me tonight, but I know I can get them there over time."

"I hear what you're saying." While I'm thinking, *You might hear me, but you're not listening to me.*

"But we really just need you to turn on them."

"But it's so obvious and desperate. They were clearly behind me the whole time."

"Can we compromise?" they asked.

I didn't want to, but I relented. "Okay, I'll figure it out."

I got with a writer and worked on something that reflected all I had gone through and the conclusions I had come to in the last few years. And of course threw in how the audience hadn't always been there for me (which they had). It was imperative that this maiden voyage promo for this new character be a success and serve as my mission statement, which was that I was tired of playing nice and waiting my turn. I was not only going to be the face of the women's division; I was going to be the face of the whole company.

It was about having the balls, for lack of a better term, to take what you want in life and no longer settling for second best.

I went out there, marinated in all my pent-up resentment, anger pouring out in every word. Maybe too much at times, but I wanted it to feel real. The anger was more at me doubting myself than at anyone else.

Then it was time to bash the audience, but the only thing I could say with a hint of realism to it was "You say that you support me. But when Charlotte won, you stood up and you cheered a new champion, so did you really care?" But they didn't buy me turning on them. It felt like bullshit to all of us.

There was an uproar online about the ridiculousness of me turning on the audience. WWE bowed to the public's pressure, immediately erasing that section of the promo from all platforms.

Rolling over and squinting in my Residence Inn hotel room, I woke up the next day to a text from a writer: "Mr. McMahon doesn't want Becky to put the audience down. Her character is similar to 'Stone Cold' Steve Austin. The look she gave proved she could draw money."

I kicked my legs under the thin blanket like a five-year-old. *Money? Vince thinks I'm money?! Hell yeah, I'm money!*

After years of my trying to prove myself, Vince believed in me. More importantly, I finally believed in myself.

I was still being booked as a heel. But I was a big ol' renegade babyface. And it wasn't just in Brooklyn either. A few weeks later, we were in Mississippi, and the "Becky" chants were as loud as they had been in Brooklyn.

Charlotte was having a hard time with this angle and our relationship was becoming strained. We had already agreed to start driving separately to keep kayfabe (the act of preserving the story line as authentic) alive. But when we did see each other, things were tense, often leaving awkward silences in the locker room and having the other members of the roster be our mediators. Charlotte wasn't happy with things I had said in interviews—for example, calling out WWE's historical preferential treatment of buxom blondes, thinking I was taking digs at her in real life, or social media posts I made. While I was trying to make this story as realistic as possible and go as far as I could with it. Which, admittedly, was often too far.

I never apologized for it or tried to squash the matter. I admittedly was rejoicing in my newfound success and thought she was being a baby. In hindsight, I could have been more sensitive, or more forthcoming.

In retaliation, however, I took her offense as a personal attack, thinking that she wasn't happy for my success and instead felt it was at the expense of her own. Business and friendship is a tough thing. All of this, I'm sure, could have been resolved with a conversation, but now we were in the midst of a power struggle. Neither of us was willing to yield control. We both wanted to be at the very top.

So much for "never let wrestling come between us."

Even as our friendship sadly started to deteriorate, with fake life causing real-life animosity, for me work had never been better. I was having a blast.

Every arena was filled with "We want Becky" chants. The creative team wrote me as though I was unstoppable. Having been on the opposite end of the spectrum, a babyface who was constantly getting her ass kicked and not following up on promises, I never wanted to go back. But also, I was being a badass at the expense of some poor good-guy shlub. I would justify that "Well, when I was in my shitty position no one was trying to look out for me," and that was enough for me to sleep at night with a big happy head on me.

It was all building to a title match at *Hell in a Cell*, where it became evident that I was ready to hold that championship.

There was no more "I just want everyone to succeed." I was the one now.

Since losing my title after my very unfortunate run in 2016, I watched everyone who held it carry it with confidence, with self-assuredness. They didn't care about everyone else's turn or how it affected the whole locker room, or if they did, they didn't show it as they went about making the most out of their run. Which they absolutely should have. You worry about you and let everyone else figure their own stuff out.

I AM THE MAN

I was going to be facing Charlotte for the SmackDown women's championship at the *Hell in a Cell* PPV.

The audience was already invested in this domestic spat between two former best friends, and I pushed it as far as I could to make sure it felt real, wanting every match to have that "big-fight feel" about it. I was hitting all platforms with intent. And that intent was to get people to care. Promos, social media, interviews, everything matched, as I was "living the gimmick," i.e., playing the character outside the confines of our TV shows. I often pushed the line, seeing how much I could get away with, and oftentimes taking terrible advice, especially as it pertained to social media and mean-spirited tweets. I do regret a lot of what I put out there during that time.

I know controversy creates cash, but it also creates resentment and feelings of self-loathing. Proceed with your mean tweets with caution.

Charlotte and I put our title match together rather sloppily. The underlying and somewhat untalked-about tension between us was like a pink elephant in the room.

I knew I was going to win in the end, so how we got there didn't bother me. Even though this was a new character and I would have to adopt a new style to fit, I wasn't worried about how to make myself look strong or outdo her. In fact, I always think it's beneficial to try to make your opponent look as good and strong as possible. That way, if you win, you've overcome an obstacle, and if you lose, well, my god, did you have a hill to climb. Taking Colby's advice from a year earlier, I had found different ways to "get my shit in."

On this night, September 16, 2018, over two years since winning my first and only title in WWE, I would be winning my second. Only now I was in a much better position than before.

I won by catching Charlotte quickly by countering a spear and turning it into a pin. One, two, three.

Creative suggested that she try to shake my hand afterward and I, cocky as ever, refuse and taunt her by rubbing the title in her face. *That'll get the people booing!* they thought.

It did not. If anything, it made them cheer more. They liked that I didn't care about anyone's approval. In real life, I wish I could be like this. I imagine a lot of other people did too. That's why it worked.

This story was outlined to go until the end of October, culminating in a last woman standing match at the first-ever all-women's PPV, *Evolution*, set to take place on Long Island. Giving Charlotte and me three PPVs to work together: *Hell in a Cell*, *Super ShowDown* in Australia, and the blowoff match at Evolution. There was enough story to give the audience something they could sink their teeth into, and likely not too much that they would be sick of it. And maybe, just maybe, we could emerge from all of this and be friends again.

We already had great chemistry, but it was getting better with every match we had. As friends, we hit each other hard, but as enemies, we beat the shit out of each other. And when I say Charlotte is strong, she is freakishly strong. With one strike in Melbourne, Australia, in front of fifty thousand people, she hit me so hard that it severed a nerve on the left side of my mouth that took almost five years to recover. Actually, I just looked in the mirror. I'm not sure it fully recovered.

I hoped the giant swollen lump that was protruding by my lower lip was going unnoticed until Daniel Bryan while midconversation after the show blurted out, "Was that always there?" while crouching down and squinting to get a close look at my slightly deformed face.

"No, I was hoping no one would notice. I got hit in the mouth."

"Yeah, I can see that. And no, it's definitely noticeable."

"Thanks, Bryan."

Fuck.

Good thing my character didn't care how she looked or what anyone else thought of her. Rebecca Quin did, though, so it took me a long time before I could watch myself talk again.

With all the steam I had been gathering since SummerSlam, the company was doing everything they could to capitalize on the momentum. They were even bringing back wrestling legends for me to work with. They scheduled a promo for me to go up against Edge—someone who had been vocal about his support of me on my rise to this point. His career had ended abruptly some years earlier as the result of a neck injury, so seeing him back in a WWE ring was a coveted event. And for me, as a fan who admired him greatly since I was an angst-riddled teen, it "reeked of awesomeness."

Edge, beloved as he was, was tasked with getting the audience to boo me. Surely with me opposite a legend like him they would decide they hated me. "What do you think about this?" he began as he sat down beside me at a table in Catering, offering suggestions on how the promo should go. I had never worked side by side with someone of his stature and experience and was willing to do whatever he wanted, but him treating me like an equal and as if my opinions mattered made me feel as if I had arrived.

"What if I warn you about the path you're going down, say that you're not going to like yourself at the end of it all?" he continued enthusiastically. "What would you say back to me?"

I was nervous to pipe up and respond. He was a Hall of Famer. A great of the industry. I didn't want to be out here chiming in shitty ideas to a legend.

"Maybe I lean into it? Like I don't like myself, I love myself?" I offered.

"Yeah! That's great!" he responded, giving me confidence to continue.

"Then, would it be too much if I said, 'Get out of my ring; don't hurt your neck stepping through those ropes'?" I asked, not wanting to offend someone who had come back to work with me specifically. Despite the fact that I had been offending my own former best friend for months in our story line.

"Not at all! That's perfect!" Edge retorted.

When the words came out of my now-deformed mouth live on TV, even with this blatant disrespect to someone the crowd loved so much, strangely, they cheered me. We had a special bond, and it was lovely. For me. Not Edge's neck.

"I tried!" Edge yelled to everyone in gorilla when he stepped back through the curtain.

"They're not going to boo her!" He shrugged as he laughed it off.

To add one legend's appearance to another, that weekend I was at a hockey game with Mick Foley. It wasn't lost on me that the same girl who had failed PE was now mixing it up with all the heroes she had looked up to on TV.

What a freakin' life.

A text from a friend at the time landed in my iPhone at the game: "You should call yourself 'The Man.'"

The idea was so simple and yet polarizing. In our industry, and so many others, there was a long-standing history of brilliant people at the top of their game who have been referred to as "The Man," but they had all been men. Now that "brilliant" person was me.

"What would *you* think if I started calling myself The Man?" I asked Mick, looking for a second opinion.

"It's genius," he responded with a grin.

I posted a picture of me holding my championship in Edge's face, with the caption "I am The Man."

We now had a slogan for the movement. It was powerful. Anyone could be The Man. It didn't matter your background or your gender or what you do. You just needed to claim your greatness and not let anyone tell you differently.

LAST WOMAN STANDING

Charlotte and I were on our way to Evolution. The final chapter in the book. Not actually the final chapter of *this* book, the metaphorical book, if you will. You know what I'm trying to say.

Anyways, they wanted me to powder (leave the ring to get away from my opponent) and cheat and do all the classic heel things. Though they didn't want me to be a heel, or a face, or an in-betweener. They didn't know what they wanted. But I knew what *I* wanted. I wanted to be the best. And so I took their direction and did it to the best of my ability. Any holes in their logic I would try to clarify on social media or in interviews.

Charlotte and I had, at the time, the longest women's match in SmackDown history, ending in me being speared through the LED board after I got purposefully counted out so I wouldn't lose my title, leading to us having a last woman standing match at Evolution.

Neither of us had ever been in a last woman standing match, but the understanding was that these matches could be hard. You don't have standard false finishes such as pinfalls and kick-outs or submissions.

But I wanted this to be the best match of my career (side note, I want every big match to be the best match of my career).

We got to Long Island early. As the first all-women's PPV, this was a big deal and they wanted to give us the best chance of success by practicing the matches a day in advance. Because of the lack of women on the main roster, they had to rely on bringing back women from the past and calling up talent from NXT to fill out the card. So it was likely beneficial to all parties to have rehearsals.

I, in a side note, didn't necessarily love that we were having an all-women's PPV. It was viewed as a female empowerment thing, but I've always wanted equality. They wouldn't be able to get away with purposefully advertising an "all-men's PPV"—that would be seen as archaic, or segregationist. Of course, at the time, they actually were forced to have "all-men's" PPVs as we had just started to run shows in Saudi Arabia and women were not yet *allowed* to wrestle over there. But in a way, to me, it felt counterproductive that we should grovel over being allowed to have our own PPV. For me, it's much more impactful for us to outnumber men's matches on a standard PPV, because there are that many good female-driven story lines. Or to main event the PPVs because we're that good and the audience cares so much that nothing can follow us. I didn't want special treatment. I wanted equal treatment. Equal opportunity.

Although when I did an interview with TMZ they asked me, "Do you think people will tune in and watch? Because don't they usually like story lines?" as if women were still relegated to having pillow fights in their underwear.

I knew we had to make this PPV extra special.

Mine and Charlotte's story was easily the best one on TV and the mentality that was stuck back in the fifties of us merely being there as a special attraction really ground my gears. To be fair, I say "the fifties," but I was looking at a poster from 2014 the other day that said: "Come see Seth Rollins, Big E, Jack Swagger, The Miz, The Big Show and the WWE Divas."

And it sickened me. There was that special attraction shit. That lump-us-all-into-one-category shit. That don't-even-call-us-by-our-names-'cause-you-don't-think-we-can-draw shit. That tits-and-ass shit.

And that was only a year before I got called up to the main roster.

I want to be viewed for the work I do. I want gender out of the picture. And not because I don't like being a woman, but because it shouldn't matter if I am one.

Where was I? Oh yes, this historic all-women's PPV.

We got to the building that day with a lot of ideas but nervous about how to deliver to match people's expectations.

We started talking about table spots and chair spots, guardrails and ladders and kendo sticks. The ring was still being put up, so we pulled the guy who handles all the props aside, giving him the laundry list of what we needed for the match and where we would like it to be placed.

"We don't have any of those things," the props guy, Mark Shilestone, warned us.

"Eh, what?" I responded in disbelief.

"No one told us we needed them," Shilestone confessed.

"It's a last woman standing match," Charlotte added.

"This is the biggest match on the card; how did no one know to get weapons for it?" I chimed back in, a bit egotistical here, but, hey, it was true.

"I have no idea. But what *exactly* do you need?" he offered helpfully.

"Chairs," Charlotte started.

"We have five, I think," Shilestone volunteered.

"We need about thirty," I insisted.

"Shit," said Shilestone.

"We need the wall set up so she can spear me through it," I went on.

"There's no walls; it's just guardrails."

"Fuck." Charlotte scowled.

That spot was out.

"Ladders?" I asked.

"We don't have any," Shilestone said, letting us down.

"Tables?" Charlotte quipped.

"Nope."

"Kendo sticks," I joined in.

"We have some of them," Shilestone confirmed, relieved.

So there was that.

Luckily, we were only an hour away from WWE's warehouse,

and because we had gotten to the building uncharacteristically early, it gave them ample time to get the hell out and get what we needed.

I was insulted. Even with the hoopla of this historic event, the attention to detail on their biggest story flew under the radar.

Charlotte and I, who were very civil throughout this whole process, got to work around the provisions we had now. There were several gaps we would be figuring out until almost bell time, but we were sure we had a banger on our hands.

We were the second-to-last match of the card. The main event was going to Ronda Rousey and Nikki Bella.

In my mind that was both misguided and brilliant. Not that Nikki and Ronda wouldn't be able to put on a great match, but there was no way that they could compete with the level of match we would have. We had a story that was years and years in the making. Plus, we had weapons, which always makes it more exciting.

But not getting the main event would seem like we were being screwed by the company again. And the fans wouldn't be too happy with that.

Although it did put a lot of pressure on the other girls.

It ended up being one of my favorite matches I've ever had. It was the first time maybe since I got to WWE that I felt completely present in the ring. I was receptive to the amazing Long Island crowd, not thinking ahead to the next spot or where my opponent should be. (I often keep an eye on less experienced talent to make sure they're in the right position.) Charlotte is so good that I didn't need to, as I trust her completely. We both talked to each other the whole way through the match to ensure everyone was on the same page.

I was also only getting used to being in a position on the card where I was trusted to have big matches and big stories.

But as Charlotte and I can *always* be trusted to do, we beat the hell out of each other. I jumped off the top of a ladder, leg-dropping her through a table and landing with all my weight on her stomach. That she didn't actually shit herself there is a strong testament to her abdominal muscles.

I piled every piece of apparatus I could find on her—shards of broken tables, chairs, announcer table chairs, anything that wasn't glued down—and sat back in delight as I waited for the ten count.

Eight, nine, and like a zombie she resurrected herself from the rubble. Only she just got to her knees and let out a T. Rex–esque roar.

Fuck, I thought.

Was the ref going to eliminate her? Technically, she was meant to get to her feet, but I don't think she was entirely clear on the exact rules of the stipulation. Charlotte is a very intuitive wrestler and so this felt like the most natural thing for her. But technically, she wasn't standing, so technically, it should have been over.

The ref let it slide. *Phew!* We had more stuff to do!

She came at me with kendo sticks like swords in her hands and beat me mercilessly.

(As an aside: Those kendo sticks don't look like much sometimes, but they hurt like hell. Unless you're me, who has my body mostly covered up, so I'll take a beating with them all day long. On bare skin, however? Excruciating.)

We got to the crescendo. She had me left for dead on a table on the outside and went up to the top turnbuckle as if to moonsault onto me. Rookie mistake. With my last bit of energy I climbed up and power-bombed her through the tables down below.

Eight, nine, ten.

I had retained my title and I had had a blast.

We came back to standing ovations and hugged and thanked each other. The spark of a friendship that might be able to recover. Especially if this truly was to be the end of the story line. I could go on to harass someone new.

After the last match, there was a curtain call where all the wrestlers went out to the stage to celebrate the success of the night. I tried to avoid it. I thought it would compromise the integrity of the match Charlotte and I had, to see us out there side by side. Or even standing after the brutality we had put each other through. Alas, I was pushed through the curtain while battling in my head whether or not going out might be an insult to the girls who had worked so hard.

I also believed that all of us going out was somewhat condescending to us. They wouldn't throw out the guys' story lines like this and pull back the curtain, so why do it to us?

Regardless, there I stood. Not smiling like the babyface of yesteryear. Just trying my best to keep my character intact in the midst of my own personal turmoil about the matter.

BLOODBATH

The *Survivor Series* PPV was around the corner and it was champion versus champion. The SmackDown women's champion, The Man Becky Lynch, versus the Raw women's champion, The Baddest Woman on the Planet, Ronda Rousey—and it was the most anticipated match in the company at the time.

Ronda and I agreed to go all out on our social media banter. She gave me some guidelines about what was off-limits and would politely reel me back in if I pushed the boundaries. And though it appeared that we hated each other, she couldn't have been more game. She understood that this was business and anything said wasn't intended to be personal. Even if it was based on sore spots.

She seemed to truly be enjoying her time here. As she already had so much pressure on her from a young age between MMA and the Olympics, and constantly being in competitive and hostile locker rooms, this was a welcomed break. We tend to have a pretty great vibe in our locker room. Especially when Charlotte and I aren't butting heads.

All this is to say, as much as I didn't want anyone to know, I loved Ronda, and I was excited that she was there and I couldn't wait to make magic with her.

The juxtaposition of the two characters was perfect. She was from another sport, getting all of the attention and special treatment, and she seemed to be a natural in the ring.

Versus me. The kid who failed PE. The one who was chosen by the audience and had to scratch and claw for every morsel that she got.

She was born tough. I was made tough. She was stronger and more skilled than I was. But I could take a beating and keep on moving forward. To quote Rocky Balboa, "That's how winning is done."

Ronda knew I was a hot commodity in wrestling. And I knew her name would put us on a level that was never seen for women in the professional wrestling world.

Week after week we would cut scathing promos on each other.

When she talked the crowd would chant my name even though she was supposed to be the babyface. I was clearly still the underdog. And it was unlikely the office would have her lose.

Before Survivor Series, we had our annual November European tour. Even though Charlotte and I were done wrestling on TV, we were not done wrestling in live events. And while we were weren't close anymore, we could talk with no awkwardness.

We, classically, beat the crap out of each other for almost thirty minutes every night for two weeks straight. By the end of the tour my body was aching and my head was pounding.

The newfound success I had acquired required me to do more media, which I loved, but meant I had no rest time—not that there was much on these tours anyway.

The morning we were supposed to return to the States, as I was getting on my seven-hour flight from London to New York, I got a text saying that me and the rest of the women would be needed for Raw that night. Travel advised me that once I landed in New York I would board a private plane to Missouri. It was past seven when we landed in the snow of Kansas City, and the show had already started by the time we made it to the arena. Mark Carrano was there to greet us and usher us in.

"Everyone needs SmackDown shirts and jeans," he ordered as he led us to the locker room.

We suited up while the producers gave us the layout for the show. We were the main event and it would be pure chaos.

As soon as I had my T-shirt and jeans on, I was rushed out to quickly film a segment with Ronda where I had her in an arm bar in the locker room while she flailed wildly. I was torn off by refs and producers alike. And that started the madness that would ensue.

The Raw women's team (minus Ronda) was in the ring after Bayley and Sasha had had a tremendous match to determine the captain of the Survivor Series team.

These invasion angles were always a ton of fun. It didn't matter if we were running on fumes.

I swaggered out as a big ol' surprise, mouthing off all the way down to the ring. Once I got to the bottom of the ramp, the women from SmackDown jumped the ring from behind and beat up Team Raw.

I slid in during the mayhem. And, well, that's when it all became a blur.

All I know was that I went to turn Nia Jax around and she punched me square in the face. Nia was our largest lady. She is more than double my weight and is as strong as an ox. And while I'm sure this was an accident, it was the best accident that could have possibly happened to me.

I remember thinking, *Ohhhhhh, I'm concussed*, as I slow-motion crumbled by the ropes. After that, I have snippets of memories.

I rolled out of the ring and went to grab a chair. Blurry doctor faces rushed me. Blood was pouring down my face. Already I couldn't even remember how it happened.

"Are you okay?" they asked as they gave me a towel to mop up the stream of blood coming from my nose.

"Yeah, I'm fine," I quickly replied as I wiped my face before throwing the blood-soaked towel back at them. "Gotta go."

I ran in with the chair and proceeded to run my spot with Ronda. She turns; I hit her in the stomach and then whack her in the back, the crowd chanting, "One more time," and, well, when they're chanting, "One more time," you gotta hit her one more time!

So I did. As cautiously as I could, though. I was with it enough to know I wasn't with it at all and didn't want to get anyone else hurt in the process.

After I did my damage, I left with the rest of my SmackDown crew through the crowd, up the stairs, as the audience went wild.

I stood there smiling and mouthing off, blood smeared all over my face, knowing that the camera was still on me and I couldn't leave until we had gone off the air.

Once I was given the cue, I walked through the doors into the foyer, where security was there to meet us.

"Where am I?" I inquired to a fuzzy face escorting us.

I had no idea what town I was in, what had just happened, or how the hell I had gotten there.

Next thing I know, I'm sitting in the trainer's room with Stephanie McMahon looking after me like a proper mom.

"I'm scared," I said to her, turning into a six-year-old and feeling like my brain would never work again.

"I know," she responded kindly, her eyes never breaking contact like she does, "but you'll be okay."

"Do you promise?" I was the direct antithesis to the person I had been in the arena.

"I do," she said, nodding encouragingly. Having grown up around the business, she'd seen things like this regularly, and often with behemoths of men. I'm not sure any of them talked to her like scared little children, though.

She guided me down the hall towards the ambulance that was waiting on-site.

Lorrie, one of our medical staff, came with me.

"I can't remember how I got here," I told her as Stephanie loaded me into the vehicle.

"That's okay. Do you know who I am?" she asked kindly.

"No," I replied as I burst into tears. I knew I was supposed to know who she was, but I could barely remember my own name.

The more I tried to remember, the more freaked out I got.

I was shaking. Possibly from fear. Possibly from having a brain injury. Probably from it being minus twenty outside.

Stephanie took off her coat and gave it to me. "Here. Stay warm." She is a legitimate angel.

The ambulance took off, sirens blaring. Which seemed a little dramatic, but whatever.

We eventually got to the hospital and Lorrie gave me my phone back. It's not ideal to be looking at blue screens while you're out of it.

I had so many "Holy shit, that was awesome!" texts.

I replied to a friend: "Did I get Ronda?"

"Get her? You became a star tonight."

That's cool, I thought. *How? What did I do?*

The hospital ran a series of tests, starting with a CAT scan. No damage to my skull, just a broken nose that I couldn't even feel. They snapped it back into place with minimum pain.

Lorrie waited with me until one of our other doctors showed up. I knew it was pretty unlikely that Ronda and I could have the belter of a match that I was hoping we would at the weekend, and I was already scheming on how I could work around my injuries.

Sasha, Bayley, and Nattie all unexpectedly showed up to check on me, which meant the world to me.

Seeing them jogged my memory.

"Do you know how it happened?" Bayley asked.

"No . . . but I do know you guys had an awesome match!"

"Ha-ha, thanks, Becks," she chuckled.

I started recalling some of the innovative spots they had. Sasha and Bayley have incredible chemistry. Both are so good and creative that their matches together are nothing short of works of art.

But recalling their match was bringing everything back into focus.

"And then I came down the ramp, but the other girls jumped the ring."

"Ohh, and then I spun Nia around! Wait a second! It was Nia."

"Yep," Sasha confirmed.

"Oh, man! Did she come to the trainer's room?!"

They shrugged. It was customary to check on whoever you may have injured, though I'm sure she just didn't want to crowd me. Or maybe she didn't even know she had hurt me.

I texted her: "It was yooooooooouuuuuuuuu."

"I'm so sorry! Are you okay?" Nia responded.

"Yeah, I'm just messing with you. I'm all good!"

It really does feel horrible when you injure someone. I would always rather be the injured than the injurer and I think that's the same for any decent worker.

There are few what you might call iconic photos in wrestling: Hulk Hogan slamming André the Giant, and "Stone Cold" Steve Austin in a sharpshooter with his face covered in blood come to mind. It was none of my own doing, but thanks to this happy accident, some might say I joined that special, "iconic photos of wrestling" club. In a way, paralleling my Rocky Balboa–esque journey on top of the steps as my supporters cheered around me.

One of our doctors arrived to drive me the four hours to the next city. I was fairly shattered after the day of travel, the time zone change, and, well, my face was literally shattered and my brain was mush.

When we showed up at the building the next day, I was fully hoping to fake my way through the day.

"I can still go," I protested to the doctors, lying right to their faces, albeit poorly. They could sniff out my bullshit easily with a simple concussion protocol test.

"Remember these five words. Apple, bubble, pencil, rabbit, banana."

"Banana, bubble, triangle? Eh, no, eh." I immediately started to cry. "I'm sorry, I don't know why I'm crying."

"Probably because you're concussed."

"I'm not; I'm okay; I might be tired," I pleaded.

"You're not, but that's okay," the doctor reasoned.

"Can I still wrestle?"

"No. Not until you heal your head."

"How long will that take?"

"A few weeks."

Now I was crying harder.

"Can I not just work around it?"

"No, it's too dangerous. Your brain isn't working properly, so this is how you could get another injury, like you step wrong and then you've got a torn ACL and you're out for even longer."

The most anticipated match on the Survivor Series card and one of the biggest matches of my career was now out the window and I was devastated.

I was reassured from top to bottom that I would be okay and that this was better for me in the long run. As Mike Mansury, an executive producer, put it, "Becky Lynch versus Ronda Rousey at Survivor Series would have been cool. But Becky Lynch versus Ronda Rousey at WrestleMania? That's a main event."

If I weren't so messed up, I would have been excited.

I was scheduled to do phone interviews that day for over an hour, only, despite WWE's medical team following procedure in textbook form, word hadn't reached the PR team to cancel them, and I sure as hell wasn't going to back out on my own. I sat in the bleachers feeling like shit, trying to sort out my head while reporters asked me questions that I couldn't understand. After two interviews I began to cry again.

"I don't know what I'm saying," I blubbered to my representative.

"It's okay. You're doing fine, but I'm going to cancel the rest of the interviews."

I was feeling more and more like a failure. Let down by my own brain.

Pushing to do a promo was probably not the best idea either.

I needed to pick a replacement for me for Survivor Series. They wanted me to pick Charlotte and hug her. Which to me felt like throwing everything we did down the drain. That suddenly we were okay with each other. I tried to fight it, but Road Dogg assured me,

"She's in a pretty shitty position; you advocating for her would help a lot," referring to Charlotte and Ronda happening on less than a week's build after having been pegged for a WrestleMania match.

I couldn't argue when my mind wasn't in the right place. I had too many thoughts and too much confusion.

It felt weird to go out there and hug Charlotte. Everyone had bought into our story. I didn't want to give them any indication it wasn't real.

And the story was far from over.

HEAVYWEIGHT

I was going to be facing Ronda at WrestleMania.

It would likely be a triple threat including Charlotte because Ronda would be leaving WWE after Mania and they felt that it would be better to have two main eventers after she left instead of just one. That or they had already promised Charlotte that she'd main event and wanted to follow through with it. Likely the latter.

The singles match would have been the better call from a story-line perspective, and it was the match most fans wanted to see. But any way you slice it, it was going to be the first time women main evented Mania and I was going to be in it; better yet, I was most likely the person who was going to win it. A year ago I was in the preshow battle royal, thrown out unceremoniously by someone who wasn't even on the main roster.

It was just a matter of how the hell do we get there? We were on two different shows and I still had the title. One idea was that I carry the title until Mania but also win the Royal Rumble and choose her.

You can't give a babyface too much these days. The fans see the machine getting behind you and they resent that. They tend to favor the underdog. The rebel with a cause. The one who rages against the machine.

That's what I had to be.

It took a few more weeks for me to be cleared to get back in the ring. My nose hadn't fully healed and I wasn't passing the standardized concussion test.

We were a long way from WrestleMania, so we couldn't keep the rivalry between me and Ronda going until then, especially with us on different shows, so Creative pivoted to me losing the title to Asuka in a triple threat (again, Charlotte was involved) in the first women's tables, ladders, and chairs match at its namesake's PPV.

While my brain was healing, so was my heart. My friendship with Colby had been growing since October. He was unhappy in his relationship and had been for quite some time and I had been unceremoniously ghosted by my latest fling. Colby and I had always had a connection, but now we were spending more time together due to booking circumstances and were bonding over our respective love life woes. His tended to be "maybe monogamy isn't for me," while I was "I love the idea of one person, but I don't seem to be matching with the right people." We talked openly and honestly about our thoughts and feelings with no judgment on either side. It was refreshing.

He was flying into LA after a tour in South America and had the day off.

"Do you have a spare room?" he asked.

"No, but I have a couch if you need somewhere to stay," I responded, being aware that as one of WWE's biggest stars, he could afford a hotel room.

"That sounds good."

I was nervous about him staying. There was clearly something there, and if not handled with care things could get messy.

I picked him up from the airport, and as we rode over to the gym for a quick workout somehow the movie *Heavyweights* came up in conversation.

"I've never seen it," I admitted.

"You've never seen it?!" he balked. "We have to watch it."

"I don't have a TV, or rather, my TV doesn't work."

"You don't have a goddamn working TV?!" he scoffed.

"I never watch it. I live in LA, man, too much to do. You can try and get it working if you like."

"Right, that's what we'll do tonight," he said, taking charge.

As we got back to my one-bedroom Marina del Rey apartment and he went to work repairing my broken television to no avail, he confided that he and his girlfriend had taken a break. I tried to counsel him through it, even though, after my shitty engagement and being recently ghosted, I was hardly feeling optimistic.

After realizing "TV repairman" was likely not something Colby could add to his résumé, he relented: "I guess we'll watch it on my laptop." Which would force us to sit closer to each other on my sectional couch as he held the laptop on outstretched legs.

The movie had just started when he put his hand on my leg.

Oh no, oh no. What do I do?! I'm not ready for this. Ahhhhhhhh-hhh, I thought on repeat for almost the duration of the one-and-a-half-hour movie. At one point, I attempted to match this body contact rather awkwardly, my hand finding its way to his arm rigidly while I hoped he didn't move any farther. How was a newly single me expected to resist this giant brooding hunk of a man? But he was also my buddy. My pal. My colleague. And I did not want to complicate that.

When the movie was over, we shifted our rigid hands and recited hilarious *Heavyweights* scenes without ever commenting on the awkward body contact.

As we both got tired and prepared to go to sleep on our respective furniture items, I gave him a hug that lingered a few seconds too long. If anything was going to happen, this would be the time for it to happen. But he would have to make the first move; I couldn't be charged with ruining our friendship.

He did not.

Probably for the best, I thought as I made way to my bedroom while he stayed on the couch.

I woke up the next morning to him poking his beardy head through the door.

"You up?" he asked.

"Yeah," I said. *I am now,* I thought, along with *Get out of here; I look awful in the morning and I haven't brushed my teeth!*

He got into bed beside me.

"Did you sleep okay?"

"Yeah, did you?" I asked as I tried to keep my mouth shut in order to preserve him from my stank breath.

"Yeah . . . I sent you a text, but you were probably asleep already."

"Oh, I didn't see it." I picked up my phone to see a "You still awake?" text from my hot friend Colby.

He admitted he had contemplated making a move. Luckily, I was already asleep.

I wasn't ready for anything. And neither was he. He was just testing the waters. And they were choppy.

We eventually got moving, already running late to meet our mutual friends for breakfast and workouts.

We were back to normal. But maybe a little closer than before. And I was hopeful that if a guy as smart, cool, and competent, not to mention handsome, as Colby was interested in me, maybe I'd find someone right for me outside of my work/friend pool.

TABLES, LADDERS, AND CANCER

I was going to have my first match back since my injury at the TLC PPV, in my first-ever Tables, Ladders, and Chairs match, and in my first-ever main event on a PPV.

I didn't have the same level of swagger as before. I was back to officially being a babyface now; the broken nose sealed the deal but immediately put pressure on me. Now I had to be likable; what if the people turned on me before Mania? Then the old imposter syndrome started seeping in. You know the one? The one that tells you you're not good enough. That someone else is better. That you're a fraud and everyone is going to find out the next time you do anything.

TLC took place in San Jose, where years earlier I had attended my first WrestleMania, hoping to one day be the main event. And while it wasn't WrestleMania, tonight we were the main event.

I watched the match before us struggle amidst chants of "We want Becky"—getting me excited. Or I would have been if that match didn't include my buddy Colby, so I looked on with conflicting emotions, hoping this wouldn't make things awkward.

The doubt that I had let set in was starting to dissipate. The crowd hadn't turned on me yet. But of course not. It was only my first match.

Colby came back through the curtain, looking dejected. He and his opponent, Dean Ambrose, had worked their asses off out there. But it didn't matter—the crowd had come to see The Man.

Colby passed me on his way to talk to Vince. "They're ready for you," he said, discouraged.

Charlotte and Asuka made their way to the ring. As soon as the music died down for a second, the chants of "*Becky*" rang through the arena before my music hit.

Piss off, Imposter Syndrome! I pronounced valiantly to my own skull.

We hadn't had enough time to rehearse or locate where all the weapons and equipment we needed were beforehand, and so when we got out there it was a bit clustered.

The crowd didn't seem to care, though. They were invested in the story, and whenever one lands on ladders or goes through tables or gets beaten mercilessly with a chair, the audience tends to forgive any additional sloppiness.

And despite our clunkiness in certain spots, there were still resounding chants of "This is awesome." It didn't feel awesome, though. It felt messy.

At the end, Charlotte and I were on top of the ladder, inches away from victory, when Ronda Rousey came barreling down the ramp and tipped us off, allowing Asuka to climb up and become the new champion.

A roar came from the crowd. Whether this was the excitement of having a new champion in Asuka or the fact that it was now inevitable that they would finally get Ronda versus Becky at WrestleMania, I'm not sure. But they sure were happy about it.

All three participants of the match came back not feeling great about ourselves. People backstage slapped us on the back and told us we were great, but we didn't feel it. Certainly I didn't; my first main event outing hadn't been the colossal success I wanted it to be.

Not the most encouraging thing while trying to aim for the main event of WrestleMania in a matter of months.

The day after TLC, as I was on my way to the next town, my brother asked me to call him.

Christmas was coming up and I was going back to Ireland, WWE camera crew in tow. They were doing a special on me for the WWE Network, making me feel like I was hitting the big time.

"Here, what would you think of going down and spending Christmas with Dad this year?" Richy asked.

My dad lived in a county two hours outside of Dublin.

I had always loved Christmas at my mom's, baking cookies, watching movies, staying in my pajamas for several days on end, and didn't want to give up that tradition.

"Can't he just come up on Christmas Eve?" I replied. That was what we had usually done, a tradition in itself, I justified.

"I just think it would be really nice and something different if we went down. He never gets to spend Christmas with us," Richy pleaded.

"But Mom always does Christmas Day," and she made a great Christmas dinner.

I could hear the frustration growing in his voice as I tried to argue with him while I wandered around the Whole Foods salad bar, trying to pick out my meals for the rest of the day.

"Becky, Dad has lung cancer," he finally blurted out.

The words walloped me like a chair to the back of the head.

"What?" I asked out of disbelief more than a lack of understanding, as the lettuce tongs fell out of my hand.

"Look, I'm sorry to tell you like this. But I just think it would be nice if we—"

Devastated by my own selfishness and inability to care about anyone else's convenience but my own, I interrupted him, "Of course we can go down to him. I'm sorry. I'm so sorry. How bad is it?"

"We don't really know. He doesn't want to do chemo or anything. He didn't want me to worry you."

"When was he going to tell me? At Christmas?"

"Yeah, I think so."

"Well, that would have been a shitty way to find out." As if there were a non-shitty way to find out your dad has lung cancer. "I'm glad you told me now. Thank you."

I was now bawling my eyes out as I walked through the drinks section.

"Are you going to be okay?"

"Yeah, I think so," I lied, not feeling okay at all. "Thanks, Richy."

I hung up and texted my mom.

"Dad has cancer?"

"Aw, Becky. I'm so sorry. We didn't want to worry you. We knew you had so much going on. Are you going to be all right?"

"How long has he known?"

"We're not sure. You know how your dad is; he wouldn't tell anyone."

"How long have *you* known?"

"Probably since October."

October?! What the actual hell?! Richy had been holding this in for over two months; his older-brother instincts of protection had him suffering in silence for months, unable to vent his worries.

It sucked. It all fucking sucked.

And I still had a town to make and smiles to fake.

It would be a long few days until I could get back to Dublin.

I called the people who were making the documentary and explained what was going on. We already had plans to film in Dublin, but now I wanted to spend time with my dad.

"Can we bring him up?"

"Of course, Becky. We'll do whatever you need," Dan Pucherelli, a real-life hero who's part of the backstage crew, assured me as he immediately went to work organizing hotels and car services for my dad so he might feel like a king.

I met my dad in the hotel bar once he had arrived. He already had a signature pint of Guinness in hand. He looked healthy. If you didn't know any better you wouldn't think anything was wrong. I got tequila. I needed it tonight.

Sitting in leather armchairs, he kept everything as breezy as he could, not going into specifics of anything. It was as if he had just been told that he'd have to get a mole removed as opposed to having stage 4 lung cancer. And bringing up his life insurance policy that he had somehow managed to maintain throughout his financial struggles, as if he were talking about the weather.

His greatest hope was, despite none of his career ambitions ever panning out, that he would have some amount of money to leave us when he left.

"Dad, I don't care about any of that stuff. I'm fine; I don't need anything. I just want you to be okay."

Through sips of stout and small handfuls of peanuts, he didn't sell a thing. As fathers tend to do. Never allowing me to get the full scope of the situation.

As a break from conversations of all things cancer, I brought up some happier news: "It's looking like I'll main event WrestleMania; I'd love to bring you over."

"What's that, now?"

He never really did keep up with the schedule or even understand the reach that WWE had across the globe. In fact, one time he mentioned to a nurse that his daughter was a professional wrestler and she produced a photo of me on her phone, saying, "Is this her?" His mind was blown.

"Becks! How did she get that picture?"

"Google, Dad."

"Ah yes," he responded, not actually having a clue what I was talking about.

Such a sweet, uncomplicated man, my dad.

I continued to explain the orbit of WrestleMania. "It's our biggest event of the year, almost like the finals of the World Cup"—the usual comparison to the Super Bowl would also be wasted on him. "And there's never been a woman that's main evented it before, but I'm pretty sure I'm going to be the first."

"Oh, right," he answered, slightly unimpressed. "When is that?"

"April."

"Well, we'll see."

"We'll see? What do you mean?"

"If I'm still here."

On Christmas Day we sat around my dad's tiny table in his modest government-appointed house, eating his deliciously cooked dinner.

Over mashed potatoes and carrots I had to stop myself from crying, trying not to let him see me upset.

This could be the last Christmas I spend with my dad, I thought.

Even worse: *This could be the last time I see my dad.*

POINT TO THE SIGN

Before we could make it to the main event at WrestleMania, there was the Rumble. I was set to get my first match with the now Smack-Down women's champion and someone I regard as one of the greatest wrestlers out there: Asuka.

She is a dream to work with. Between broken English and sweet giggles, she comes with a plethora of ideas, and the most amazing footwork and finesse I've ever seen. When she goes through the curtain she transforms from the sweetest human on earth into an absolute killer, and it was my honor to face her for the title, and more so to put her over for the title. I was going to lose to her in the first match of the night and then enter the Rumble later that night.

I needed this match with Asuka to go well. If it didn't, then people might not care to see me again that night. Or as the annoying voice in my head said, *They won't care to see me* ever again.

When I landed in Arizona, the home of the Royal Rumble that year, Colby kindly offered to pick me up from the airport. He had gotten in earlier that day and rented an Airbnb to stay at. "You're welcome to join," he offered. I declined. I had to concentrate on my matches, damn it, and needed no man with a body built by the gods distracting me.

Though I may have topped up my makeup upon arrival and given myself a little perfume spritz before getting in the car.

The drive from the airport to the hotel took only ten minutes, but we stayed talking in Colby's car for almost two hours. I hated how easy it was and would sporadically question what it would be like if we kissed. Derailing my own thoughts by arguing that his beard would likely leave a rash on my face and that would be very uncomfortable indeed. *Indeed.*

It was getting late and I had an early start time the next day. We hugged a hug that once again lasted a few moments longer than it should have before I retreated to my room, texting my friend Jay: "I think I may be in love with Colby."

To which he responded: "I just turned on my phone and it appears to be broken. What? You literally just gave me a laundry list of all the reasons that would be a bad idea THIS MORNING."

"What can I say? Single Becky is unpredictable."

It is *a bad idea*, I would remind myself.

But you're single, Becky. You can explore whatever you want. No attachments. You get what you want out of it. You strong, independent woman you!

Hell yeah. I wasn't getting feelings. I was starting a goddamn movement. I was a regular Gloria Steinem, thank you very much.

The following day, which was the night before Rumble, Colby invited me out to dinner, but I didn't finish my appearances until midnight. So he tried to entice me to come to his Airbnb with a selfie.

It's the selfie game we're playing, is it? Truth be told, I wasn't much into the selfie game. I often scoffed at the kids for their willy-nillyness to send selfies. *Quite conceited, are we? Arrogance, is it? Look at me; I'm soooo beautiful that you will fall madly in love with me from my beautiful yet only slightly edited picture of me pouting like a duck* is how I imagine the inner monologue of the selfie sender goes. Whatever happened to wooing someone with wit? And intelligent quips? A joke, perhaps? I'm not quite sure. But this was how the kids were doing it these days, so I decided to get hip with the kids. And by "kids" I mean Colby, a full-grown adult male. I wasn't sending any selfies to kids.

Anyway, my midsection had a hint of abs on this day, should I flex correctly under the right lighting, and I thought I should share them with someone. Even if I was thinking, *I really shouldn't*, but that's usually how the best stuff starts.

To which he responded with heart emoji eyes and we continued texting like excited teenagers.

I barely slept that night. Selfie adrenaline, nerves, and anticipation of what was to come combined were all taking chunks out of sleep time.

The date was January 27, 2019. The Rumble where The Man came around.

It took place in Chase Field, a large baseball stadium that held upwards of forty thousand people. I walked out to a roar from the crowd. Fans holding "The Man" signs illuminated the arena and I was overwhelmed with gratitude. My favorite PPV of the year and this time I would be winning the Rumble at the end of the night. Thirteen-year-old me wouldn't believe it. Thirty-one-year-old me barely could.

Asuka and I took lumps out of each other for nearly thirty minutes straight.

We knew we would go over our allotted time, but towards the end we were being yelled at by the ref, "Take it home! You gotta take it home," meaning we had to cut out a bunch of our false finishes and go straight to the end. There were still a lot more matches to come, including two-hour-long Royal Rumbles.

She hooked me in her finisher and bridged over to a chorus of boos. The Man couldn't do it. I tapped out. There's a weird thing about tapping out. That it can be argued for weakness, and especially with a strong character like "The Man." But I also didn't want to be "that guy." The one who makes a fuss about tapping out or losing. At the end of the day, I was going to go on to win the night and potentially main event WrestleMania. The least I could do would be to make Asuka look strong on my way there.

And I still had to go out again in a little over an hour! The adrenaline dump and exhaustion from not sleeping the night before were catching up to me.

The plan was for Lana to be attacked by Nia on her way to the ring, thus rendering her unfit to compete and by proxy leaving a spot open in the Rumble. I made my way out summoning the energy of Zeus to a chorus of cheers, saw Lana crumpled on the ground, and wondered if anyone would mind if I joined her momentarily for a quick nap before getting on with business. No napping would be allowed, as I argued with Fit Finlay, who was attending our fallen comrade Lana and had suddenly become the authority on who was allowed in the Rumble for some reason. Whatever, it's wrestling; we make up the rules as we go.

In the end it came down to me and Charlotte. However, not before I got pushed off the stairs and my knee was injured by a salty Nia, who had just been eliminated. I would have to overcome as many obstacles as possible on my way to the top.

The referees were about to call the match, declaring Charlotte the winner, before I valiantly hobbled my way into the ring and, after a series of blows, tossed her over the top and did the one thing that every wrestling fan turned wrestler dreams of doing: the classic point to the WrestleMania sign. Once you feel as though you've done it ad nauseam the referee will yell at you, "Keep pointing!" It's a helluva shoulder pump, I'll tell you that.

I came back through the curtain to an abundance of congratulatory hugs and back pats. As I made my rounds, I looked over to see that Charlotte was crying. I didn't ask why; we weren't close like that anymore. I assumed she thought her WrestleMania moment was dead and buried now. But I knew she would be included and knew she would always be okay. Not because she was Ric Flair's daughter. But because she was good. And she had a work ethic that would never let her down.

The night was not yet over, though. I still had to watch Colby win his Rumble.

It felt so serendipitous that these two flirty friends were both having the biggest Rumble nights of their lives. A true love story . . . even if one of the characters in this particular story didn't believe in monogamy anymore and the other was skeptical and guarded of the other's intentions.

Anywhooooo. Colby had been having problems with his back; he had fractured his spine in a match a little while ago but hadn't told anyone about it because he's a machine that can fight through just about anything and didn't want to miss out on this opportunity. He was also competing for that WrestleMania main event spot. I watched nervously, knowing he was going to go through a table mid-match, and I prayed to the heavens that he didn't mess himself up too bad. That would have really put a dampener on all the flirting.

When he came through gorilla, there were camera crews there to capture him. I hugged him as I awkwardly tried to get out of frame. This flirtiness had become pretty obvious and I didn't want to give the game away on camera.

"You coming to get food?" he asked.

"I've got friends in town, so I'll probably go see them, but let me know where you end up."

I was going to have to go to Raw the next day to choose my opponent for WrestleMania, and again, I didn't want any distractions, so I knew this was a false promise of meetuppery, but one must keep one's options open.

While out for dinner he was sending me pictures of his food, which looked far more appealing than ours.

"We're still eating, so I might have to pass on tonight," I finally bailed.

"I was supposed to get a red-eye tomorrow after Raw, but should I stay and hang out?"

"Yeah! Do that; that would be cool."

"Except I have to be out of my Airbnb by tomorrow morning. . . ."

"You can just stay with me," I responded while I'm thinking, *What are you doing, Rebecca! This is a terrible idea*, and then the devil on my shoulder would chime in, *Relax, you don't have to do anything. It's just your friend Colby. You love hanging out with your friend Colby.* It's true, Mr. Devil, sir, I do.

"Cool. I'll bring my bags over when I check out if that's okay."

"Sure is. See you tomorrow. Sleep tight."

I was working out in the hotel gym when Colby said he was on his way. Flustered, I finished my set and ran upstairs to shower before meeting him at the elevator. My body language was signaling my nervousness as I desperately tried to fight it. *You're The Man, remember. You're The freakin' Man. Goddamn it, why can't you just be The Man in real life?* I argued with myself.

What the hell are you so nervous about? It's your friend. You know it's not going to go anywhere. Just have some fun and stop being so uptight.

"Mind if I get changed?" he asked as we got into my room.

Why do you need to get changed? I thought, but I responded, "Make yourself at home," my voice cracking like that of a prepubescent boy.

He didn't go into the bathroom or attempt any other form of modesty, just stripped down to his underwear there in front of me, quads glistening as the sunlight cascaded into the room.

Fuck. Well, it's gonna happen, Rebecca. No use in fighting it now. Assert dominance! I thought.

"Would you like a kombucha?" I asked, the most millennial pickup line ever.

The minifridge in my room was just beside the bed, which was exactly where he was sitting.

"Sure. What you got?"

"Mint mojito, strawberry serenade, raspberry hibiscus . . ."

"I'll try the raspberry hibiscus."

I bent down to get the bottle, then stood up and gave it to him. The kombucha, that is.

Now is the time. You got this, Quin. You. Are. The Man!!!!!!

I stood directly over him, straddling his legs while he was seated on the bed.

He had talked a good game. Time to see if he could back it up.

He looked nervous.

I could tell I was right by the way he said, "I'm nervous."

Our lips met and soon we were in full make-out mode.

So this was what it was like to kiss him, beard tickling, tongues rolling. My heart pounding. Years of sexual tension and energy went into this one moment.

"I wasn't expecting that," he said after.

Bitch, of course you were. You were laying the groundwork for months. Possibly even years, I thought. But I responded, "Me neither."

We were both liars.

"We should go," I said, finally putting an end to its progression. We had a whole night ahead of us.

Raw had an early call time and I was feeling like the new kid at school. I was a SmackDown resident and being in this new environment had me a bit on edge.

Colby and I didn't see each other throughout the day but stayed texting and flirting, recalling those tender hotel moments earlier that day.

But back to the task at hand. This was the moment everyone was waiting for. I was choosing Ronda Rousey as my WrestleMania opponent.

Coming off the highs of the night before and events earlier in the day, I was feeling pretty darn good about myself.

Unfortunately for Ronda, she had just had a promo where the crowd had chanted for me and derailed her train of thought, followed by not her best match. However, it did make my entrance that bit more exciting. And we needed all the excitement we could get to earn that main event spot on Mania. But considering my emotional butterflies, what was at stake here, and days running on no sleep, I was jittery to say the least. Somehow I managed to deliver a promo that at least seemed like I was calm, cool, and collected, which was followed by a riled-up promo from Ronda in retaliation. This time, the anger she felt for the crowd and their unapologetic favoritism, and probably a bit for me, lit a fire under her.

And thus, my double duty on both *Raw* and *SmackDown* began and would remain in place until *WrestleMania*. TV time is prime real estate to a performer, but as a babyface, if you get too much exposure, you run the risk of the audience getting sick of you.

Which is also the risk I was running with escalating things with Colby. *We work together; what if we get sick of each other?!*

Nonetheless, I waited for Colby to be done in the hallway of the Phoenix arena, trying to make it not so obvious we were leaving together.

We made it back to my room, shut the door, and immediately began pawing at each other. Clothes were thrown across the room, and I kept thinking, *Ahhhhhhhhhhhhhhhhhhhhhh! My friend Colby's gonna see me naked. What if he's not into it and then it's all just awkward from here on out? Abort mission! Abort mission, Rebeccaaaaaaahhhhhhhh! Oh, but it feels so nice and he looks too good. You're in too deep now, Beck. Well done, you failure.*

But on the outside I tried to feign confidence and fumble my way through. This new level of intimacy could change everything between us.

Lying beside him felt so comfortable, but I still couldn't wrap my head around the fact that I was in bed with such a longtime friend and had just experienced him in a whole new way.

I was less thinking, *He's the one*, and was more thinking, *I wonder how we'll get out of this not feeling weird around each other.*

THE SLAP

"Do you want to hang out again?" Colby texted me about the up-coming loop we were both on.

This is already too much, I thought, but of course responded: "Sure, let's do it."

I arrived in Portland, where he was watching the Super Bowl with Bayley and a tag team called The Revival, everyone polite enough not to say anything, even though we were obviously getting cozy.

Later, I tried to fight my instinct to get close to him. I knew I needed to keep my distance. But being with him was so effortless. Everything clicked. Conversation, interests, outlook. We had every type of chemistry firing on all cylinders. And while we lay there talking, he interrupted me to tell me I looked gorgeous. "Aww," I cooed as my heart melted—feeling like a princess. Maybe there was potential there.

But I was worried about getting distracted. I needed to be well rested, head fully in the game. And though it was also easy to have someone who understood my concerns, in many regards he was my competition. We were both aiming for that top spot, and the main event of WrestleMania.

The next day at Raw, I was set to do a promo with Stephanie Mc-Mahon. Usually you're onto something big when the McMahons are in the story line. It is the ultimate rub from the company.

The story was that my leg was clearly hurt from the Rumble and

she needed me to sign a hold-harmless agreement, which my character's paranoid mind took as them trying to screw me over.

It was so awfully orchestrated that I'm not actually sure what
it was intended to do. Stephanie couldn't look too much like the
bad guy, but in turn, I looked like an asshole. She came across as
compassionate and concerned about my well-being, whereas I was
fired up about her being a rich daddy's girl and refused to sign the
hold-harmless agreement. In turn she took me out of the match and
I attacked her mercilessly.

I will say, even though the story and the execution made me look like
a petulant child, I was pumped to be in a story line where I got to beat
up Steph. She nails every role she plays and is a dream to work with.

All this is to say, my immense violence against Vince's daughter
and the chief brand officer of WWE forced Vince to suspend me in
story land, giving me yet another obstacle I would have to overcome.

That night, Colby found a hip vegan Portlandy spot for us to go where
we could go incognito. As we chatted and played footsie over hummus
and cucumbers, he asked what my expectations were in all of this.

There were none, really, other than I expected not to get hurt
at the end of it. I was concentrating on wrestling and that had to
be my number one priority.

"When I said you were gorgeous yesterday, and I saw the look on
your face, I thought, 'Oh no!'" he said, implying that he was worried
about me catching feelings.

It felt like a revelation: *Well, that's it, then. We really shouldn't
go any further.*

He asked if I wanted to stay the night and drive in the morning,
but I declined. Despite the fact that I was about to drive in a wild
snowstorm that just hit the area, I thought it better to begin my
distancing now.

Especially because this episode of *SmackDown* was going to
be a big one for me. Because I had been suspended the night before, I was going to make my entrance through the crowd tonight
and interrupt a promo by the one and only HHH.

Was I dreaming? A promo with Stephanie McMahon and Triple H in the same week? The most powerful couple in all of wrestling? HHH had gone from the person I had watched at home as a kid and despised because of his great heel work to the person I loved because of his booking of women in NXT, and I was about to go face-to-face with him. And slap the crap out of him.

I was led up to the stands and hid out in a janitor's closet with all of its glamour and jumped up and down like a giddy three-year-old about to get ice cream.

I got my cue and started to make my way down through the stands, feeling like the most badass person on the planet. And the crowd kindly treated me like I was too. Thankfully, the awful segment the night before hadn't done too much damage.

I got in the ring running my mouth, Triple H and me trading shots back and forth until it was time for my big moment. The slap that was going to set the world on fire. I cocked my arm back, ready to deliver the slap of a lifetime. I lined up my target, taking bearded surface area into the equation.

As my hand got closer, I realized I had completely underestimated my own wingspan, missing the mark, with only the tips of my fingers gracefully fluttering against his cheek—*ah, fuck*.

God bless him, he's a pro. He sold it like I clattered him, the crowd graciously cheering as if I had drawn blood and taken out an eye.

I swaggered back through the crowd, back through the swanky janitor's closet, and made my way to gorilla.

"That was great!" Vince remarked, giving me a hug before adding, "But we're gonna need Steph to teach you how to slap."

I left content regardless. My shameful night on *Raw* had been turned around by a big victory on *SmackDown*.

The next day, at home in LA, I took a hot yoga class to sweat the remaining stench of Raw out of me. When I had complete clarity, I needed to tell Colby immediately that we couldn't continue any more of this malarkey. It would be the biggest mistake ever! I can't do casual and he isn't looking for anything serious. But I could be the best friend he ever had! We just had to end this right this second and be BFFs forever!

Mid–downward dog, I became so consumed that I grabbed my mat and water bottle, dabbed the sweat off my body, and rushed out of the studio to text Colby.

"What are you up to?"

"Just teaching class," he replied. He owned a wrestling school and taught there regularly. "How are you, sweetheart?"

Ugh, swoon. I loved that he called me sweetheart. But still, clarity! I now had clarity!

"I'm great! So great! I won't bother you. I'll talk to you after!"

"You're never bothering me. What's up?"

"Well, I just had an epiphany. We can't do this anymore! We just have to be friends!"

"Wait, what? No! Why?" he responded.

"You don't want to get into anything and this has the potential to get messy, so we're better off ending it now!" I was so excited to tell him how terrible this all was.

"That's not what I want! Is it something I did? If you don't like me you can just tell me."

"No, I think you're the best. But it's like this. If I go in with no armor, I'm begging to be pummeled, but if I go in all suited up, I don't feel anything, so what's the point? This is a great thing! You're not looking for anything right now and this way we can be the best of friends and you can sow all your wild oats."

"I guess you're being smart. I hate that you're being smart."

He might have hated that I was being smart, but I loved it for me and went to bed happy as a clam.

When I went to go train with our mutual friend Joshy G the next day, he had already heard about our conversation.

"What are you doing?" Josh asked me judgingly.

"He's not interested in me, Josh! He wants to be single for a while. This is the smartest thing!"

"You guys just make sense, though."

"Nooooo. Honestly, this is the best for everyone!" I argued.

Colby texted me later that day, still downtrodden by this decision.

"Can we still hang out this weekend?"

"Of course!"

"Do you want to stay in my room?"

"I can do that." *I love a slumber party! Who doesn't love a slumber party? That's totally something BFFs do!*

And so, after a loop where, because I was suspended, I would just show up and beat some people up and then leave, which really is a great gig if you can get it, I rocked up to the Hilton in Grand Rapids. He had left me a key at the front desk and had prewarned me: "This room is huge." *Great*, I thought, *all the better for the separation!*

I put my key in the door. True to his word, the room was huge. I walked down the hallway and rounded the corner to find him in bed already. In *THE* bed already, I should say. No twin beds, as would be customary for this grown-up slumber party. And he had his shirt off. His pecs sitting above the sheets, an acceptable amount of chest hair highlighting his definition. My god, he looked good.

Maybe this wasn't going to be as easy as I thought.

"I'm gonna shower real quick," I said while thinking, *Fuck, fuck. Stand your ground. It's better to just be friends. You're smart, Rebecca. Be smart.*

I came back and hopped in dangerously close beside him. I had already gone too far, pheromones acting like unstoppable magnets. My body had a mind of its own. A horny mind of its own.

We talked for over an hour, our faces being drawn together until we were mere centimeters apart. And that was it. We were passionately making out. Clothes were off.

We were in too deep. The connection was too strong. And it felt so right.

The next day, as we walked through the icy Grand Rapids street en route to coffee, we actually held hands. He didn't strike me as the hand-holding type.

"What happens from here?" he asked.

"Ah, I don't know. Fuck it, we'll figure it out."

SUCK IT

Raw was all about The Man. The McMahons had invited me to come back and I could get my WrestleMania match back if all I would do was apologize.

I had multiple segments with different characters, old friends, including Fergal, and foes, including Ronda, advising me to apologize.

It was a bit of a catch-22, whatever way you looked at it. I had made a point of ensuring the character came across as smart and aware, but considering the previous week's emotional outburst, smarts wasn't exactly what I was selling. Seeing as I did in fact beat up Stephanie, I should apologize, but also, the McMahons were notorious for screwing people over. What's a gal to do?

Life was imitating art—I fought to try not to apologize, considering the likelihood it would be futile. The least my character could do was stick to her convictions, however skewed they may be. I lost that battle. They thought it would be more impactful to see how reluctant I was and then have it taken away.

And so in the main event segment, I did it.

"But if all it's going to take is two words, then . . ." (I would have loved to say "Suck it"— HHH's famous catchphrase, but no dice.)

"I'm sorry."

With that Vince came bounding through the curtain in classic Mr. McMahon swagger. Even though I had no love for this creative, that was pretty friggin' cool—to be the focal point of a promo with Vince, Hunter, and Stephanie. It was like I had transported myself back to the Attitude Era, the peak of my fandom.

Of course, Vince didn't come as a messenger of joy, and reprimanded me for being the asshole that I was, and said that I could never lay hands on his daughter. Which, hey, man, you're right: I'd do the same thing!

But now I was suspended for sixty days, which naturally would take me up to the day after WrestleMania.

WHAT???!!! Ronda and I were (story line) pissed! We were gearing up to destroy each other once and for all in a sanctioned match at WrestleMania.

However, Vince came up with a suitable replacement. What he called "the epitome of the embodiment of a WWE superstar". . . my archnemesis . . . Charlotte Flair!

The crowd booed their faces off.

There was no way Charlotte was being left out of the Wrestle-Mania main event.

I didn't mind her being in there. Triple threats are some of my favorite types of matches. It's like putting together a jigsaw puzzle. But also, I knew that it would be an extra layer of heat, which always helps the babyface. It would also leave something on the table for me to have at a later date, seeing as we hadn't given away Becky Lynch versus Ronda Rousey.

The other part of me, the part that, despite the ups and downs of our friendship, has nothing but love for Charlotte, was happy that we would get to do this historic match together, and should we rekindle that bond it would be a special memory to share.

But as the obstacles in the story kept mounting, the next night I showed up—again, regardless of my suspension—on *Smack-Down* and was attacked, leading to me being on crutches for the next few months. I suppose I had that one coming. The Man had become a bit of a dumbass.

To turn things around, at least in my personal life, when I got back to LA, Colby surprised me at my apartment with a beautiful bouquet of flowers and some fancy dark chocolate. (I may have a slight obsession with dark chocolate.)

It was the week of Valentine's Day and he had all sorts of outings planned. Including going to see Bring Me the Horizon in the Forum in LA, and a dinner together for Valentine's night, where the exclusive conversation came up.

"What do you want to do here? Do you want to date?" he asked.

"No, I don't think so. You're not ready for it." I put the heat on him when in reality, I wasn't sure I wanted to.

I had never been in a relationship that hadn't broken up. If we were an item it would eventually become public, and if we broke up it would be awkward. Everyone would have their input on it. What would work look like? From what I had seen, when people at work broke up, one always came out looking worse than the other and eventually someone would have a meltdown and either leave or get fired.

I didn't want to go through all that.

"But maybe I am. Maybe I wasn't with the right people before," he conceded.

"You'll regret it if you don't go and sow your wild oats," I said, still putting the heat on him, though I wasn't ready to commit. I wasn't even ready to commit to not committing. It was all too scary.

I left the next day for an autograph signing in Houston, Texas, ahead of the Elimination Chamber PPV.

I didn't have a match at the PPV, but I was going to appear and beat the soul out of Ronda and Charlotte, doing terrible at this being "suspended" thing. But I was a rebel with a cause. And pretty dumb, apparently. But so were the security guards, who couldn't stop my crippled crutch-wielding self from entering the ring.

But before all of that went down, I had babies to kiss and hands to shake. While doing so, I began to notice that whenever someone came up and either brought Colby's name up or perhaps was wearing his shirt, I got overwhelmingly excited to talk about how great and talented, kind, smart, and funny he was. How gosh darn handsome he was. I swooned as little cartoon love hearts popped out of my head as the fans smiled and nodded awkwardly.

Shit. What are you doing, Rebecca? I'd stop myself as I tried to shoo away the butterflies that seemed to be populating my organs. The conversation in my own mind was going something like this:

You're really into him, aren't you?

No!!!

Why not?

'Cause he's so . . . so . . .

Perfect? And gets me and is the most incredible human I've ever met?

Damn it!!

I was into him. Fuck.

I got to the arena for Elimination Chamber. Colby hadn't even landed in Houston and I was texting him that I missed him and couldn't wait to see him.

"What happened? Are you okay?" he asked, confused by my sudden affection, a departure from the somewhat aloof game I had been playing.

"Why are you all about it all of a sudden?" Colby asked as we drove after the PPV.

I was already showing more affection than I had before, stroking his arm as he drove, smiling at him nonstop.

"Earlier, at the signing, whenever someone or something reminded me of you, I got this weird subconscious excitement. I just wanted to talk about how great you are. It made me realize I might be kind of into you."

"So do you want to do this? Like, do you want to be a thing?"

"Yeah. I think I do."

"So we're doing this, then."

"We are."

"Oh, that's wild, man," he said, stamping our officialness into the cosmos.

It was wild and it felt so right.

We now just had to figure out if we cared about this becoming public.

I wondered if The Man should have a man, and if that would do anything to my mystique. If I even had mystique. Best to just keep it on the down low for the time being.

We were having coffee that morning in a cafe near the arena when Fergal walked in while we were all cozied up. Fergal and I were so far past any sort of romantic relationship that there was zero weirdness, but it did make it obvious that Colby and I wouldn't be keeping this a secret for very long. And that was okay too.

KAYFABE

The next few months were a battle to stay hot while on the road to Mania. I ran the risk of being overexposed by being on both shows, coupled with the nonstop appearances I had once sought after so badly. The thing that had gotten me over in the first place was that people sympathized with me being overlooked. How long would they stay with me now that I was clearly being backed by the company? And would they care to see us in the main event of WrestleMania?

As enticing as our match had the potential to be and as popular as the story had been, there were several other viable options that made sense.

For example, Kofi Kingston, who had been with the company for ten years, was gaining even more popularity with the crowd. It was Kofi Mania! That man is one of the kindest and most genuine people you could ever meet. It was impossible not to root for him. And with him about to get a well-earned title shot at Mania against Daniel Bryan, that could very easily make sense as a main event.

There was also Colby versus Brock Lesnar. Lesnar was a well-tested main eventer and a proven draw. Colby was the best wrestler in the world, who has arguably had the biggest Mania moment in recent history when he cashed in his Money in the Bank briefcase in the main event of WrestleMania 31; he was beloved and respected by the crowd.

Nothing is guaranteed.

To bolster my anxiety, my dad started to take a turn for the worse. They had put him on an experimental medication and every side effect they could possibly warn him about was affecting him.

His liver function was rapidly decreasing and the doctors let him know that unless that improved, there was no way he could travel.

My mom also made a point about insurance. In America he would not be insured, while in Ireland he was completely covered by governmental health care.

I didn't want him to miss this. Maybe that was self-serving. Maybe he wouldn't care. I just wanted my dad to get out the other side. The guilt of not being able to be there for him if anything went wrong was consuming me.

I would be given the opportunity to win my way back into the WrestleMania match at the next *Fastlane* PPV. It would be me versus Charlotte once again, and if I won, the match at Mania would turn into a triple threat. Only this time I had the added obstacle of being on one leg. Though I had already beaten her on one leg before, at the Royal Rumble. I could do it again.

Only in the story, I couldn't. She picked me apart by going after my "bad" leg relentlessly. The odds were insurmountable and it would take a miracle for me to pull out a victory.

Well, either a miracle or a little pouty angel in the form of Ronda Rousey to come down and interfere. If Charlotte were to lose via disqualification by way of Ronda interfering on her behalf, then I would be back in the match.

Ronda came down, bulling as ever like the human weapon she is. However, she hit me with a laughably weak punch to make her point that she was doing this as a way to get me in the match. Where she was *really* hoping to destroy me.

I rolled to the corner as they made the announcement: "Winner by disqualification, The Man, Beeeeeeckyyyyyyy Lyyyynch!"

I laughed as the audience cheered. We were getting closer to the main event of WrestleMania, where it would officially be a triple threat match between Becky Lynch the RAW women's champion, Ronda Rousey, and the SmackDown women's champion Charlotte Flair—and the winner would take all. I just needed to stay healthy and relevant until Mania.

The latter being the harder of the two.

THE BUILD

WrestleMania 35. It was a nice number. It seemed like a good year for women to be the main event. We were still running hot. People still cared. But one can never bank on anything until the actual day. Card subject to change is a very real thing.

However, on Sunday the twenty-fourth of March 2019, I got my answer.

I had just finished a show in Buffalo, New York, and had a nearly seven-hour drive to Boston for Raw.

It was on that drive that I got a text from Vince to myself, Charlotte, and Ronda.

I pulled over to the side of the road to read the most glorious text I had ever received:

YOU WILL BE THE MAIN EVENT OF WRESTLEMANIA 35. WE ARE GOING TO ANNOUNCE IT TOMORROW. CONGRATULATIONS!

Holy shit.

What am I reading? Is this real? Did I hit a deer on the drive and I'm deep in a coma, dreaming all of this?

I shook my head. I wasn't misreading it or misinterpreting it, was I? I didn't think so. There was only one way you could interpret that. We were the main event of WrestleMania. Historical. First time ever.

I needed to tell someone. As great as this little dance party I was throwing myself alone in the car on the side of the 495 was, there was too much excitement to keep to myself.

I texted Colby: "Vince just texted! We're the main event of WrestleMania, they're going to announce it tomorrow."

"That's interesting. I wonder why they would announce it."

"Because it's never been done before and it's a big deal!"

I wanted someone to share in my excitement, but I wasn't getting the reaction I wanted from him. Of course, I was being selfish. I didn't consider how upsetting that news would be for him. He had always wanted to main event WrestleMania and he had a chance to do it this year . . . until his girlfriend took it away from him.

I became cold and distant, hurt that he didn't congratulate me right away. There was still at least three more hours on my drive. He was already in the hotel in Boston, waiting for me. But I had plenty of time to find a new one for myself.

"Yeah, I suppose this year is different. I think I'll stay somewhere else tonight. It'll be late when I get in."

"What? No. What's wrong?" he asked.

"I just gave you the biggest news of my life and you didn't even say congratulations."

"Sorry, you know how I like to analyze things, especially when it comes to wrestling."

"This isn't one of those things. This is the biggest deal of my life," I responded, upset.

"You're not staying somewhere else. Just come here."

I arrived three hours later. Still cold and distant.

"Why are you getting so upset about this? I'm sorry, I should have said congratulations; it was my own jealousy."

"Because I feel like you don't think I deserve it," I said through tears.

He hugged me tight.

Though the fact was, it wasn't him not believing I deserved it. *I* wasn't sure I did.

There was my imposter syndrome again. A syndrome that is maybe never more rampant than in the sport of professional wrestling. A profession where you literally have to fake it to make it.

In an industry filled with larger-than-life characters, muscle-bound athletes, and charismatic enigmas, how was this once pudgy, awkward girl from Dublin going to be on the same marquee that once boasted "Stone Cold Steve Austin vs. The Rock"?

However, in good news, the doctors had switched my dad's medication and his liver was rejuvenating rapidly. He was going to be allowed to travel after all!

My whole family was going to be able to make it out!

The only problem was that I had so many appearances that week, I would barely be able to see anyone.

When I got to the hotel for WrestleMania week, it was jam-packed, filled with wrestlers and fans alike. I barely had time to put my bags in my room before I was shuttled off to the warehouse in Connecticut for our match rehearsal.

Charlotte, TJ, our ref, Spider, and I sat in the warehouse waiting for Ronda, whose driver had taken her to the wrong spot.

While we waited, all running on fumes after months of going nonstop in the lead-up to this historic match, TJ read out the creative direction for the match. I was to win via arm bar on Ronda and me and her should barely touch. This would leave Charlotte to be relied upon heavily. Hearing the direction, Charlotte was on the verge of tears as TJ went on.

"It just feels like I'm the third wheel!" she cried.

While TJ and I looked at each other, both considering how to carefully and compassionately broach the situation, Spider, flamboyant and brash, blurted out, "Bitch, you *are* the third wheel! That's the heat!"

He was right. HHH had made a career out of being the one

in the middle, whether it be between Rock and Austin or anyone else who was over. But that made his job no less important. If anything, it made him even more valuable, as he could be inserted anywhere and added value.

Eventually we came up with a few ideas of false finishes. One idea was that I have Ronda in an arm bar and she is almost about to tap when Charlotte comes in and stops it.

When Ronda finally arrived over an hour later, TJ gave her the rundown of the ideas.

"And then it looks like you're about to tap, but—" he explained.

"Oh no. My mom would never talk to me again if it looked like I was about to tap."

TJ and I looked at each other. If her mom wouldn't talk to her if she looked like she was going to tap, we would have a hard time selling her on actually tapping for the finale.

"Okay, we'll come back to that."

I didn't feel the need to fight it. Whether it be a pin, a roll-up, or a submission, I was going to be walking out of there holding two championships in the air, having been the first woman to win the main event of WrestleMania.

We left with one or two things nailed down, but the majority of the match was still up in the air.

By the time I had driven the hour back to the hotel I was filled with doubt about how good this match was going to be. With all of our busy schedules, it didn't look like we would have a moment to talk about it before the big day.

Colby held me while every doubt and insecurity I had ever had about wrestling and my ability gushed out of my mouth like a waterfall.

"It's not about the moves," he reminded me. "The story is all there; you just have to tell it."

He was right, of course. He had the best mind for wrestling of anyone I knew. And even though I was in the spot that he wanted, he wanted me to do my best and own it.

But it felt so big. Because it was. It could change the wrestling business for women forever.

While the next few days were a blur of appearances, early-morning media, and late-night shoots, I was grateful to come back to Colby every night and have that comfort. I had never had that before, nor had I wanted that before.

At first, I was even reluctant to share a room with him that week. I was used to my own way of doing things, which is to isolate myself, dwell, write, and concentrate on envisioning how I want everything to go. I viewed having someone else there as a distraction. Not him, though. He was the greatest addition to my life and the best decision I ever made.

THE MAIN EVENT

The day that felt like it would never come was here: April 7, 2019.

This was my WrestleMania. I was the headliner. My name was on the marquee. This day would never happen again and I didn't want to miss a thing.

We arrived at MetLife Stadium before 10:00 am. It would be a long time before I would go out. In recent years, WrestleMania had become upwards of eight hours long, including the preshow.

They had a tent set up with two rings, so we had a place to iron out our match; however, because everyone was so busy, we had to put the match together in small increments. We would come together, throw down a few ideas, and then be pulled away to do rehearsals or an appearance or try on our gear for the night.

Ronda had Joan Jett play her in, live, and Charlotte would arrive via a helicopter.

I wouldn't have anything special. But that was also part of the appeal. I was raging against the machine. It would have been odd if they went all out on this for me.

As I walked the hall on the way to the tent between obligations I passed The Undertaker and Hulk Hogan. I had watched both of them main event and I was now in the same spot. Only I still felt like an excited kid, and I wondered if that's how they felt too. Maybe they didn't. Maybe it wasn't a big deal to them. Or maybe how big of a deal it was was lost on them. Maybe not. All I knew was I had left my nerves in the hotel room. I was enjoying every minute of this day.

The main show was about to start and we still didn't have our match planned out.

Suddenly a ref came in and put a new run sheet up. Colby, who was set to face Brock Lesnar, had gone from being right before me to the first match on the card.

"Shit, I gotta go watch this! I'll be back in a few."

I ran out of the tent and up to gorilla just in time to catch his entrance.

Brock had arrived late and didn't like his spot on the card and thought their match would be better as the opener. What Brock Lesnar wants Brock Lesnar gets. I knew Colby was meant to win the title from Brock that night but wasn't sure if that had now changed also.

Colby went out there, the star that he is, and took some gnarly bumps that had my heart jump into my mouth, considering his back was still feeling awful and I wondered if he'd even be able to walk tomorrow. I couldn't relax until the match was over. Eventually, as I watched through my hands, he hit the curb stomp (his finisher) and pinned the beast one, two, three, to become the new Universal Champion!

I jumped up and down in my own little corner in gorilla and waited for him to come back. Once I saw him walk through the curtain safely, I left gorilla and stood just outside to allow him to have his moments and thank everyone. Plus, we weren't officially out yet.

He came out and wrapped me up in a big sweaty hug. "I couldn't have done it without you," he said as camera crews swarmed us.

Of course he absolutely could have and would have. Even worse, he might have been the main event. Regardless, I felt special that I got to experience it all with him.

But now that he was done, I had to finish putting my match together, get into my gear, and get my makeup done. It was just after 7:00 pm, so I knew I would have at least four hours before we went out.

By the time we had finished putting the match together, I was proud of what we had come up with.

"This could be match of the night," I said to Charlotte as we sat in one corner of the ring.

"Do you think?" she asked.

"I do."

I was genuinely proud of what we had put together.

It was almost midnight when I stood in gorilla, makeup on, gear looking exactly as I had imagined it.

Fergal walked back after finishing his match. He too had just won the intercontinental title. It felt like all my people were having their nights made tonight.

"Enjoy it, sis. Go get 'em," Fergal said as he walked past me.

It was now time for the main event! The moment that felt like I had been building to my entire life.

The women's roster had now congregated in gorilla, I imagine watching with equal parts hope and envy. It was the spot everyone wanted.

"Bad Reputation" had just begun and as Ronda went to exit through the door that had replaced the standard curtain in gorilla to the stage, the door fell with a giant thud on the ground, nearly crushing our star!

I hope that's not a bad omen, I thought as Ronda made her way to the ring, Joan Jett and the Blackhearts playing her down as the exhausted crowd came to life. The energy was clearly dwindling after so much wrestling.

Then it was Charlotte's time.

"Let's kill it," I said as she walked out through the now-gaping hole in gorilla.

Her music finished and I heard the sound of eighty thousand people chanting my name, awaiting history.

My music hit and I strutted out, ensuring I took my time to soak it up. The stadium was packed to the brim; the dark night sky was cold and crisp. I looked to my left to see Joan Jett kindly smiling at me as she clutched her guitar.

Walking down the ramp to the ring felt like it took two hours and two seconds at the same time as I tried to take in as many faces as I could.

I looked out into the front row and immediately spotted my brother and dad. My dad, covered in a blanket to keep him from freezing, nodded at me with a warm smile on his face. My brother winked and smiled with a proudness about him. I wouldn't be doing any of this if it hadn't been for him.

Usually the friends and family of the performers get brought to the front row when their match is on. I looked for my mom, slightly nervous about how her and my dad would relate now, being in the same space for the first time in twenty years, but I couldn't see her anywhere.

"I'll find her later," I said to myself, while also being relieved that I didn't have to worry about any parental confrontations right now.

The bell rang and the match started, the tired crowd graciously serenading me with chants of "Becky, Becky!"

Midway through the match I was sensing it was too long, considering the hour, and tomorrow was a school day after all.

It wasn't going as smoothly as I had hoped for. It's true that sound escapes in stadiums like that, but as a performer, and as a human, I was aware that that crowd had now been there for nearly nine hours.

We also hadn't taken into account that Ronda had never done a triple threat, so some things that we knew from doing many of them she wasn't aware of, such as rolling out of the ring and to the floor when you're not in a portion of the match.

Eventually we had reached the crescendo. Charlotte was out of the picture, having gone through a table, and the crowd got riled up for the moment they had waited for. At last, it was Becky Lynch versus Ronda Rousey one-on-one.

We circled and then went in throwing fists before she cut me off to lead immediately to the finish, not giving them much of anything. She picked me up for one of her slams, but I rolled through to a pin. One, two, eh, three.

She had picked her shoulder up off the mat before the three count. Whether that was by accident or deliberate, I suppose we'll never know.

But the ref, knowing this was the end of the match, counted to three regardless of Ronda's shoulder coming up, in one of the most anticlimactic finishes in WrestleMania main event history. We were making all sorts of history that night!

Poor Spider even paid a $1,000 fine for his sin of counting three when a shoulder had come up. Vince was strict on these things.

The crowd jumped to their feet regardless. They were happy to see me win in this historic match but I'm sure also partially happy to get the hell home!

All the people who got me to where I was flashing before my eyes as I crumpled over with disbelief.

When I stood up, I saw my dad and brother clapping.

Where was my mom? Why wasn't she there? She was supposed to have been brought down to the front.

I saw my friends Jay and Jen. Maybe my mom was on another side of the ring.

I surveyed the fringes of the crowd. I couldn't see her anywhere.

My search was called off by fireworks going off to celebrate my win. I got fireworks!

Soak it in, I repeated to myself.

Am I soaking it in enough?

Is this the right way to soak it in?

No matter where you go, there you are. There will always be insecurities; there will always be doubts. But on this night, I had proved to myself, despite it all, I would find a way to overcome them.

I got out of the ring and ran to my brother and dad. "I'm proud of ya, kid." Richy beamed.

"Well done, Becks," said my dad as I hugged him.

I began to walk up the ramp, looking out to the crowd, afraid to even blink should I miss a second of this, the two titles I was holding becoming heavy on my shoulders.

Tomorrow I would worry about what would come next for me, but for tonight I was The Man.

I texted my mom when I got back to the changing room: "Where were you? Why weren't you in the front?"

The last time she had seen me perform live in New York I had fallen flat on my face. Now I was holding two titles in the air, doing what no woman in the history of wrestling had ever done before.

"No one came to get us, but that's okay. I'm so proud of you."

Even The Man yearned for the approval of her mother. And to put her mind at rest. All those gambles were worth it.

THE NO-SELL

It was the *Monday Night Raw*, right after *WrestleMania*, and I returned to gorilla after my segment.

"What the fuck was that?" Vince asked me.

"Eh, I'm sorry, sir? What do you mean?" I responded, confused.

I had just won the historic main event at WrestleMania, and Vince was making sure I knew how little that mattered and I better not be getting too big for my britches.

"What did I tell you?" Vince asked, turning it on me.

"To go down on the punch," I answered, it dawning on me why he was upset at me.

"Then why the fuck did you no-sell it? You fucked everything up."

"Sir, honestly, I didn't mean to no-sell it. I thought I did sell it, I just didn't go down, I wasn't expecting it to land the way it did, and I was a little stunned," I explained my reasons, which, once they came out of my mouth, I realized, sounded like fabricated excuses.

"Do you fucking think I was born yesterday?"

Well, no, sir, I certainly don't think you were born yesterday.

I had never been cussed at by him before. This was real top guy shit. But I was completely unprepared. And also, I was not in any way trying to fuck him, or anyone for that matter, over.

We were less than twenty-four hours removed from WrestleMania. I was running on about an hour of sleep, having done media in the morning, and had just delivered a promo with a new chantable catchphrase and future merch shirt.

How about a thank-you?

Instead, Vince was very upset that I, who had just won both titles in the first women's main event of WrestleMania in its history of thirty-five years, didn't sell the punch delivered to me by Lacey Evans, the brand-new lady on the roster who had only been seen walking down the ramp in high heels, a dress, and nice hats.

Should I have been selling for her in this manner the night after such an occasion? Fuck no. But that's not why I didn't. She hits a punch to the jaw, which, though safe, can be a little jarring, and as this was my first time feeling it, I got a little rocked and instead of falling to the ground as one would with a "sell," I caught myself from falling in the moment as was my natural reaction.

I would chase after her and get the upper hand in the segment regardless, so there was no "no-selling" necessary on my end anyway, considering I would overcome and conquer, which had been my path to the top thus far.

Vince, however, could not be swayed from the fact that he had made me a top star, given me the keys to the castle, and now I was a big-time arrogant asshole who thought I could get away with whatever I wanted, and no pleading with him could sway him otherwise.

In fact, when I tried to explain myself, he yelled at me, "You're not fucking listening to me!"

So many f-bombs.

Shaken, I walked out of gorilla and looked for solace in my friends backstage.

Colby was right there to help me. "You've gotta understand. He's been burned so many times by people he's made stars. And plus, it's kind of a good thing. He thinks of you as a top star, as one of the guys; he'd never talk to a woman like that otherwise," Colby comforted me. But it hurt me that Vince thought I was doing that intentionally.

In reality, Lacey should not have been my first opponent. She was brand-new, green, and it would be my job to make her. As I was the champ, double champ, and someone who had just made momentous history, there should have been someone built up on the back end so that people would be excited about what I do next. But these were the creative oversights WWE had continued to make.

"What do I do?" I asked Mark Carrano, the head of Talent Relations.

"Look, you fucked up the spot. That's it. You tell him you fucked up the spot. But talk to him before he leaves; otherwise it's going to sit on you and him all week long," Mark advised.

"Okay, yeah, you're right. When should I talk to him?"

"Wait till after the show. I'll be walking him out of here and I'll let you know so you can get him while he leaves."

I camped outside of gorilla, waiting to pounce, and occasionally being deterred as I'd confided in another confidant about the situation.

"Fuck him, don't bother. You know you didn't mean it."

But perception is reality in this joint.

As soon as the show was over, Mark gave me a nudge to let me know he'd be coming through and told me exactly where to stand so I could get Vince on his own.

When I saw him rounding the corner, I pounced, his demeanor still indignant.

"Look, Vince, I'm really sorry. I mean it. I didn't intend to do that. I fucked up the spot. I'm sorry. I want to say it won't happen again, but shit, sometimes I fuck up."

He immediately softened. "I'm Irish too. I fuck up all the time!" He laughed.

I laughed too (nervously).

He gave me a big hug that I hadn't anticipated but sure as hell appreciated. It gave me a rare glimpse into the human being who resides behind the skin of the mythical Mr. McMahon. The man who seemingly wants everything so controlled that he is perturbed by the act of sneezing, as it means he has lost momentary authority over his own body.

We were cool again. And it was nice to know that even billionaire tycoons like Vince know they fuck up all the time, but move on regardless. Not dwelling in the shit.

THE INTERGENDER TAG

"Seth says to Corbin, pick any ref you want. So, he picks Lacey 'cause she has a vendetta against you and tries to screw Seth out of the title; that's when you come out. What do you think?" Ed Koskey, the head writer of *Raw*, pitched me on an idea.

"Gosh, I don't know. Is it weird for The Man to have a man, ya know?" I wondered.

"Think about it," Ed said.

Colby and I weren't even together six months. Our relationship had barely been public for a month. Working together could be fun, but would it work?

"The way I see it, it's like seeing Daredevil and Elektra fighting side by side: if you know they're together, that's cool, but if not, it's no big deal," argued Colby.

"I suppose as a fan I'd want to see that," I answered.

"Exactly, and it'll be fun," Colby reiterated.

"I'm worried that they're just going to turn me into your girl-friend, like that's what I'll be relegated to," I confessed.

"Nah, you're too big for that by now," Colby comforted me.

The summer months right after Mania and before Summer-Slam can be a bit of a lull in WWE. Look at it this way: Mania is Christmas. There's so much buildup, anticipation, preparing, then the big day comes, you get all your presents, and then you move into the cold dreariness of January, where nothing much of significance happens.

Joining forces with Colby would either be exciting or ruin us. Both from a career standpoint and a relationship standpoint.

After much deliberation, and with the earth-shattering excited love energy between us, we gave the creative team the all clear to go ahead with the story line.

But I had one condition that needed to be drilled into Vince's head. "Becky can't just be Seth's girlfriend."

"Ha-ha! Becky's not Seth's girlfriend! Seth is Becky's boyfriend, ha-ha-hah-ha-haa-hah!" Vince exclaimed, laughing in hysterics.

It was all so nice in theory. Two of WWE's top stars, both champions, fighting side by side in the face of evil.

We made our side-by-side debut at the Money in the Bank PPV and quickly found out that, in reality, it was a damn mess and not in the slightest bit cool.

Commentary reminded the good folks watching every two minutes that "Becky and Seth are in a real-life relationship"—so much so that it was both uncomfortable and off-putting.

We also had no idea how to interact with each other on-screen. I was used to being a badass. He was too, and in this mushy, muddled TV relationship we were just plain awkward. Or, more appropriately, I was plain awkward. Or "cringe," as was often the word used to describe it online.

Blending the two worlds didn't work for me, as I was two completely different people in each of them.

In the ring I said what I meant, didn't take any shit from anyone, needed no one, and showed no level of vulnerability or humility.

At home, or with Colby, rather, I needed no mask. He was very aware of the insecure, strange, often shy girl I was who would struggle to say how I feel or speak up. He knew all of my vulnerabilities for better or worse. He knew I was not the person on-screen . . . unless I was pissed off. Then The Man would be scared of Rebecca Quin.

When the story line was over, I think everyone was relieved. Him. Me. The audience.

Colby and I learned a lot about ourselves and each other in that short time. We hadn't been dating long, but we were thrown into the deep end.

Even if we weren't a good pairing on-screen, I had found the perfect person for me off-screen.

Two months after the TV story line had ended at the Extreme Rules PPV—and after us having our first tag match together, which, despite the awful story line, was actually a great match—we took our first vacation together to Hawaii.

On our second day on Maui, we got lost on the way back from a day trip and stumbled across a beautiful secluded beach. No one was there, only the sun drifting behind the cliffs, the sound of the ocean crashing against the shore, the odd bird chirping in song. I was taking photos of Colby as he was looking at the sunset, his jacked back and sleek tattoo a more beautiful sight than the picturesque scenery. All of a sudden, he pivoted and dropped to a knee.

I stopped snapping as my jaw hit the sand below.

"Will you marry me?" he asked.

"What? Is this real?"

"Yes," he said.

"Yes! Yes! Of course!" I exclaimed, happier than ever.

As if by magic, a lady with a professional camera showed up a minute later. Colby hadn't planned any of this, but when we came across the ideal scenario he figured it was perfect. And the magic lady took my iPhone and angled us into the best lighting.

As we got unlost and found our way back to the hotel, I texted everyone I knew to tell them the good news.

There was no shame, no worry, no doubt.

As a friend, I had never thought Colby would be the marrying type, but two months into dating he was already calling me his wife. We never really discussed marriage; it was more of a foregone conclusion that we would be together forever.

My mom didn't stop talking to me for three weeks when I told her. In fact, she was over the moon.

When you know, you really do know.

GIMME A HELL YEAH

Things were rolling at lightning speed. In the space of a year, every wrestling dream I had ever had was coming true. I was put on the cover of the WWE video game—the first time ever for a woman.

I was on the cover of magazines, even becoming the first wrestler on the cover of *ESPN The Magazine*. I did *SportsCenter* commercials.

I went for a week straight sleeping only on airplanes because I had so many appearances literally all over the world.

I got to work with The Rock, John Cena, Edge, film with "Stone Cold" Steve Austin.

I was on *Billions* on Showtime.

I filmed with Marvel.

I got a book deal. (Hi!)

I became the longest-running Raw women's champion in history.

I bought my first house.

I had great matches. I had awful matches. I had underrated matches. I had mediocre matches.

I was getting to travel the world and work side by side with my best friend and now fiancé, and paid to do it.

Life was a series of ups with the odd down and little time to process anything or even be aware of what was happening.

However, I now had many voices in my head and my ear offering different advice. Some voices more dominant than others, with some

ideas that were better than others. It was my job to navigate between
all the noise; I was The Man after all. But sometimes I fought the
wrong creative battles and listened to the wrong people. I got worked
up over insignificant promos or outcomes. Approaching everything
as if it were do-or-die. I felt the need to conform to what I had been
doing on social media, i.e., being an asshole, leaving me feeling not
so great about myself. Like I hadn't been true to myself, and to use
the quote from the beginning of the book that my dad had always repeated to me (which he misquoted from the Bible, but I liked his version better): "If you bring forth what is within you, what you bring
forth will complete you. If you do not bring forth what is within you,
what you bring forth will destroy you."

I loved my work. I hated how worked up I would get at every
single week of television or every single creative direction. As if
the wrong story would send me back to the pit of irrelevancy from
whence I came.

I had worked so hard to be the first woman to main event Wrestle-
Mania and send the business in a different trajectory, but once I
reached the top of the mountain, the first question was "What
next?"

The company came and offered me a somewhat lofty contract,
but now that I had achieved my ultimate goal I wondered if it was
time to think about my next goal. One outside of the confines of the
ropes: being a mother. I had badly wanted a family one day; I had
found my perfect partner.

In work, I was becoming increasingly more anxious worrying
about my booking. Having reached the top of the mountain didn't
mean that I could enjoy everything more—it meant I was concerned about staying at the top. And I'm positive I was a pain in
the ass for the creative team. It's so clichéd that it's all about the
journey and not the destination, but it was true. The destination
was only the beginning of a new journey. But while I was worried
about what was going to happen next, all of a sudden the world
shut down.

We were supposed to fly out to Canada when we got word of the global shutdown because of Covid-19.

"Is the show still on?" I asked the travel department.

"Yes, for now. Just take the flight anyway."

"But what if we get stuck in Canada?"

It was March 2020 and you couldn't sit down to get coffee anywhere, but in WWE the show must always go on. Vince was the first person to put a show on after 9/11; he has run shows after the tragic passing of coworkers: he loves wrestling more than anything but also truly believes that wrestling is the distraction people need during hard times, such as a global pandemic. So unless the government made him cancel, those shows were going to run.

The government did indeed make him cancel that show, and many to follow, but they couldn't stop him running a TV show, on a closed set, in front of no one.

And that's what we did. All of our travel was changed to Orlando, to the Performance Center, where I had trained for all of those years.

In the classic, never-say-die Vince McMahon way, the show carried on as we hurtled towards WrestleMania. After all, this global shutdown couldn't last more than two weeks, could it? No way? Even two weeks seemed like an eternity.

"Do you think we're gonna have to cancel WrestleMania?" I asked Paul Heyman.

"I think you're looking at the venue for it," he responded nonchalantly.

"This? PC Mania? No way! You think it's gonna last that long?"

"October at the earliest before we have fans back," he prophesized.

I walked away, shaking my head, thinking what an alarmist he was. There was no way it could last that long.

This wasn't any Raw, though. This was the return of "Stone Cold" Steve Austin on 3:16 Day—so-called after his famous King of the Ring promo where he notoriously said, "Austin 3:16 just whooped your ass"—leading to a global phenomenon and the best-selling T-shirt in wrestling history.

"Stone Cold" Steve Austin in the PC, drinking beers and giving the finger to no one, seemed so very weird.

All of this felt weird. Just a week earlier we were wrestling in front of fifteen thousand screaming fans in Washington, DC. Now it was us in our bodies, bereft of adrenaline, taking bumps to no reaction but still with the duty of entertaining millions of confined viewers the world over.

I had pitched doing something with Steve because we had been compared so much and it was a hard-and-fast no.

That was up until ten minutes before he went out for the main event segment of the show. Even though there was no one in attendance, we still went live, because that was the only system we had in place.

A writer came and grabbed me. "Hey, we might need you to come out and drink with Steve if we go under time."

"Well, shit. That's cool. Would have been nice to have planned something earlier—but sure!"

"Okay, great. There'll be a cooler full of beers waiting at gorilla; bring that down and you guys can cheers or whatever."

I stood behind the curtain, watching Austin, the coolest wrestler to ever lace up a pair of boots, in the midst of an awkward segment. That even seems weird to type. An oxymoron, if you will. "Austin" and "awkward" are just not two words that go together. It was simply so un-Austiny.

No people. Him holding cue cards. Bantering back and forth with Byron Saxton.

This shit was weird. And it was about to get a whole lot weirder when my music hit. Down I walked, cooler in hand. We cheered. We stunned Byron Saxton too many times; we accidentally kicked him in the dick too many times. Drank too many beers 'cause the music kept playing and there was nothing else to do.

By the time the segment was over, I was suitably shit-faced.

The company had never filmed a Raw in front of no one and I had never gotten drunk live on TV, but here we were. The year 2020 was wild in all the worst ways.

And it was about to get even wilder. . . .

⤜⤛●⤜⤛

Post Raw and in the throes of drunken passion, Colby and I took less caution than usual. Even though I did want to be a mother, I was still the champion and I fully envisioned it would take an eternity to become pregnant, even though I was only thirty-three, considering the damage I had done to my body over the course of nearly twenty years. Between taking bumps and eating disorders, I figured there was no way in hell that my insides would be working properly.

Oh, boy, was I wrong.

When we returned home from filming WrestleMania at the PC two weeks later, I was already feeling nauseous.

No, it couldn't have happened that quickly, could it?

Holy shit. But what if it had?

There won't be any fans for months. What will I be missing? If ever there was a time to be pregnant, this is it.

But then again, what if I lose all my momentum? Everything I have worked for could all come crashing down.

This has never been done before. How will Vince react? How will the fans react? How will my mom react? Out of wedlock and all that jazz.

Only one way to find out.

Take the damn test, Rebecca.

I bought one of those early response tests; "6 days earlier," it said.

I peed on the stick. The control line showed up immediately, but not the second line, the "You're pregnant" line.

Without waiting the full time, I threw it in the bin because I was so certain I was not pregnant.

Off I went to the gym, still nauseous as a sailor.

When I came back, I noticed the stick again, only this time there was a second line.

"Oh, shit."

"Don't read after 10 minutes," the box said.

But that's a second line. I could swear that's a second line.

I showed Colby.

"Oh, shit. That's a second line!"

"Right?! But it says don't read after ten minutes."

"When did you do this?"

"Before the gym."

"Did you not read the instructions?"

"You know I'm not an instruction reader."

"Well, fuck. Do another one."

So I did.

Another faint line.

"I think that's positive."

"It's very faint."

I texted Rachel the next day, showing her.

"It looks negative," she said. "Don't be disappointed. It usually takes a long time."

"But I feel it! I feel like shit."

"Might just be your period. My sister was trying for a full year."

I'm getting a goddamn digital test!

Life hack: always go for the digital test.

I went into the pharmacy to pick up the test. The man behind the counter offering me a "Good luck" as I walked out, box in hand.

After I actually read the instructions, Colby and I camped out in the bathroom, waiting for the little digital window to inform us of our fate. Those three minutes felt like we were waiting the entire duration of *Schindler's List*.

"Pregnant," Colby read out as he threw his arms up in the air! Proud of his seed. "Yaaaaaaaaaaaaaaas!"

Holy shit! Yes! But also no! What if I'm not actually ready?!

I'M NOT READY!!!

Now all those questions were real. "*What* will *Vince say?*" I asked, while simultaneously arguing that I shouldn't have to care. I was a woman and had a right to become a mother. Sure, it wasn't ideal that I was currently the champion. The men in our industry don't have to skip over the important part of life choice that is starting a family; why should I have to? Apart from obvious reasons of the time away. But this is a new world, and these things should be taken into consideration. For better or worse, I was going to be the crash test dummy. Could women in wrestling have it all?

Colby sent his mom a picture of me with the test. She rang immediately and went as far as to start opening up her closet, showing all the baby clothes she had already purchased in anticipation for this day.

"Damn, Holly! We ain't even been together that long."

"I thought I had more time; that's why these are the only things I have," she said as she pulled out an entire wardrobe for a newborn.

Oh, man. I'm about to be someone's mom.

We did the rounds.

We called Colby's dad.

We called my mom.

We called my dad.

The dads cried.

Our lives were about to change forever.

TAKE A WALK

The tears streamed down my face.

"I'm not saying this! This is the biggest announcement of my life and I'm not going to have two old men tell me how I'm going to say it! We agreed on this weeks ago! Why the hell has this all changed? Why is no one listening to me?"

The doe-eyed writer looked back at me. "I'm sorry, I don't think you have to say it exactly as is."

"What the fuck is the sword of Damocles and why the fuck would I be talking about it now? And why am I starting a fight with Charly?! Or anyone, for that matter?" (Charly was our backstage interviewer.)

"I, eh, well, you don't . . . It's—"

"It's not what we agreed on!"

I'm pretty sure I was turning crimson while I ugly cried, yelled, and rained spit drops all over the poor writer, who was trying to console me. This was the epitome of my "difficult to work with" era—only now amplified by the multitude of hormones circulating in my body.

There's a custom in the backstage politics of professional wrestling where you must maintain your best poker face at all times. Emoting is seen as a sign of weakness, and this business is survival of the fittest.

Ironically, beyond the curtain, the opposite is true. The best wrestlers are the ones who emote authentically, who allow the audience to feel what they feel. They sell, i.e., react to something in such a way which makes it appear believable and legitimate to the audience, usually referring to the physical side of wrestling, but it stretches far beyond that. We're selling stories, characters, hopes, dreams, and, most importantly, merch. Okay, maybe it's not "most important," but in the eyes of the company, it's pretty darn important.

Anyway, back to my meltdown.

"Vince is almost done; go in there as soon as Jamie's out."

On most days, even though I had built a good relationship with Vince McMahon, there was still always a nervous anticipation of approaching his door to ask for something. Today, however, was no ordinary day. I had no filter, no restraint, and absolutely no couth whatsoever.

There was no deep breath or blessing myself to protect myself against his ability to mind control before I knocked on the door. In fact, I didn't even knock on the door. I kicked that mother down, metaphorically speaking, of course. Clearly, I had enough rage on my face that our director of Creative at the time, Paul Heyman, gathered his papers and bolted out of there as quick as he could.

I had long since hypothesized that pregnancy was accompanied by a free pass for bad behavior, and on this occasion my theory had been proved correct. I was only nine weeks pregnant, but I was bad to the bone.

Vince, still miraculously delighted about the fact that his current longest-reigning women's champion and arguably biggest star was leaving to go have a child, was oblivious to the fury I had brought into his office, as he greeted me with a welcoming hug that ended up tear-soaking his fancy Armani blazer.

"What's wrong?!" he asked, finally reading the room.

What came out of my mouth next was barely comprehensible, but between sobs I managed to get out, "Iuh don'tuh wantuh touh do thisuh! No oneuh isuh listuhehninguh touh meuh!"

"What are you talking about? Calm down now here a second. What don't you want to do?" Vince consoled me like a grandpa.

I composed myself for long enough to explain why I didn't want to go out and start a fight with Charly, who was simply interviewing me, and then pick a fight with Asuka, who, unbeknownst to her, would become the next Raw women's champion. I was The Man and all, but I wasn't a dumbass pregnant lady who would pick fights for no reason.

He listened before asking, "What do you want to do?"

"I want to go out there with the title in the Money in the Bank briefcase and talk about how much this has meant to me but say I need to go away for a while. Then Asuka comes out screaming at me, looking for her contract. I tell her that I put a lock on the case and that she hadn't just won a chance at the title, she had won much more. She opens it—then I say, 'Now you go be a warrior, because I'm going to go be a mother.' "

"Well, that's much better. Why don't we do that?"

"Really?" I was now sobbing because of how nice he was being.

"No one told me this idea. It's great! Let's go do it now," Vince said with a warmth that tends not to be associated with the mythical billionaire.

I had somehow managed to keep my makeup intact in the midst of my breakdown, and Vince guided me to the empty warehouse to give my farewell speech in front of nothing but a camera and a skeleton crew. Such was the covid era way.

It was a long way from where I started. I'd left my family years ago to make this dream work. Now I was leaving my dream work to make a family.

The announcement was received with overwhelming positivity. Of course there was the odd "How irresponsible" comment here and there. But hey. Go fuck yourselves.

I knew the timing was perfect, as if I'd been guided by the universe. But the daunting reality that now I'd be sitting at home by myself several days a week with a growing belly and hormones aplenty was sending me into a deep anxiety.

I'm not the world's best at doing nothing. But if nothing else, I'd be doing nothing with the rest of the planet.

Except maybe I'd try to write this book.

I AM THE MOM

The week before I was due, I got unearthly terrified. I. Am. Not. Ready.

Everyone would ask me, "How are you feeling? Are you excited?"

I'd respond with an "Oh my god, I can't wait," while inside I was trembling with fear.

What if I didn't bond with her? What if I got postpartum depression? I tend to veer on the side of the depressive as it is.

On a rare day off from the gym Colby and I sat down in his coffee shop and were relaxing as we watched a couple of young girls play on the couches there.

"We're going to have one of those."

"I know!" I responded with a hint of anxiety.

Not a moment later, the phone rang.

"Hi, is this Rebecca?"

"It is."

"Hi, this is Dr. Jones."

"Hi, Doc, what's up?"

"We tested your liver enzymes and they've become elevated. You have what we call cholestasis. So we're going to bring you in to induce you."

I grabbed Colby's arm as he was mouthing, *Who is that? What's going on?* as I clearly had a terrified look on my face.

The doctor continued, "Because if it passes through the placenta it will stop the baby's heart. Seeing as you're at thirty-nine weeks, it really is best to just get her out now."

I quickly responded, "Oh, shit. Okay, we'll head right there," before telling Colby, "We have to go have the baby now. They're going to induce me."

Panicked, he loudly replied, "No! What?! No! What's happening?! No!"

"We have to! Actually, Doc, could you just explain this to my husband?" (We weren't married yet, but "fiancé" is such a fluffy word.)

One minute later, he hung up the phone. "We're going to have a baby! Ahhhhh."

I guess I wasn't the only one who was nervous. Though I was now visibly shaking. The reality that life would never be the same again had come.

We rushed home and got our bags for our stay at the hospital. People had told me to eat as much as I could before getting to the hospital because once I was there I couldn't eat.

I stood at the kitchen counter shoveling leftover pad Thai into my mouth, my whole body quaking in fear, my appetite nonexistent, forcing the food down regardless, though swallowing felt like throwing up in reverse.

The next time we'd be coming home, we'd have our little girl with us.

—◦◦◦◦◦—

I was in labor for twenty-four hours without pain medication and was now puking and spasming uncontrollably from the pain. Though I think the most painful experience of the whole thing was the annoying high-pitched nurse telling me, "Each contraction is bringing you closer to meeting your baby."

Shut up, bitch! I'm puking over here. What if I don't like this baby?! It sounds cold and heartless, but I'm 98 percent sure that plenty of women have felt the same way on the brink of giving birth. Going from someone's child to someone's parent in one fell swoop.

I had told myself that if I could get through this without an epidural, I would be able to do anything else in life that I wanted. I

would have the will and determination and fortitude to achieve anything. For I am the creator of life, the fortress of pain, the willer of
wills. Or something like that. Point is, I hadn't had a challenge in a
while and I was getting pretty damn bored chilling at home.

The Pitocin swam through my veins, never letting the agony break
for a split second. The sensation was compounded temporarily by the
loud crunch of chips and the ratchet smell of salsa as Colby dug into
his snack. A serpent's tongue temporarily popped out of my mouth
as I hissed, "Go away."

"What's that, honey?" he replied lovingly.

"Go away, please."

"Huh?" He sounded befuddled.

My head felt too heavy to even look up.

"The chips. Go away. Just go away, please."

He put the crinkling bag away as he sighed. "I'm so hungry."

I was passing the threshold. Shit was happening.

You know, movies give a real bad indication of labor. I thought the
pushing part was the hard part. But as soon as I had the urge, it felt like
a release, like finally my body was working with me and not against me.

Sure, the guttural sounds that came from me were like something
you'd hear on Animal Planet. But it wasn't painful.

After I had been pushing for five minutes the doctor informed me
the baby's heart rate was dropping.

"We have to get this baby out now," she directed me firmly yet
shockingly calmly.

I was done waiting for contractions to push; I bore down and
pushed that child out with every fiber of my being.

Only she wasn't crying.

Why wasn't she crying?

I had never been more scared in my life. After spending nine
months wondering if I would bond with this baby, I was immediately ready to die for her.

The nurse had a cloth over the baby's mouth as they hit her on
the back.

"She can't breathe!" I yelled at the nurse, moving the cloth away from my baby's nose and mouth, completely forgetting how umbilical cords work.

Thirty of the longest seconds of my life later, I was calmed as with one final whack to her back, she started the most adorable, most amazing little whimper I had ever heard. My little baby girl was here. She was the most beautiful thing I had ever seen and I loved her with every cell in my body.

Nothing would ever be more important to me than her.

We named her Roux. I thought that was such a cool name.

But when she cried, she looked like a little grumpy old lady; she looked more like an Agnes than a Roux. Still, we called her Roux.

I couldn't believe that this most perfect baby, who, by the way, I had no idea how to look after, was mine to keep.

Two days later, we went home. My perfect little family.

THE SUBMISSION

Should I kick off the mortal coil, there is no point in you even trying to come back as, actually, I won't be here and there certainly won't be much craic in these quare times. —Dad

And so, at 4:00 am I lay in bed in Los Angeles, my iPad on my chest, and watched as my brother carried my dad's coffin into the funeral home in Limerick.

I had to be careful not to wake the three-month-old lying next to me.

Ten people max, six feet apart, masked up. This was his send-off.

Twenty fucking twenty-one.

No craic indeed.

And then Roux started crying. That makes two of us, baby.

His health had gone down rapidly. Or at least that's what he had let on.

He never wanted me to worry. He didn't tell me that the cancer had returned. Or that he had passed out in the doctor's office. Or that he had become so swollen that his clothes had to be cut off of him.

After all, I was a new mother and had enough to be worrying about.

Every time he called me, I was short. Talking about how stressed I was. The lack of sleep I was getting.

I had nothing but time and the luxury of being at home with my beautiful healthy baby. Why the fuck was I acting like this?

Why did I become so self-centered that I neglected to call him back for three weeks? *I'll get around to it*, I thought.

When I finally did, I was complaining about how tough I was finding it. How stressed out of my mind I was.

"Enjoy it, missy." That's all the advice he could give me.

I became mad at him for brushing me off like it could just be that easy. "I can't enjoy it, Dad. I'm so stressed. I don't have any help. She won't sleep. I don't know how I'm gonna go back to work."

"It's an adventure, missy. Enjoy the journey."

Now I get it. I get that he was on his way out and he wanted me to enjoy this part of my life—every part of life, really. Especially that which was his favorite part of life—being a parent.

Richy was the good kid, the one who looked after him always. I could provide the money. Richy provided the things that were priceless. Care. Affection. Time.

Richy suggested that we do a FaceTime so that Dad could see his granddaughter. That was the last time I saw him.

He looked skinny and frail. His arm was in a sling. He said he fell. I knew things weren't quite right, but not for a second did I think, *I'll never see my dad alive again.*

I just chatted and played with Roux till the conversation had run its course and we hung up, not thinking anything of it until Richy said, "He's not doing too well. Would you think of coming home?"

I got stressed again. There were two-week quarantine procedures. There were no direct flights and hardly any going into Ireland at all. How would I figure all of this out, and with a three-month-old and a fiancé who was on the road?

"How long do you think he has?"

"I don't know. It could be six weeks."

He didn't even have six days.

I tried to talk to him every day after that. His voice becoming increasingly more fragile. His mind unable to comprehend the things I was saying. Not yet admitting he was exiting the world.

It was a Monday, four days later, when me and my dad had our last conversation.

"I'm on my way out, Becks."

"I know, Dad," I said as I broke down in tears.

I did weird things. I played nervously with a makeup brush.

I cradled a teddy he gave me.

I ran downstairs half-dressed, looking for Colby's hand to hold.

I scrolled my phone looking for a way to record the phone call so that I could still have my dad's voice to listen to.

All while he was talking.

"I'm sorry, Dad. I know I was trouble. I know I wasn't a good daughter."

"You were always a joy, Becks."

How could he forgive me? He was dying and I hadn't even returned his calls. He was dying and all I could talk about was myself.

He truly loved me unconditionally.

"I wish I could be there, Dad."

"I should have been there when Roux was born."

"But you couldn't, Dad."

"I know."

"I love you, Dad."

"I love you, Becks."

Richy took the phone from him.

He lost his ability to talk the next day. The day after that he was gone. He never got to meet Roux. He would have adored her. He would have loved her uniqueness, how she knows exactly what she wants and will not be dissuaded. He might see expressions that remind him of me, but he'd know that she is an individual and he'd encourage her originality.

In the pain of loss and the crippling guilt I've felt since, I still write messages to his phone as if he's here. Updating him on Roux. Telling him all of my worries that he'd never judge me for. It makes me feel like he's not really gone. He's just back in Ireland and I haven't seen him in a while. Like he's getting back at me for not returning his calls by not writing back.

It's hard to know what to say when someone dies.

Always there with the wisdom of a sage, and knowing the perfect thing to say, The Rock, whom my dad always loved watching when he was wrestling and who had become a good friend and confidant to me in recent years, offered the most comforting perspective. In his signature voice, kind and compassionate, he gave me the greatest amount of comfort in one sentence.

"And now, he's always with you."

And now, he's always with me.

AND NEW

I was en route to LA, eight months after I had had Roux, when Vince McMahon called me.

"What would a comeback look like at SummerSlam?"

"Well, damn, I don't know. You just called me. What are you thinking?"

"Well, I'm thinking you show up and you cost Charlotte the title. And then go away again."

"What's the story behind it?"

"There is none, just a one-off and then we don't see you again until the draft."

I was insulted.

They had originally told me I was coming back at SummerSlam; then they changed their minds and told me I wouldn't be returning until October. Now they had changed their minds again.

I had plans to make. A baby to take care of.

"Can you give me a night to think about it?"

"Of course, of course."

As soon as I got off the phone, I told Colby, "This fucking guy . . . ," and started to explain the phone call.

To my surprise, he responded, "Ha-ha! I kind of like it. Just the idea of you fucking someone over and then disappearing. Sounds like something Austin would do."

"You think? Like, they don't have any sort of plan. Feels like it's just a waste of my return."

"Nah, man. It's not your real return."

With an outside perspective, I thought about it. Let it simmer and went to sleep getting pretty excited about being in the mix again. Let's fucking go.

Only to wake up to a text from Vince the following morning saying: "I've changed my mind. But be ready."

"Well, that's disappointing. I had come around to the idea. But don't worry, I stay ready," I replied.

I had done all the in-ring training, gotten in the best shape of my life, but at least I had more time to prepare.

Only a day later, on a Saturday, Colby, who was doing live events, texted me to say: "Sasha's out."

She was set to face Bianca for the SmackDown women's title.

SummerSlam was only a week away. I was going to get the call that they needed me.

Sunday came. No call.

Monday came. No call.

Tuesday came . . . *brrring, brrring.*

"Hello?"

"Hi, Becky." It was Bruce Prichard, the creative director of *Raw* and *SmackDown.*

"Hi, Bruce."

"How's it going?" he asked.

"Going good. What's up?" I responded, knowing exactly what was up.

"Well, we have a bit of a problem. . . ."

"Oh, yeah?"

"Sasha might be out for SummerSlam," Bruce stated.

"I heard that was a possibility."

"And you gotta either give them the match or something bigger"—not that this would be necessarily a "bigger" match, but the element of surprise made it most intriguing.

"So, what are you thinking?"

"Well, Bianca comes out, says Sasha can't make it. We go to a two-on-one match with Carmella and Zelina. She beats them. Then you come out and beat her quick. You win the championship and we turn you heel. Then we don't go back to you and Bianca till Mania."

"Ohhhh, that would make her a huge babyface! I like that!"

"That's option A."

"What's option B?" I asked.

"Option B is you interfere in the Raw title match and cost Charlotte the title, then we don't see you till the draft."

"So you're saying either way you need me for SummerSlam?"

"We need you for SummerSlam."

"All right, see you there."

"Thanks, Becky."

But now, shit. Who was going to look after Roux? With such short notice, we had no nanny situated.

We had discussed our friend Jen, but she was going to SummerSlam as a fan and was excited about her first big event. I didn't even know what I'd need for this damn comeback. New gear? I didn't have any of that.

Thank god I had dyed my hair a week earlier.

Turning heel was a huge move for me. I had spent the entirety of my career in WWE as a babyface. The one time they tried to turn me into a heel, I became an even bigger babyface. But this was different. It might work this time. Because I was given so much before I left to have Roux, the online crowd was already beginning to turn on me as a babyface, and if I screwed over someone they genuinely cared for, like Bianca, someone who was new and exciting, and the crowd was genuinely behind and happy for the push she was getting, it would be the most dastardly thing I could do. And I was excited to try out a new character, one that was the exact opposite of "The Man."

By Friday night I still wasn't sure what I was doing! Communication was minimal out of both uncertainty and trying to keep this a big secret. Thankfully, being the angel that Jen is, she said she would miss the show to help us out, relieving my greatest source of anxiety.

At around noon on Saturday afternoon, Johnny Ace, now head of talent relations, and Bruce came to see me on my and Colby's tour bus that we had recently acquired. There was no way we could travel fifty-two weeks a year, different town every night, with an infant without one.

Bruce, Johnny, and I chatted formally amid the chaos of what was about to be everyday life on the bus. Important business meetings going on while Roux scooted around the floor, cooing and crying, Jen picking up toys, Colby cooking food, and our bus driver, Andy, pottering about, looking for things to fix lest he be still for a single second.

Sasha was out and I was in. It turned out they had a little problem with their original idea. They had forgotten to book Zelina on the PPV. So instead of it being a two-on-one match, it would just be Bianca versus Carmella.

I would then come out, beat up Carmella, and throw her out of the ring and into the steps. Cut a promo challenging Bianca to a title match that would "blow the roof off the place" and then beat her lickety-split.

Bruce started, "Vince just wants one thing."

"Well, I can do that!" I responded, relieved that I wouldn't have to have a full match right away with someone I'd never worked with.

Johnny added, "So you go to shake her hand, punch her in the throat, and then one thing—what would that be?"

"Probably a Rock Bottom?"

"Sounds great. We'll tell Bianca and get her in here soon so you can go over it with her."

"What about Carmella? Does she know?"

"No, we're going to tell her in gorilla. Trying to keep this as secret as possible."

I get kayfabe, but not telling a performer what was actually going to happen was pure fuckery, and the last thing I wanted to do was put Carmella, whom I adore and respect, in that position.

I texted her right away: "Hey, I know they're trying to kayfabe you on this. But your match doesn't actually happen. I come out and they want me hitting a few things on you and throwing you into the stairs. I'm so sorry."

She knew that it was likely my return was happening. She's a great worker and didn't mind that being her role. But understandably, she did not appreciate being kept in the dark by the office.

She did, however, appreciate the heads-up so at least she wasn't blindsided in gorilla. I felt guilty that my return put her in that position, though. A new feeling to add to the already bubbling melting pot of emotions. Anxiety, excitement, doubt, apprehension, suspense—you name it, I felt it.

Bianca came in to see me a few hours later. The chaos of the bus was now amplified as we had added a hair and makeup person, Megan, to the equation, Roux constantly trying to take brushes out of Megan's hand as soon as she came near my face.

I got up as Bianca came in the door; she gave me a huge hug as she smiled and welcomed me back. I didn't really know her, having only met her a handful of times, but she could not have been more gracious.

"We'll make you a huge babyface out of this. Thank you so much for being so cool," I told her, trying to ease her mind of any potential fuckery on my end.

"I know how it goes. I'm just excited I get to be a big part of this moment."

I knew she was being honest. I can also imagine she is not an android and was also extremely disappointed. She had been doing a fantastic job as champion.

It was my goal to make sure that she got her moment back in a big way at WrestleMania.

It could have been easy for her to bitch and cry about being buried, to be mean to me and not want to work with me, and it all would have been understandable. She was nothing but pure class and tact and deserved her next championship to be even bigger.

I retreated from the chaos in the front of the bus to the back bedroom and made a call to The Rock to make sure it was okay that I used the Rock Bottom, not wanting to just straight up thieve his finishing move. Never mind he's the most successful movie star on the planet, he's also like Batman: if you need him, he's there in a flash.

"Of course," he said, in his wonderful way of saying everything that he has ever said. "This is your moment. Take it in. And when the time's right, I want you to look into the camera and say, 'I'm back'—just that."

He's the freakin' best.

⌘

It was almost show time. . . . I fed Roux one more time and handed her off to Jen, ready to do the damn thing.

I was rushed past everyone in gorilla, including John Cena, HHH, and Stephanie, who all gave me big smiles and stood at the curtain, waiting for my music to hit.

All the thoughts were going through my mind like *What if they don't remember me?* and *What if it's not that big of a pop?*

My worries vanished almost right away when my music hit and the crowd cheered like we were still good buds, sending a shock wave of gratitude down my spine.

I was too happy and excited to act cool. To use HHH's term that he used with me years earlier, I was on "excitement crack."

Once I kicked Carmella out of the ring—which, by the way, didn't get much of a pop, mostly because I imagine to most people she didn't deserve it and it was mean-spirited to the woman who had shown up to cover up the absence of another. . . .

It was game on: the crowd became electric, feeling the intensity of what was about to unfold. This wasn't the match they were prepared for, but by god was it the match they wanted now. I soaked up all their excitement and love for one final second, knowing that in about one minute they were going to despise me. *Alas, ol' pals*, I thought, *it's been a good run, but I have done all I can as your friend; it is time for me to see what I can do as your foe.*

We had a little bit of good sportsmanship with a handshake, then bam! Right in the kisser! Slam! Right on her back! *One! Two! Three! "Annnnnnnnnddddddddd neeeeeeeewwwwwwwwwwww!! SmackDown women's champion! Becky Lynch!"

The air was sucked out of the arena. The pop had faded to boos, or mostly shock and confusion. *What the hell just happened? Did they just squash Bianca? Why? How?*

My heel turn had begun. People were genuinely angry.

It was going to be hard for someone who had been a fan favorite to all of a sudden be a bad guy. But if they felt that the machine was behind me, that I didn't give a fuck about anyone else and wanted to keep my spot by any means, then they would surely be mad. And they were big mad.

When I came back, I saw Bianca crying. Understandably. She felt like her momentum had been killed, not that she would sell it, though. She's a real-life champion and passed it off as being happy for me. I tried to reassure her that I would do right by her, but she didn't know me and had no reason to believe me. I would have to prove it to her.

As I made my way through the sea of wrestlers and colleagues whom I hadn't seen in nearly two years, welcoming me back and offering hugs, I was eager to find my baby. Show her my new title—"Look what Mama did!"—as if she'd give a shit. This was my new reality, the perfect blend of the thing I love and the people I love most.

Instead of going out to dinner to celebrate my comeback, or hanging out with my friends, talking shop and making jokes, I popped a frozen meal in the microwave and ate it while nursing my child; then it was time to give her a bath and put her to bed. I couldn't imagine a better way to celebrate. Or a better way to live my life from here on out.

THE DARK MATCH

What followed SummerSlam in 2021 and into 2022 is what I consider my favorite year in wrestling. As a heel, I finally felt the freedom to do what I want. To say what I want. To not take myself too seriously or have to answer to anyone's expectation.

I had a new perspective on life and work. I was there to build my opponent and tell the best story I could and hopefully take an entertaining ass kicking while I was at it.

Wrestling is my art. And I'm damn good at it, even if I'm not the most technically proficient artist in the world. My body is my paintbrush, the ring is my canvas, and the moves are my paint. Within there are my opponents—different strokes with different folks—but it's all art, and whatever the onlooker thinks of it is up to them. But for me, I just want a body of work and a portfolio I am proud of.

Even though I was back to being on the road four days a week, every week of the year, I had my new little family with me the whole time. Sure, it meant dragging a tiny baby to Saudi Arabia and back again twice, or to and from the UK several times and on planes several times a week. It meant not sleeping through the night one single night all year. Or sometimes not sleeping at all the night before big PPVs. I was juiced up on all the love I could handle . . . at home. . . . The audience mostly hated me or at least played along. Twitter is where the real hostility happens. Where avatars in droves told me how awful I was. I might hate me too. What with my beautiful little baby, hot-ass husband, and dream job, life has been fucking good.

Of course, it was not without its hiccups. I fractured my goddamn trachea. Mine and Charlotte's heated rivalry reached the boiling point when we had one of the shittiest segments in *SmackDown* history, when during a title exchange I felt she deliberately went off script, leading to me yelling in gorilla that she was a, to use my exact words, "crafty fucking cunt" right in front of Vince and a plethora of onlookers and her denying it was intentional emphatically.

And yeah, Sasha and Naomi walked out of *Raw* right as it went on air when we were meant to main event that night, leading to a whole bunch of chaos, but they had their reasons and that is their book to write.

Vince suddenly retired from the company, after being all I'd ever known of WWE and in many ways is responsible for the life I have now and my lovely little family.

I was able to have my dream match with my teenage hero and friend Lita in Saudi Arabia, where once women weren't allowed to have matches at all.

Bianca and I were able to pay off her quick loss by stealing the damn show, if I do say so myself, at WrestleMania 38 in Dallas, the same place I had my first WrestleMania match six years earlier, and I got to give her her championship back. Ultimately, our feud continued to SummerSlam that year, where I would finally turn back babyface but also separate my shoulder. Which in a weird way was a blessing.

And my little girl has been there to see it all, oblivious to her unique way of life. I get to be her constant. When everything around us is shifting, through never-ending airports and hotels, living on buses and in different cities every night, her momma is always there to put her to bed at night, to comfort her when she wakes up.

I have learned many things on my journey, many of which are your usual clichés. That it's always about the journey and not the destination. That change is always possible, and things are only impossible until someone does them. That nothing outside of ourselves can bring lasting happiness. More than anything, I have learned that my biggest enemy has always been self-doubt and that when I have been able to free myself from its irritating shackles and had the courage to trust my inner compass, wonderful things can happen.

I had never considered myself successful, always striving to do more, be more, chase more. That hamster wheel had become pretty exhausting until I realized I have everything I wished for since I was a kid. My family, my dream job, my friends. For the girl who was always so average in every aspect of life—average height, average weight, average anxieties, average grades, average upbringing—I have gotten to do some most unaverage things.

I am not your average average girl.

ACKNOWLEDGMENTS

I wanted to write paragraphs about the people I need to acknowledge for being big parts of my journey. As the deadlines snuck up on me, I realized that, unfortunately, I would have to condense this section and simply say thank you and I love you in no specific order to:

My mom, Annette Quin; my dad, Ken Quin; my brother, Richy Quin; my daughter, Roux Lopez; my husband, Colby Lopez; my stepdad, Chris Muir; Loretta and Kevin Quin; Courtney Quin; Holly Franklin; Bob Franklin; Ron Lopez; Aaron Blitzenstein; John Stokes; Paul Stokes Jr.; David Stokes; Melissa Stokes; Paul Stokes Sr.; Seamus Walsh; Eunice McMenimum; Jake, Lilly and Martha Walsh; Judy, Walter, Morgan, Leah and Emma Walsh; Catriona, Nigel, Aisling and Oisin Warrengreen; John Quin Sr.; John Quin Jr.; Brandon and Jeanette Lopez; Arleen Lopez; Kim and Jim Lopez.

Joe Cabray, Joshy Gallegos, Mick Foley, Jen Houston, Rachel Walker, Steve Austin, Andy and Jackie Rowe, Dan Cohen, Lisa Black, William Regal, J Eatedali, Dave Feldman, Kim and Jeff Drusch, Steven Brown, Michael Gordon, Alan Doyle, Adam and Sinéad Leahy, James Roday, Maria Menounos, Seth Green, James Swan, Brian Koppleman, Tom Draper, Katie Stewart, Grainne and Gerald Boyle, Kate and Holly O'Reilly, Aisling Hughes, Mary and Patricia Byrne, Seana Keogh,

Michelle Purcell, Vanessa Strafaci, Duke Van Fleet, Paul Burke, Holly and Alex Dearborn, Fiona Shannon, Jay and Jen Ferrugia, James Nunn, Audi Langang, Shannon Corbally, Jessica Suver, Mel Berger, Guille Cummings, Flo, Chris Skehan, James Inglehart, and Clayton Thomas.

Fergal Devitt, Paul Tracey, Andre Baker, Johnny Moss, Robbie Brookside, John Ryan, Danny Garnell, Paddy Morrow, Sean Brennan, Niall Ebbs, Jordan Devlin, Scotty Mac, Juggernaut, Allison Danger, Canyon Ceman, Lexie Fyfe, Peter Farrell, Danny Butler, Paul Behan, Kev Daly, Jason McCormick, Robert Morrissey, Keith Loughman, Davey Loughman, Phil Boyd, Adam Burke, Ross Browne, Ian Kelly, Daragh Cleary, Carl O'Rourke, Jaffa, Neil Keegan, John Caufield, Marc Deegan, Leon O'Neil, and Joe Duignan.

Kevin Owens, Sami Zayn, Khadija Sebai, Big E, Paul Levesque, Stephanie McMahon, Vince McMahon, Nick Khan, Matt Altman, Chris Legentil, John Cone, Mark Carrano, John Cena, Dwayne Johnson, Brian Gewirtz, Ed Koskey, Ryan Ward, Cathy Morrell, Jenna Loeb, Sheamus, Bianca Belair, Bayley, Xavier Woods, Kofi Kingston, Nikki and Brie Garcia, Natalya, TJ Wilson, Petey Williams, Billy Kidman, Amy Dumas, Trish Stratus, Charlotte, Sasha, Naomi, Asuka, Iyo Sky, Dakota Kai, Kairi, Piper Niven, Nia Jax, Alexa Bliss, Paige, Emma, Alicia Fox, Ronda Rousey, Shayna Baszler, Lacey Evans, CJ Perry, Liv Morgan, Jessie McKay, Cassie Lee, Jojo Offerman, Maryse, The Miz, Jamie Noble, Michael Hayes, Arn Anderson, Ric Flair, Dean Malenko, Jim Ross, Kevin Egan, Michael Cole, Jerry Lawler, Bray Wyatt, Road Dogg, Ryan Callahan, Drew McIntyre, Miro, Adam and Beth Copeland, Cody and Brandi Rhodes, Sara Del Rey, Claudio Castagnoli, Norman Smiley, Ryan Katz, Billy Gunn, Nick Dinsmore, Johnny Russo, Joey Mercury, Bill Demott, Matt and Farah Bloom, Tyler Breeze, Luke Harper, Amanda Huber, Meagan Sackrider, Vanessa Caldwell, Zoey Stark, Tiffany Stratton, Lyra Valkyria, Tamina, Ashley Sebera, Ruby Soho, Zelina, Sarah Logan, Carmella, Nikki Cross, Chelsea Green, Sonya Deville, Mia

Yim, Shotzi Blackheart, Mandy Rose, Lilian Garcia, Chad Allegra, Luke Gallows, AJ Styles, Randy and Kim Orton, Jason Ayers, Danillo, Renee and Jon Good, Ivory, Mickie James, Bryan Danielson, Dr. Robinson, Dr. Pescaseo, Dr. Amman, Dr. Daquino, Moonlight, Peaches, Tara Halaby, Byron Saxton, Sarah Schreiber, Mackenzie Mitchell, Booker T, Shawn Michaels, Vic Joseph, Mauro, Wade Barrett, Corey Graves, Frenchy, Bull Dempsey, Joel Redmond, Mojo Rawley, Cory Weston, Shawn Daivari, Molly Holly, Ian Maxion, Jackie Stakel, Kristen Bacino, Jet Emini, Joey Maloney, Anthony Notoreli, Anthony Santaniello, Candice Lerae, Indi Hartwell, Tegan Nox, Tavia Hartley, Rod Zapata, Jim Kelly, Matthew Johnson (MJ), Chad Patton, Bobby Roode, Ben Saccoccio, Joe Hickey, Lambchop, Pumpkin, Lumpy, JJ, Chase, Adam Pearce, Chris Parke, Aja, Eddie Orengo, Shawn Bennett, Matty Cox, Kasama Bhasathita, Shinsuke Nakamura, Jolene, Sarath Ton, Stu, Rico, Sweaty, Marty, Kristin Prouty, Matt Boyd, Jacq Lefevre, Adrian Tadle, Tomerio, Scott Zanghellini, Michael Kirshenbaum, Alex Varga, Zachary Hyatt, Eric Thompson, Jimmy Jacobs, Kristin Altman, and Stacy Depolo.

Chelsey Goodan, Neil Strauss, my team at Range, my writing group, the WWE fans, the cast and crew at *Young Rock*, the cast and crew on *Billions*, Nate Moore, Eric Tannenbaum, Morgan Lehmann, Brad Slater, Shima, Sumie Sukai, Dave Prezak, and Erin O'Brien.

Thank you to my entire team at Gallery Books: Jennifer Bergstrom, Aimee Bell, Sally Marvin, Jen Long, Mackenzie Hickey, Rebecca Strobel, Anabel Jimenez, Bianca Ducasse, Lucy Nalen, Eliza Hanson, Caroline Pallotta, Lisa Litwack, John Vairo, Chelsea McGuckin, Davina Mock-Maniscalco, and Steve Breslin.

If I have left anyone out, which I likely have, I apologize. Please remember that I hit my head for a living.

ABOUT THE AUTHOR

Rebecca Quin is best known as one of WWE's biggest superstars: The Man, Becky Lynch. She is also an actor, writer, and mother. Rebecca was born in Ireland and, despite failing physical education and dropping out of college, she quickly ascended to wrestling superstardom. She was the first ever SuperGirls champion, the first SmackDown women's champion, and the first woman to win the main event of WrestleMania. She has competed all over the world and has been instrumental in driving change in a traditionally male-dominated sport.